Monuments of the Incas

1 Altar or "funerary rock" and "watchman's hut," Machu Picchu.

Monuments of the Incas

Revised and expanded edition

Text by
John Hemming

Photographs by
Edward Ranney

With 174 duotone photographs and 31 site plans and maps

Thames & Hudson

First published in two separate volumes in 1982 by the
New York Graphic Society and in 1990 by the University
of New Mexico Press

Second edition published in 2010 in hardcover in the
United States of America by Thames & Hudson Inc.,
500 Fifth Avenue, New York, New York 10110

thamesandhudsonusa.com

Library of Congress Catalog Card Number 2009902028

ISBN 978-0-500-05163-4

Printed and bound in Singapore by CS Graphics Pte Ltd

Contents

Maps and Plans

Photographer's Preface

PHOTOGRAPHIC DOCUMENTATION OVER THE LAST 150 YEARS has played a major role in helping us understand the many different qualities and spaces of archaeological sites around the world. In the Andean region, the first photographic views of Inca sites around Cuzco date from between 1864 and 1865, made by E. George Squier using a stereographic format, but it was not until the 1920s that a significant number of well-executed, large-format pictures of Inca sites became available to travelers and specialists in Cuzco. When I first began to photograph in the Cuzco area in the mid-1960s, there were few available references to earlier photographic work in the Andes, and as part of my photographic exploration of Andean archaeological sites over the last forty years, I have examined in depth the work of my predecessors, in particular that of Martín Chambi and Juan Manuel Figueroa Aznar. Both of these Cuzco photographers, working in 1928 with Peruvian archaeologist Luís E. Valcárcel, produced extremely fine 8×10 views of Machu Picchu, as well as other Inca sites, which were published in 1934 in the little-known volume *Cusco Histórico*. While some of Chambi's images are reproduced here, and his archive survives virtually intact in Cuzco, Figueroa Aznar's work is available for study only in the Luís E. Valcárcel Library in Lima and has been reproduced exclusively in historical studies on Peruvian photographic history (see notes on page 222).

My own use of 4×5 and 5×7 inch black-and-white film, first in the highlands, and for the last twenty years at archaeological sites in the Andean desert, speaks of my preference for the specific qualities provided by the large-format camera over more portable formats. For me, the view camera continues to render the complex spatial qualities of landscape and architecture far more convincingly and interestingly than smaller formats. Used with a moderately wide-angle lens, it is ideally suited, I think, to conveying a sense of the intimate relationship of Inca archaeological sites to the surrounding landscape. It makes possible a different way of entering what might be called the Incas' sense of visual space, of referencing just how organically much of the architecture, particularly at sites in the Urubamba valley, is integrated with the rock outcrops and shapes of the surrounding topography. The view camera has been particularly important in my exploration of the Incas' "in situ" carving of rock shrines in the Cuzco region, and in helping me to see how certain landscape features such as sacred peaks, caves, springs, and rivers influenced their way of configuring sites within the landscape. Outstanding among these, of course, is Machu Picchu which, with its unusual shaping of white granite outcrops, has survived as one of the great achievements of pre-Columbian sculpture and architecture. No fewer than six major stone shrines, each carved to follow the unique characteristics of the rock and its specific location, mark different ways of showing reverence for the surrounding landscape. It is well known that the highland Quechua people have for hundreds of years revered aspects of the natural landscape, and practiced religious rituals at selected shrines in the vicinity of Cuzco. The simple, though to us often obscure, carving which marked many rock shrines as special should be seen as part of a unique visual language. Like the patterns and concepts still evident in the best contemporary Quechua weaving, the forms of the rock carving are intimately related to the natural world, where they were first seen. The patterns and motifs created in both cloth and stone may strike us now as primarily abstract in form, but within their original context both undoubtedly held very specific religious and cultural meanings. The achievements of pre-Columbian weaving continue to be studied in great detail, revealing a highly evolved sense of craft, design, and symbolism. The legacy of Inca rock carving lends itself less to in-depth study, but nevertheless stands as one of ancient America's most unique artistic achievements—one crucial, I think, to our understanding of both Inca architecture and the culture as a whole.

The religious beliefs of the Quechua people certainly contributed to the Incas' architectural and sculptural achievements, but there was a definite split between the poetic vision that marked certain aspects of Inca religion and the rigid utilitarian mentality that so efficiently organized and controlled the expanding empire. Ultimately the monuments came to serve two contrasting functions, and distinct types of sites speak to us in different ways, as a comparison of the remote administrative settlement of Huánuco and the gardenlike sanctuary of Machu Picchu makes clear. Huánuco provides important answers in our desire to know what kind of political organization enabled the expanding empire to flourish, while the unique achievements of Machu Picchu speak profoundly of the possibilities of art, religion, and culture.

2 The upper stone of Saihuite, carved with terraces, houses, animals, and divination channels.

QUITO

Latacunga
Ambato
Riobamba
Alausí
Cañar ▲ **Ingapirca**
Tumibamba
(*CUENCA*)

Tumbes ▲ **Saraguro**
Cusipampa

Sullana ▲ **Aypate**
Piura **Huancabamba**
Cajas
Serrán

Motupe

Amazon

Marañón

CHICLAYO
Zaña ▲ **Cajamarca**
Cajabamba
▲ **Huamachuco**
Antamarca
Chan Chan Corongo
TRUJILLO Conchucos
Huaylas
CHIMBOTE Piscobamba
Yungay ▲ **Tantamayo**
Casma Huari
Huaraz ▲ **Huánuco (Pampa)**
Recuay *HUÁNUCO*
▲ **Tonsucancha**
Cajatambo
Paramonga Oyón ▲ **Pumpu**
Huaura *Lake Junín* Chacamarca
Tarma ▲ **Tarmatambo**
Chancay ▲ **Jauja**
▲ **Wari Willka**
LIMA Huarochiri
Pachacamac Yauyos
Mala **Vilcabamba**
Huarco **Machu Picchu**
▲ **Incahuasi** Vitcos **Ollantaytambo**
▲ **Vilcashuamán** ▲ **Paucartambo**
Pisco Saihuite **CUZCO** Pisac
▲ **Huaitará** Abancay Urcos
Tambo Colorado ▲ **Curamba** ▲ **Raqchi**
Ica ▲ **Soras**
Andahuaylas
Nazca Ayaviri
Azángaro
Pucará
Colca *Lake Titicaca*
Sillustani Island of the Sun
Hatuncolla + *Mt. Illampu*
PUNO ▲ **Coati Island**
Chucuito
AREQUIPA Chuquiabo
(*LA PAZ*)
Tiahuanaco + *Mt. Illimani*
Desaguadero
COCHABAMBA
To Lake Poopó *Pocona*
Incallacta ▲

Marañón
Chachapoyas
Huallaga
Ucayali
Urubamba
Apurímac
Mantaro
AYACUCHO
Cañete
Pisco

TAWANTINSUYU
THE INCA EMPIRE

(North–central part)

Inca towns	○ Corongo
Inca ruins	▲ **Saihuite**
Inca roads	——
Modern cities	● *LIMA*

(All modern names are in italics)

N

0	100	200	300

KILOMETERS

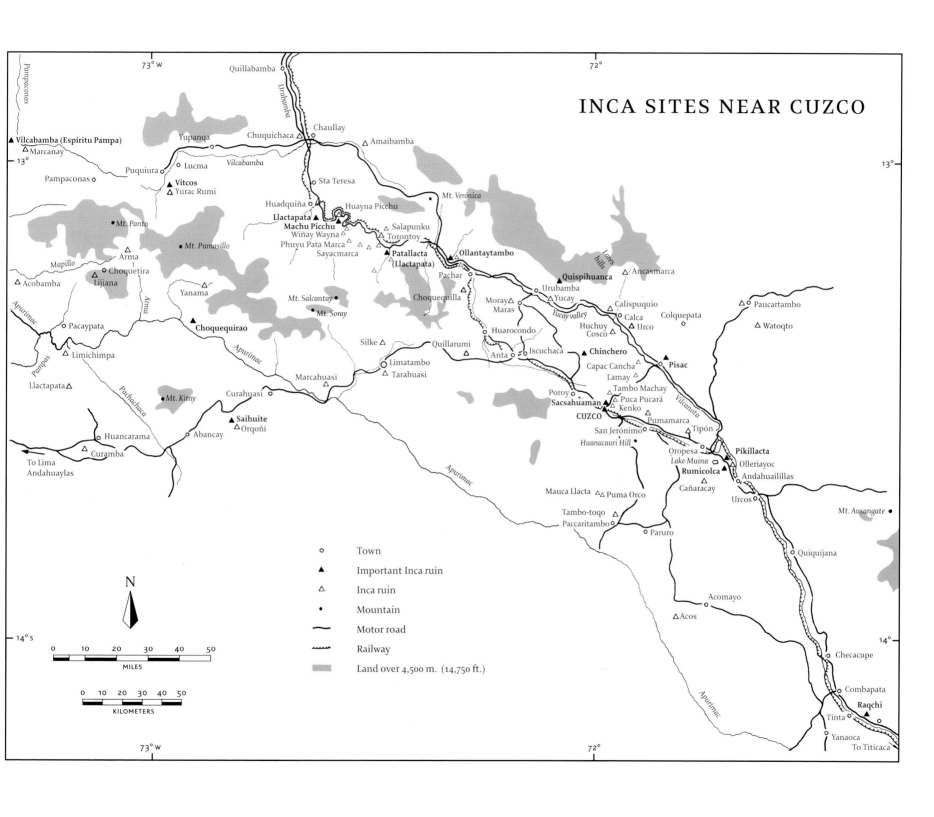

INCA SITES NEAR CUZCO

Town ○
Important Inca ruin ▲
Inca ruin △
Mountain •
Motor road
Railway
Land over 4,500 m. (14,750 ft.)

N

0 10 20 30 40 50
MILES

0 10 20 30 40 50
KILOMETERS

5 Soccllacasa pass, near the rock shrines of Saihuite.

1. Inca Architecture

THE INCAS WERE AN AUSTERE MOUNTAIN TRIBE, one of many Andean peoples who flourished during the millennia before the European conquest of the Americas. The name Inca would be known only to archaeologists but for two things: the accident of history by which Francisco Pizarro's Spaniards invaded Peru just as the Inca empire was at its zenith; and the architectural legacy left by that energetic society.

The Incas were the Romans of the Andean world—efficient administrators, disciplined soldiers, fine engineers, but with little of the artistic brilliance of the more flamboyant civilizations that preceded them. Their ceramics, metalwork, and textiles were competent and beautiful, but sometimes derivative and stereotyped. Their greatest artistic triumph was in architecture, or more precisely in masonry. Inca buildings were simple in plan and design, but their stonework was technically and aesthetically astounding. It is a durable legacy and it impresses modern visitors just as it did the first conquistadors. The Jesuit chronicler Bernabé Cobo wrote that "the only remarkable part of these [Inca] buildings was the walls, but these were so amazing that it would be difficult for any who have not seen them to appreciate them."

We know that the military and political expansion of the Inca empire was short-lived, a mere ninety years before its defeat by Spanish invaders. To modern observers, the *quantity* of building achieved during so brief a span is as impressive as its excellence. To understand this great achievement, we must know the historical and geographical context of Inca architecture.

The Incas themselves recorded eleven rulers—called "Inca" like the tribe itself—in the history of their rise from obscure origins to control of the vast empire overthrown by Pizarro. Under the first seven of these chiefs they were an insignificant tribe, one of hundreds that farmed, hunted, and fought one another along the length of the Andes. Inca origin legends indicated that the tribe migrated northward from the high plain near Lake Titicaca and settled in the rich vale of Cuzco. They built a town and temple. Their huts were simple structures of adobe bricks or fieldstone set in clay mortar, roofed with thatch tied to a wooden trellis. Their town probably had no organized plan. Its streets were simple paths between the houses, all that was needed by a mountain people with no draft animals or vehicles. The tribe gradually established an ascendancy over the people already settled near Cuzco. The Incas expanded under their early rulers, often by intertribal skirmishes, by marriage alliances between chiefs' families, or by wealth generated by successful farming. The tribes they absorbed near Cuzco left remains that are now excavated by archaeologists; and when the Spaniards interrogated survivors of these pre-Inca tribes, they found surprising resentment of the Inca conquest that had occurred little more than a century before the arrival of the Spaniards themselves.

By the 1430s of our Christian era, the Incas were in control of the valleys around Cuzco. Their territory was fertile hilly ground between the canyon of the Apurímac and the deep valley of the Vilcanota–Urubamba rivers, which flow north toward the main stream of the Amazon. To the north and east lay mountains, with the endless forests of the Amazon basin beyond; to the west, the main chain of the Andes separated Cuzco from the deserts along the Pacific coast of Peru. The chronicler Miguel Cabello de Balboa tells us that the event that transformed Inca history occurred in about 1438. Pizarro's official secretary Miguel de Estete roughly confirmed this. He wrote, in 1533, that "by the reckoning of the most ancient men, this land has been subject to a prince for only ninety years."

The turning point was an attack or invasion by the Chanca tribe from beyond the Apurímac. The Chanca advanced to the heights above Cuzco itself. The Inca army was on the point of collapse, but rallied under a younger son of the ruling Inca. The Chanca were defeated and pursued back across the Apurímac, across the territory of the Quechua and into their homeland near modern Andahuaylas. The Inca victory was complete, and so unexpected that in the Inca legend the rocks of the battlefield transformed themselves into warriors to turn the tide of battle. Those rocks, known as *pururaucas*, were later venerated in gratitude for their timely help.

The prince who commanded the victory of 1438 soon established himself as Inca with the title Pachacuti.* In Quechua, the Incas' language, *pacha* means land or time, and *cuti* means to turn around; so that the title Pachacuti could mean reformer of the world. This one man is credited as the architect of the

---

* "Pachacuti" is the old Spanish spelling. I generally use such spelling in this book, since these versions appear on maps and are easier for visitors to read. More modern, phonetic spellings of this and other Inca or Quechua words and names are given in the glossary on page 220.

ELNOVENOINGA
PACHACVTIINGA
IVPANCVI

6 Pachacuti Inca, as drawn by Guaman Poma, the sixteenth-century Indian chronicler.

drained marshes below Cuzco and channeled the Huatanay and Tullumayo streams that cross the city into stone-lined culverts. He conceived the center of Cuzco as the body of a puma, the mountain jaguar that had been the sacred animal of Chavín, Tiahuanaco (Tiwanaku), and other pre-Inca civilizations. The hill above the city was deemed the puma's head, and the Inca started to build the temple-fortress of Sacsahuaman there, with zigzag ramparts symbolizing the puma's teeth. The sloping ground between the two streams represented the feline's body, and the sharp triangle where the streams met was a district known as *pumachupan*, "the puma's tail" [ill. 30].

In reorganizing Inca religion, Pachacuti established existing practices in a calendar of ceremonies and ritual. He ensured that the Inca, as spiritual head of the empire, played a leading role in each element. There was an ancient agricultural tradition with festivals marking the seasons of the farming year, puberty rites for Inca boys, and veneration for the wonders of nature—in rocks, caves, springs, waterfalls, mountain passes, or any plant or animal that, in Cobo's words, "differed from others of its kind through some extraordinary or exaggerated feature... They reasoned that if nature had marked them out there must be something miraculous involved." The Inca himself directed many of the seasonal ceremonies, leading the chanting. Plowing throughout the empire could begin only after the Inca had turned the first sod of earth with a golden foot-plow. The chronicler Garcilaso de la Vega, whose mother was an Inca princess, wrote that in her people's origin legends agriculture and architecture were linked, as symbols of civilization itself. By their agricultural terracing and buildings, the Incas tamed wild places and brought order to the less sophisticated peoples who preceded them.

Another canon of Inca religion venerated the sun, *inti*, and to a lesser extent the moon, stars, thunder, and rainbows. Pachacuti also claimed divine status for the Inca ruler—he himself was the son of the sun, and his presence dazzled onlookers with the brilliance of the sun. This was the same identity with the sun that Egyptian and Japanese emperors claimed, to enhance their majesty. A consequent element of the Inca religion was ancestor worship. Here again, traditional beliefs were elaborated and ritualized for the greater glory of the royal family. The body of each dead Inca was mummified and his spirit was represented by a *huauque* (totem). His lineage of male descendants, called *ayllu*, or for royalty *panaca*, was responsible for maintaining his possessions and for parading his mummy and huauque at frequent ceremonies.

Legends surrounding the start of the Inca tribe assumed religious importance. One tradition was that a godlike figure, Viracocha, had created the world and then disappeared westward over the Pacific toward the setting sun. Pachacuti's own father was called Viracocha, so that a cult of Viracocha was elaborated alongside worship of the sun and celestial bodies. Viracocha was

Inca civilization and social system. Flushed with success over the Chanca, Pachacuti embarked on a rush of conquests that transformed the Incas into an imperial power. He was one of those protean figures, like Alexander or Napoleon, who combined a mania for conquest with the ability to impose his will on every facet of government. Cobo wrote that it was Pachacuti "who instituted the state with a code of laws and statutes. He set everything in order: he abolished some rites and ceremonies and added others. He expanded the official religion, instituting sacrifices and services by which the gods were to be worshipped. He embellished the temples with magnificent buildings... In short, he overlooked nothing and organized everything efficiently."

Pachacuti galvanized the people of Cuzco to rebuild their town on a monumental scale, with a plan worthy of the capital city of a budding empire. He

7 A ceremonial stairway in a sacred outcrop near Chinchero, north of Cuzco.

believed to have started his creation of the world at Lake Titicaca, and it was from here that the founders of the Inca tribe had taken their people north to Cuzco. The exodus was led by the four mythical Ayar brothers and their sisters. Places involved in this migration became venerated shrines: the islands in Lake Titicaca; Tambo-toqo, the cave from which the brothers emerged after traveling underground; and Huanacauri, the hill near Cuzco on which one of them was transformed to stone. Sites connected with the legendary first Inca, Manco Capac, were equally holy.

This sketch of Inca religion does not begin to embrace the complexity of its rituals, sacrifices, prayers, and ceremonial. Andean Indians are highly spiritual and profoundly superstitious, so a basic understanding of Inca religion is essential to understand them and appreciate Inca architecture.

The Incas, like so many other peoples, built spectacular temples in the name of their religion. Other triumphs of Inca masonry were for the semidivine Inca and his government. Anyone who contemplates imperial Inca architecture is awed by the devoted labor and thousands of man-hours it must have consumed. We have to remember that much of this labor was inspired by religious zeal. There was the same intensity of faith that has produced glorious religious architecture in all parts of the world. There was also patriotic devotion to a divine monarch: a desire that this venerated ruler should enjoy the very finest available workmanship.

As their empire grew, the Incas harnessed and organized labor levies from all parts of the Andes. They exacted tribute in kind and in personal service. There was occasional reluctance or armed rebellion against these demands, but most of the labor levies went willingly, proud to serve their religion and their ruler. After the Spaniards had conquered Peru, they held official inquiries into taxation and tribute under their predecessors. One such inquiry has survived from the town of Acora on the shore

8 Lake Titicaca from the Island of the Sun.

of Lake Titicaca. Aged chiefs were asked about the tribute they had paid to the Inca, and "they replied that they gave him many Indians for warfare and to build his houses and chacaras [agricultural terracing] in Cuzco." A long list followed, of other duties of tribute laborers (male and female), of produce to feed, clothe, and arm the Inca court and army, and gold, silver, textiles, and featherwork for ornament. The list ended with "copper bars for the Inca's buildings, and everything else that the Inca requested of them, for they were very obedient to him."

After the defeat of the Chanca in 1438, the Incas' conquests moved steadily north and south from Cuzco. They advanced beyond the Chanca into the highland valleys of central Peru. Another campaign swept southward, up to the plateau of the altiplano around Lake Titicaca to conquer the region of the tribe's legendary origins. Being a mountain people, the Incas were more at ease fighting along the ranges of the Andes. But with the Peruvian highlands secure, they were able to encircle and descend upon the rich kingdoms of the coastal deserts. Their most powerful opponent was the artistic, sophisticated, and by then somewhat

9 Adobe retaining walls below the temple dedicated to Viracocha at Pachacamac, overlooking the Pacific Ocean.

decadent kingdom of Chimor on the north coast. This was the region that had built the largest structures of South America in the adobe-brick pyramids of Moche and the vast city of Chan Chan—one of the world's largest urban complexes of its period. Under Pachacuti and his equally brilliant and belligerent son Topa (Tupac) Inca Yupanqui, Inca armies were well drilled and equipped. They had little difficulty in defeating Chimor, and then conquered southward along the Pacific coast. They took the ancient shrine of Pachacamac near modern Lima, a place so venerable and venerated that they incorporated its god into their own Viracocha cult.

The Incas were effective empire builders. They preferred to absorb tribes into their empire by negotiation rather than by force. Many Andean peoples chose to join the Inca hegemony, attracted by the obvious efficiency of Inca rule. But the Incas fought hard against any who offered resistance. There was a long campaign against the Chuquimanco people of the southern coastal valley of Lunahuaná. Another fierce campaign against the Cañari of southern Ecuador ended with the slaughter of most of the adult males of that tribe. A

revolt by the Colla of Lake Titicaca was ruthlessly suppressed by Topa Inca Yupanqui. However, campaigns eastward into the Amazon forests generally failed because phalanxes of Inca warriors with their slings and battle-axes could not maneuver in the confines of the forests and were defeated by the archers of jungle tribes. By the time Pizarro's Spaniards began to explore the Pacific coast of South America in the 1520s, the armies of the eleventh Inca, Huayna Capac, were fighting on the distant marches of a vast empire, against the tribes of what is now southern Colombia, the Guarani of eastern Bolivia, and the Araucanians of southern Chile.

The Incas instinctively adopted many practices of other successful imperialist powers. They left pliant local chiefs with a measure of pomp and prestige, but reserved real power for their own centrally appointed officials. They brought the sons of such chiefs for education at the court of Cuzco. They were reasonably tolerant of the deities of conquered tribes: such idols were transported to Cuzco, partly for the honor of inclusion in the empire's central pantheon, but also as hostages for the subject tribe's good behavior.

10 The royal highway, here winding through uplands toward Huánuco.

11 The fortified town of Incahuasi, built by the Incas to administer the coastal Cañete valley south of Lima.

12 Adobe and pirca construction of the post-Conquest palace for Manco Inca's son Sayri Tupac at Yucay.

As the empire expanded outward from Cuzco, the Incas secured its communications with a magnificent network of roads and bridges. They relied entirely on the mobility of their armies for military control of their federation of tribes. Bridges were a key element in Inca expansion: expert bridge builders, the Incas directed their roads to strategic river crossing-points. The main imperial highway, the Capac-Ñan ("road of the lord" or "chief road"), ran northwestward from Cuzco, across the Apurímac on a great suspension bridge, past the territory of the Chanca, and on toward the coast. At Vilcashuamán this trunk road turned north and ran through intramontane valleys for over 1,600 kilometers (1,000 miles) along the length of the Andes to Quito and the northern marches. Another important road traversed the coastal deserts beside the Pacific Ocean. There were feeder roads through the mountains and down the main coastal valleys. The southern part of the empire was served by a road past Lake Titicaca, across the altiplano, and into Chile. Subject regions were governed from administrative centers built at regular intervals along these roads.

The history and geography of Inca expansion are of fundamental importance in understanding Inca architecture. Historically, we have to keep reminding ourselves of the relative speed of the conquest. Allowing for consolidation after the Chanca war and for time lost in civil wars, there were only about ninety years between the start of the expansion and the arrival of the Spaniards. This was not long enough for a significant chronological change of architectural style or technique. Nineteenth-century observers of Inca architecture used to equate the huge stones of the temple-fortress of Sacsahuaman [ill. 46] or of Hatun Rumiyoc palace in Cuzco with the cyclopean walls of Mycenaean Greece. They wrongly concluded that these had been built by a megalithic culture, perhaps a race of giants far older than the Incas. We now know that all Inca building was done during the burst of creative activity of the empire's expansion. The great German traveler Alexander von Humboldt declared in the early nineteenth century that: "Simplicity, symmetry, solidity: these are the three characteristics that so admirably distinguish all Peruvian buildings... You could say that a single architect built this great number of buildings." Graziano Gasparini and Luise Margolies—the first modern scholars to analyze Inca architecture—added that the "single architect" of Humboldt's observation was "the State, which selected and imposed the repertoire of solutions."

There were variations in Inca building due to differing function or geographical location rather than to stylistic evolution. Provincial centers tended to be on flat ground, and they needed a range of structures for colonial administration. Gasparini and Margolies noted that the Incas used this "architecture of power" to impose their rule throughout the vast empire. However, closer to Cuzco, the chronicles attribute certain buildings to each of the last three Inca rulers. There was some evolution in detail—the adoption of new ideas in roof gables, more elaborate (and often wider) niches and lintels, larger halls (some with open ends), the use of pillars and false domes. Pachacuti seems to have preferred mountainside locations and close identity between buildings and the rock from which they rose; whereas his grandson Huayna Capac preferred a flat site with level expanses of terracing, enclosing his rural estate in a high rectangular wall, and making greater use of adobe on top of stone masonry.

Different styles of stonework were used to denote the function and relative importance of a structure. Temples and royal lodgings naturally deserved the finest masonry. Freestanding or load-bearing walls were built with a different technique from retaining or terrace walls. Surfaces that were going to be plastered and painted might be built with less care than those where the stone itself was exposed. There were obvious variations in architectural needs for different geographical regions—the rainy, humid Amazonian foothills, the cold Andean plateau, and the hot desert of the Pacific coast. Although essentially uniform, Inca architecture did admit some local variation by regional craftsmen and to allow for the availability of different building materials.

Any observer will notice at least four types of wall construction in Inca buildings. There were sun-dried adobe bricks which are still so common

13 Coursed masonry, with tightly fitted joints and a drainage outlet, of the acllahuasi (house of chosen women), Cuzco.

throughout South America. When building Cuzco, Topa Inca Yupanqui "ordered adobes to be made of mud and sticky earth. A great quantity of straw was mixed into these adobes—a straw like Spanish esparto grass. The earth and straw were kneaded in such a way that the adobe bricks would be well made and compacted. These adobes were to be used above masonry, for buildings to reach the desired height and appearance." The American archaeologist John Rowe found some Inca adobes in one of the palaces in Cuzco. He noted that they did have a high straw content, and that they were generally long and flat, measuring some 20 centimeters (8 inches) across by 80 centimeters (32 inches) in length. He also observed that they were of different shapes and evidently not made in standard molds. The Incas did not disparage adobes or regard them as inferior to stone. They used them in some of their most holy buildings, including the sun temple Coricancha in Cuzco (where they were used on top of walls of incomparably fine masonry), the Viracocha temple

at Raqchi [ill. 190], and the temple that is now the parish church of Huaitará. Adobes have survived quite well where they are protected by some form of roof. But where stone ruins are now bare, we must often appreciate that they were once higher, topped by courses of adobe that melted when the roof collapsed. Adobes were the obvious and normal building material on the rainless coastal desert plain. Adobe structures of Inca date can be seen at Puruchuco near Lima, at Pachacamac, at Tambo Colorado in the Pisco valley, and at Incahuasi in the Cañete valley.

The majority of Andean buildings were built of *pirca*: roughly shaped fieldstones set in clay mortar. This is a natural building method in the stony, rather treeless Andes, which is reflected in the use of the Quechua term *pircani*, meaning "to build an ordinary wall." It was used in the very earliest buildings in Peru, thousands of years before the ascendancy of the Incas. Pirca differs according to the nature of the local stone—limestone breaks more neatly

14 The famous twelve-cornered stone in Hatun Rumiyoc, the palace of the early Inca Roca in Cuzco.

the stones interlock at random, with the convex of one fitting into another's concave. Every visitor to Cuzco is shown the famous stone of Hatun Rumiyoc with no fewer than twelve corners on its outer face; and at Machu Picchu there is a huge block with thirty-two fitted corners in three dimensions. To modern onlookers accustomed to rectangular sawn masonry, polygonal is baffling. It seems impossible to explain how the Incas could shape heavy stones into these irregular but highly accurate shapes. Polygonal masonry is strong, and was always used for containing walls holding back earth platforms or terraces. The style evidently derived from agricultural terrace walls. But instead of using roughly shaped fieldstones, Inca masons demonstrated their virtuosity by creating a stone jigsaw puzzle.

Father Cobo marveled at the size and brilliant fit of some Inca stone blocks: "These clearly show the human effort that must have been required, to transport and erect them in their present positions. Even though these are so extraordinarily large, they are cut with amazing skill. They are elegant, and so finely positioned against one another, without mortar, that the joints are scarcely visible. With the rusticated, polygonal walls, I can assure you that although they may appear rougher than walls of [coursed] ashlars, they seem to me to have been far more difficult to make. For, not being cut straight (apart from the outer face which was as smooth as on ashlars), and yet being so tightly joined to one another, one can well appreciate the amount of work involved in having them interlock in the way we see. Some are large and others small and both sorts are irregular in shape and structure; but they are still positioned with joints as precise as those of coursed ashlars. Thus, if the top of one stone makes a curve or point there is a corresponding groove or cavity in the stone above that fits exactly into the other. Some stones have many angles and indentations all round their sides; but the stones they meet are cut in such a way that they interlock perfectly. Such a work must have been immensely laborious! To interlock the stones against each other, it must have been necessary to remove and replace them repeatedly to test them. And being of such great size, it is obvious how many workers and how much suffering must have been involved!"

Every modern observer shares Cobo's awe at the sight of polygonal masonry. The chronicler was right to stress that it was the product of days of patient human effort. There was no secret formula, no magic chemical, concentrated solar beams, or extraterrestrial intervention that could shape stones, nothing but the skill and dedication of Inca masons. The Inca state efficiently mobilized, housed, and fed the levies needed to perform this labor. The official religion and the mystique of the Inca monarchy inspired the workers. Subject regions of the empire were proud to send tribute labor, and most of those skilled artisans took delight in serving their semidivine rulers.

than granite, while shale and mica form long, thin stones. Some pirca builders worked their stones with more care, chipping or cutting them to interlock tidily or making the visible outer surfaces smoother. Most of the houses in any Inca town were built of pirca. These rough stones are the basic material of most of the ruins of Huánuco, Machu Picchu, and even the capital city Cuzco itself. Anyone walking around the side streets of central Cuzco can observe the foundations of former Inca houses, with rounded stones that fit together snugly but without the uncanny precision of the masonry of important buildings. These wall bases had upper walls of adobe. Pizarro's secretary Pedro Sancho wrote to the King that "most of the buildings [of Cuzco] are of stone or faced with stone, but there are also many adobe houses, very well built and arranged in straight streets on a rectilinear grid. All the streets are paved and have running water in a stone-lined culvert down the middle. The only drawback is that these streets are narrow and allow only one mounted man to pass on either side of the gutter." Agricultural terraces, one of the glories of Inca engineering, were invariably made of fieldstone set in clay.

The most famous Inca buildings were of tightly fitting masonry of two types: either "polygonal" or "coursed." Blocks of stone were pounded until their outer surfaces interlocked with absolute precision. In polygonal masonry,

15 Polygonal masonry in the foundation terrace wall of Hatun Rumiyoc palace, Cuzco.

16 Loreto (or Inti Kijllu) Street, Cuzco, with coursed masonry of the acllahuasi on the right and of Amarucancha palace on the left. Photograph by Martín Chambi, 1925.

The incomparable Cobo inquired about this problem, and observed native-born builders at work in post-Conquest Peru. He wrote: "The thing that impresses me most when I study one of these buildings is the question: what tools or machines can have brought these stones from the quarries, cut them, and placed them in their present positions? For the Indians had no iron tools or wheeled vehicles... This consideration really does cause one to be justifiably amazed. It gives some idea of the vast number of people needed [to build] these structures. We see stones of such prodigious size that a hundred men working for a month would have been inadequate to cut one of them. By this standard, the Indian claim that it was normal for thirty thousand men to work during the construction of the fortress of Cuzco becomes plausible...for a lack of tools or clever devices necessarily increases the volume of labor, and the Indians had to do it all by brute force.

"The tools that they did use for cutting and working stones were hard black [obsidian] pebbles from the streams. They employed these more by pounding than cutting. They transported stones to where they were needed, by pulling them. Having no cranes, wheels or lifting devices, they made a sloping ramp up against the building and lifted the stones by rolling them up this. As the building rose, they raised the ramp proportionately. I saw this system being used in the building of Cuzco cathedral. Since the laborers engaged in the work were Indians, the Spanish architects and foremen let them organize their work using traditional methods. They made these ramps to raise stone blocks, piling earth up against the wall until it was level with the top."

The other great masonry style was "coursed," in which rectangular ashlars are laid in even horizontal courses. The Incas themselves probably valued this coursed system more highly than the polygonal that so impresses modern observers since they used it for the walls of their palaces and temples. The most famous surviving stretches are the side of the *acllahuasi*, the house of the Inca's chosen women (*acllas* and *mamaconas*) and now the convent of Santa Catalina, and the superb east wall of the sun temple Coricancha [ill. 55]. Coursed masonry was used for freestanding walls. For aesthetic and technical reasons the stones became smaller higher on the wall. The walls themselves taper at the top and slope inward, so that the top of the inner surface overhangs its base. The respective uses of polygonal and coursed masonry are demonstrated on the ruin of the *ushnu*, a stepped platform, at Vilcashuamán [ill. 185]. The visible part of each tier is faced in coursed masonry, but the buried section of these same walls is polygonal.

The surface of each ashlar was allowed to bulge so that the joints were slightly countersunk. The effect of this rustication is magnificent, with each stone outlined in a frame of sharp shadow in the clear Andean air. There is a ripple of chiaroscuro over the gray or tawny beauty of the stone. It is thrilling to see the accuracy of the masonry joints. Heavy blocks of stone interlock like putty, but with the strength to resist successive earthquakes. The degree of bulge varies from building to building. In the splendid walls of Coricancha it is very subtle and slight. In the great blocks of the temple-fortress of Sacsahuaman or the famous polygonal terrace of Tarahuasi [ill. 182] the bulge is more pronounced. It is almost too prominent in the late-Inca or post-Conquest walls of Colcampata palace in Cuzco.

The high skills of Inca masons cannot have been developed during the decades of Inca ascendancy. Architecture anywhere in the world evolves from precursors. The Incas borrowed techniques or actual skilled artisans from all parts of their great empire. The earliest cut stones in Peruvian ruins were in the temples of Caral and Chavín de Huántar (respectively on the coast and in the mountains, north of Lima) and these cultures antedated the Incas by over two millennia. But the Incas' stonecutting skills clearly came from the region of Lake Titicaca—home of the Inca tribe in its original myths. Rectangular ashlars, huge blocks, tight polygonal joints, metal clamps between stones, and bevel-ing of junctions are all found in the buildings of the Tiahuanaco–Huari (Wari) civilization that swept across Peru from its cult centers south of Lake Titicaca and in the Chanca region west of the Apurímac. That cultural "horizon" was in the tenth century of the Christian era, five centuries before the rise of the Incas. Masonry skills were kept alive in the Titicaca region, whose Colla and Lupaca tribes were conquered by Pachacuti and his son. Stone burial towers at Sillustani near Puno and at other places near the lake show continuous use of many techniques that were adopted by Inca masons. A familiar Tiahuanacan motif was a zigzag step design, and this is found on doorways of the Inca palace on Coati island in Lake Titicaca itself. A similar design is carved in relief on a monolith of the temple in Ollantaytambo [ill. 85].

The chronicler Pedro Sarmiento de Gamboa tells us that Topa Inca Yupanqui was so impressed by Tiahuanaco that he took captives from the Colla tribe to labor on his magnificent buildings at Ollantaytambo. We know from post-Conquest interrogations that districts in the Colla had to provide labor for "the houses of the Inca in Cuzco" whereas other parts of the empire provided workers for other purposes. In addition, Bernabé Cobo made it clear that "the Indians themselves tell that the Incas used [the temples of Tiahuanaco] as a model and design for the great structures of Cuzco and other parts of their empire." Incas also learned some bonding systems from Tiahuanaco. They occasionally held stones together with copper clamps: they cut a T-shaped groove in each stone, so that the clamp holding them was H-shaped. They also copied the Tiahuanaco device of cutting blocks to turn at the corners of build-ings. This prevented the structural weakness of having a line of joints at the angle of a wall.

17 The Incas learned masonry from the Tiahuanaco civilization of the Titicaca region. In a chullpa burial tower at Sillustani near Puno, perfectly fitted curved stones surround a core of mortar.

All the chroniclers' observations about Inca stonecutting have been brilliantly confirmed by Jean-Pierre Protzen, professor of architecture at the University of California at Berkeley. Protzen realized that the way to solve these enigmas was to get into the Incas' quarries himself and learn first-hand how they operated. He found that the quarries were littered with round hammerstones, often of harder stone brought from river beds—just as Garcilaso de la Vega and Cobo had noted. Protzen learned empirically that "pounding was the predominant technique for dressing and shaping stones." Very rarely, for special needs such as fountain spouts, they may have used saws or files, but no such tool has been found. Pounding away for days on end, the professor discovered that "the extensive experiments I made with hammerstones found on location in the ancient quarries…demonstrate that the process is relatively easy, effective and precise, and not as time consuming as one might imagine." Extrapolating from his own work rate, he calculated that the largest block in the quarry near Ollantaytambo would have taken a team of twenty quarrymen two weeks to pound into shape. Thus, the 150 blocks lying in those quarries would have taken 300 men (perhaps in fifteen crews of twenty each) about eight months to shape. Inca stones were covered in pitting scars from this pounding—a technique that the art historian Carolyn Dean prefers to call "nibbling," because according to the earliest Spanish–Quechua dictionaries (of 1560 and 1608) *canincakuchini* meant "to work a wall well" and *canini* meant "bite" or "nibble." Protzen took only fifteen minutes to grind away these nibbling marks from a block, using a piece of andesite with water and soil.

Protzen's experiments and observations explained many more aspects of Inca masonry. He discovered the reason for the beveled joints that add such beauty to Inca walls. These indentations occurred as each block was shaped to fit into its neighbors. This was done with smaller hammerstones, striking oblique glancing blows away from the worker. In coursed rows, each ashlar's side and top were rough until shaped—by trial and error—to fit a new block beside or above it. The uncannily tight joints were on the surfaces of blocks: further back, out of sight, they could be slightly rougher. Protzen found that teams of masons worked toward one another from either end of a course. At the point where they met, a keystone would be pushed into the rectangular gap. Knowing this, it is often easy to find the keystone; and these occasionally fall out of their slot in both coursed and polygonal masonry.

Another American architect, the explorer-scholar Vincent Lee, postulated that the shape of one stone might be "scribed" onto another with a stick and plumb bob, as is done by log-cabin builders in the Rocky Mountains. Lee also tried to rig up a gantry for positioning the gigantic 300-ton blocks used in Sacsahuaman, but his experiment was not successful enough to solve that enigma.

As efficient engineers and disciplined planners, the Incas liked rectangular plans for their buildings, streets, and courtyards. These right-angles were a departure from the round houses and irregular streets of most pre-Inca cultures around Cuzco and of the Incas' contemporaries, the Chanca and Huanca of the central highlands. The inspiration for rectilinear plans may have come from the conquered coastal kingdom of Chimor, whose vast cities such as Chan Chan had a complex grid of adobe enclosures. They might otherwise have been inspired by sites of the Tiahuanaco horizon period—Huamachuco in the northern Andes, Huari near modern Ayacucho, or the mysterious Pikillacta a few miles from Cuzco itself.

Whatever its origin, a square or trapezoidal enclosure became the favorite planning unit of official Inca architecture. Known as *cancha*, this courtyard evolved from corrals for animals and formed a meeting place for people who spent little time inside their dark thatched houses. Even in Inca religion, much of the daily ritual took place in the open air, in temple canchas or larger town squares. Inca houses hardly ever had internal chambers or doors. As Cobo said: "Each room or apartment was a separate entity—they did not interconnect or follow one another." But he stressed that courtyards were a sign of rank. Ordinary peasant dwellings "are so narrow and humble that they should be called huts or cabins rather than houses. Only the chiefs' houses have large courtyards, in which the people gather to drink at their parties or celebrations, or a greater number of rooms."

Although almost all Inca buildings were rectangular, there were a few round plans, generally for sacred structures. Some funerary towers (*chullpas*) continued to be round. Walls surrounding altars or sacred outcrops might be curved, like the famous torreón [ill. 107] at Machu Picchu or at Runcu Raccay on the nearby Inca Trail, as were parts of sun temples such as Coricancha in Cuzco [ill. 52], in Pisac, or Ingapirca in Ecuador [ill. 203]. There was a round tower called Muyuc Marca in the temple-fortress Sacsahuaman, whose circular foundations were excavated in the 1930s [ill. 47], and another outside the Amarucancha palace on the main square of Cuzco. Hundreds of *qollqas* (storehouses) were round; and some domestic huts continued to have this traditional shape throughout the Inca era.

One element of Inca architecture was the Incas' own invention. It was so common and so peculiarly Inca that it became their symbol, a sure sign that a structure was built during their era. This hallmark was the trapezoidal shape for doorways, niches, alcoves, and even ground-plans. In a trapezoidal opening, the lintel is shorter than the sill and the jambs slope inward toward the top. It used to be thought that this was done to reduce the weight supported by the lintel stone and to minimize the thrust on either side of the opening. However, Professor Protzen found that the shortening of the lintel was too little to support this explanation. He argued that the Incas used trapezoidal openings because they are aesthetically satisfying. Rows of tapering doors or niches relieve the austere simplicity of Inca buildings, and the sloping sides of these openings balance a slight inward lean of the walls themselves. In coastal buildings with adobe walls and flat cane roofs, the trapezoidal shape of doors and windows is often the only proof that the structure was of Inca date.

For all their brilliance in masonry, in mobilizing huge contingents of labor, and often building on recklessly steep locations, the Incas were conservative architects. Their structural solutions were repetitive. Their empire expanded so rapidly and they wanted to impose Inca rule so fast that there was little time for architectural innovation. They preferred simple designs and proven techniques. This is most evident in their cautious approach to woodworking and roofing. It is remarkable that a people who could shape stone with such virtuosity did not develop carpentry beyond the rough shaping of roof beams. The Incas had no specialized carpentry tools and did not use nails, although they did use wood effectively in making beakers (*keros*) and vessels.

We know little about Inca doors. The Spanish conquistadors regarded them as insubstantial—chroniclers marveled at the honesty of a society that possessed no locks and in which a man leaving his house simply placed a bar across the opening to indicate that he was away. In strategically important walls there was something more solid. We see stone sockets beside the bases of doorways at Machu Picchu and other sites: these evidently held swiveling upright beams. Such doors in defensive walls or important enclosures had stone pegs sunk into the masonry of either jamb. A stone ring was often fixed above the lintel on the inner side. The side pegs probably secured a defensive crossbeam, and the top ring may have been used to support a

18 Defensive devices in a gateway at Machu Picchu: a stone ring above the lintel and side pegs were used to secure a door.

hanging doorframe. Normal doors were of cloth or hide on a wooden frame—as were the battle shields carried by Inca warriors. Whatever their construction, some doorways of fortresses were effective. During the siege of Cuzco in 1536, Francisco Pizarro's youngest brother Juan was killed while trying to force a gate into Sacsahuaman; the temple-fortress finally fell to an attack by siege ladders. A similar attack on the terraces of Ollantaytambo, by Hernando Pizarro during the same campaign, also failed to penetrate any gates into that town.

Inca conservatism seems most marked when it came to roofing. A modern observer is struck by the incongruity of having magnificent masonry topped by thatched roofs. Although pre-Columbian Peru had a long tradition of pottery, there was no attempt to use ceramic tiles for roofing. No pre-Conquest American culture discovered the Romans' great achievement, the arch. There were corbeled roofs in Peru, starting with the temple of Chavín de Huántar which dates from two millennia before the Incas. The tomb towers of Lake Titicaca had corbeled false domes over the central burial chamber, and the Incas used a similar technique to roof small rooms in the Pilco Caima palace on the Island of the Sun in Lake Titicaca. Storehouses for perishable goods were roofed with stone in this way. Flat stones were used extensively to make flights of projecting steps between agricultural terraces, and corbeled flat stones were used to support the ends of short bridges. Although slates exist in Peru, they were not used for roofing. Most Inca buildings, however important, were therefore roofed in thatch on a wooden frame.

The idea that thatched roofs were too humble for royal palaces or the most venerated temples is misleading. Inca thatch could be very elaborate. The American traveler George Squier saw a surviving Inca thatch during his travels north of Lake Titicaca in the 1870s. He remarked that "the thin, long, and tough ichu grass of this mountain region is admirably adapted for thatch, lying smoothly, besides being readily worked." He then described and illustrated the suntur-huasi, a circular Inca building, 5 meters (16 feet) in diameter, in the town of Azángaro. In Squier's drawing the damaged thatch looks like a steep conical haystack, but his description showed its vanished splendor: "The dome of the Suntur-huasi is perfect, and is formed of a series of bamboos of equal size and taper, their larger ends resting on the top of the walls; bent evenly to a central point, over a series of hoops of the same material and of graduated sizes. At the points where the vertical and horizontal supports cross each other, they are bound together by fine cords of delicately braided grass, which cross and recross each other with admirable skill and taste. Over the skeleton dome is a fine mat of the braided epidermis of the bamboo or rattan, which, as it exposes no seams, almost induces the belief that it was braided on the spot. However that may be, it was worked in different colors, and in panelings conforming in size with the diminishing spaces between the framework, that framework

itself being also painted... Over this inner matting is another, open, coarse, and strong, in which was fastened a fleece of finest ichu, which depends like a heavy fringe outside the walls. Next comes a transverse layer of coarser grass or reeds, to which succeeds ichu, and so on, the whole rising in the centre so as to form a slightly flattened cone. The projecting ends of the ichu layers were cut off sharply and regularly, producing the effect of overlapping tiles." Azángaro's magnificent Inca thatch has now gone—I myself once searched in vain for it—but the roof seen by Squier is confirmed by descriptions in the chronicles.

Garcilaso de la Vega recalled seeing a huge hall in the estate of the last Inca, Huayna Capac, at Urubamba. Its walls were three times the height of a man; but above them towered a conical thatched roof *twelve* times a man's height. This thatch was 2 meters (7 feet) thick, and half its width projected as eaves to keep the walls dry. The chronicler Pedro de Cieza de León said that Inca thatched roofs were so densely woven that they lasted for many years unless destroyed by fire. It was such a fire that consumed the roofs of pre-Conquest Cuzco. In May 1536 there was a desperate attempt to drive the Spanish invaders from the imperial capital, led by Manco, a son of Huayna Capac whom Pizarro had elevated to be a puppet Inca. Manco's men fired stones wrapped in burning cotton from their slings. According to one eyewitness: "There was a strong wind that day, and as the roofs of the houses were thatch it seemed at one moment as if the city was one great sheet of flame." And: "They set fire to the whole of Cuzco simultaneously and it all burned in one day, for the roofs were thatch. The smoke was so dense that the Spaniards almost suffocated." Only one thatch survived the conflagration: that of a great hall called suntur-huasi. The beleaguered Spaniards were huddled inside this hall, and when its thatch failed to ignite they attributed their escape to a miraculous intervention by the Virgin Mary or by Santiago (Saint James) of Spain on his white charger.

The buildings of Cuzco all had flat-topped walls, for their roofs were built on frames without the benefit of gables. This style is known as a hip roof. A frame of wooden beams sloped inward from the four flat walls and supported a central roof beam along the building's axis. The process was described by Garcilaso de la Vega: "The timber that served as roof beams was laid on top of the walls and lashed down with strong ropes made of a long, soft grass... instead of being nailed. Over these main timbers they placed those which served as joists and rafters, binding them together in the same fashion." The royal palaces of Cuzco and even the most holy sun temple of Coricancha were covered with thatched hip roofs. After the roofs of Cuzco burned in the siege of 1536, Manco Inca's attackers ran along the flat tops of the exposed walls, firing missiles down at the dreaded Spanish horsemen in the streets below. For once the indigenous warriors had the advantage of height in the unequal battles of the Conquest.

19 A restored house at Machu Picchu, with bosses along its gables to tie down the thatch.

This device was convenient when a building was on steep ground—common enough in the vertical world of the Andes—so that the front roof needed to be longer than that at the rear.

In the hot Urubamba valley and in sites near Machu Picchu, some buildings have one side open like an urban bus shelter. In longer buildings of this type there might be stone or wooden piers along the missing wall. Such structures were presumably for assembly or administrative purposes: their interiors are sufficiently light for daytime use, although too cold and exposed for sleeping. The Peruvian architect Emilio Harth-Terré called these open-sided buildings *masmas*. There are fine examples at Machu Picchu, notably the famous "temple of the three windows," the "watchman's hut" near the cemetery, and the house whose thatch has been reconstructed on the path toward Huayna Picchu.

The space within the beams of a pitched roof was an obvious storage area. Any indigenous hut had objects stored on the rafters or hanging from them. A natural development was to floor this attic area. Two-storied houses thus evolved among the Incas, with access to the upper story invariably from the outside: there might be a flight of external projecting stone steps or, on steep slopes, doors to the upper story at a higher level. There are various examples of this in Machu Picchu: the famous "house of the ñusta" ("house of the princess") in the torreón group, or an imposing three-storied house in the "prison group" which has entrances to its three levels cunningly fitted into rock outcrops. There are curious two-storied storehouses on the steep slopes of Pinkuylluna, opposite Ollantaytambo—curious because the door levels of the upper floors do not correspond to the walls of the lower floors on the opposite sides of the buildings.

As Garcilaso de la Vega remarked, the Incas did not use nails. Their thatched roofs were therefore tied down with fiber or osier cords to bosses projecting from gables or to stone loops ("eye-bonders") sunk into the tops of walls. Protzen found that Inca masons made stone rings by pounding rather than drilling. At Choquequirao (Choquequirau)—a recently restored Inca city south of Machu Picchu, on a mountain spur high above the Apurímac canyon—a terrace has a row of full-length niches with massive stone rings fixed between them. The first modern explorer to find this site, the Frenchman Léonce Angrand in 1847, wondered what could have been tethered to these curious rings. He guessed pumas, the only dangerous wild animals in the Andes. Other bosses or pegs were fixed along internal walls, often between storage niches. The same boss that secured the thatch could also be used for hanging household articles or fixing the ends of body looms. One of the many triumphs of Inca stonemasons was the skill with which they sculpted these utilitarian pegs and sank them into their fine stone walls.

By contrast, most of the buildings in Machu Picchu—in a wetter climate than Cuzco's—have roofs resting on gable ends. The main roof beam rested on these gables or, in longer halls, on a series of roof beams running the length of the building and supported by pillars. One variation was for the roof to rest on a solid wall which divided the house into two units without internal communication. Another variation was for the gable slopes to be of unequal length.

20 A masma beside the "sacred rock," before restoration. To support the roof on the open side, a beam fitted into slots in the gables.

There is another type of boss in Inca architecture. Some stones have one or a pair of low bosses protruding from their surfaces, or even a long barlike ridge. The bosses seem to have been used to lever blocks into position or pull them with ropes. Protzen found that many blocks in the quarry at Ollantaytambo had bosses for handling, but none that had left the quarry still had them. However, some stones fitted into magnificent buildings still have bosses, including examples at Sacsahuaman above Cuzco and the unfinished double-jamb gateway to the temple at Ollantaytambo. Masons as skillful as the Incas could easily have removed them. They no longer serve any purpose. We can only conclude that they were left for artistic reasons. A famous Zen Buddhist garden in Kyoto, Japan, is decorated only by a pair of low cones of gravel. The Inca projections are aesthetically just as satisfying. They provide sharp points

21 Bosses on the wall of niches on the uppermost terrace at Ollantaytambo.

of shadow to relieve the pattern of smooth surfaces and tight sunken joints of the best Inca stonework.

The other favorite device for decorating Inca walls is a line of niches. These niches must have had a strong appeal to the disciplined minds of the Incas. They were functional, useful, and decorative—breaking the monotony of a bare wall with the symmetry of a row of classical columns. Domestic or temple buildings have simple niches at chest height around their inside walls. These were obviously useful for storage or display. Almost all niches are of the standard trapezoidal shape, tapering upward toward the lintel, but Inca masons occasionally allowed themselves variations on this standard type. At Huaitará, which lies in the Andes between Pisco on the coast and Ayacucho, an important Inca building has survived as part of the town church. One interior wall has ten large niches with triangular plans; the side walls converge to form angles in the interiors of the niches. Other niches in this same building are of conventional plan, but some have small window openings set into their back walls. A few Inca buildings have two rows of niches, set either directly above one another or in a diagonal arrangement. Such double rows are found at Incahuasi, a large coastal site in the Cañete valley south of Lima thought to have been a camp used by Inca armies when they subdued this region in about 1470 at the end of Pachacuti's reign. More elaborate and presumably later double

rows of niches are at Choquequilla in the Anta valley west of Cuzco [ill. 140]; and there are diagonal arrangements in some houses at Pisac, Ollantaytambo, the coastal Tambo Colorado, and at Incallacta on the eastern edge of the empire in Bolivia. The British archaeologist Ann Kendall has sought to demonstrate that these are architectural evolutions that can be dated from the reigns of Pachacuti's successors.

Terrace or retaining walls of important Inca buildings are sometimes decorated with lines of tall trapezoidal niches. It is easy to imagine a row of brilliantly uniformed attendants standing guard in these "sentry-box" alcoves. My favorite row of full-length niches is on the platform at Tarahuasi [ill. 182] which was the great ushnu or temple Limatambo, where the road from Cuzco dropped toward the Apurímac canyon and suspension bridge. There are also fine examples at Vilcashuamán, at Topa Inca Yupanqui's estate Chinchero near Cuzco, and at Paullu Inca's palace of Colcampata above Cuzco itself. An elaboration in these tall niches was to sink one niche inside the outer frame of a larger niche, so that there were double or even triple jambs and lintels. The Colcampata niches are double in this way, as are those of the Pilco Caima palace on the Island of the Sun in Lake Titicaca. On the Island of the Moon, Coati, also in Lake Titicaca, is a building where the inner niches have stepped lintels reminiscent of a favorite Tiahuanacan motif—a decoration that makes it look decidedly Moorish to Western eyes.

An architectural device used sparingly by the Incas was the pillar or column. It was sometimes necessary to use pillars to support the roofs of open-sided masma buildings. These were generally wooden piers, but some were mono-liths—notably at the "temple of the three windows" in Machu Picchu. There were adobe pillars under the flat roofs of coastal buildings. However, the main use of columns was to support the roofs of huge ceremonial halls. Such halls in palaces of Cuzco, nearby royal retreats, and Tumibamba (modern Cuenca in Ecuador) have disappeared. So too have barracks-like kallankas at Cajamarca and elsewhere. But where kallankas survive—at Incallacta near Cochabamba in Bolivia, at Chinchero near Cuzco, and most impressively at Huánuco in the central Andes—there are circles of stones at regular intervals that once secured the bases of great wooden piers. The most famous Inca columns are in the empire's greatest temple, the extraordinary Viracocha shrine of Raqchi [ill. 192], midway between Cuzco and Lake Titicaca. The temple there has a high central wall that runs along its axis and supports the slopes of its enormous roof. Halfway between that central wall and the side walls are lines of columns that evidently helped the girders support this roof. These round columns, eleven of them on either side, have stone bases rising 3.3 meters (11 feet), above which they are made of adobe. They helped cover the largest building in the Inca empire.

22 The church of Huaitará (between Vilcashuamán and the coast) was built on an Inca temple with elaborate trapezoidal niches.

Modern archaeologists are concerned to identify the *function* of Inca buildings. There is a paradox about Inca ruins. On the one hand they are very obvious. The Incas tended to build in new locations, so that their provincial towns are uncomplicated by earlier occupation. Their ruins are relatively recent—only five centuries before the present—and, being solidly built, they survive well unless destroyed by later human abuse. There is also a reasonable fund of written information about the Incas by the Spaniards who conquered and destroyed their civilization. Spanish chroniclers tell us much about Inca daily life and about certain famous buildings. Interrogations of aged Indians during the sixteenth century add useful details, particularly about the administrative and taxation systems. But despite all this evidence, surprisingly many mysteries remain. It is often impossible to assign precise function to individual buildings in an Inca site. We know that regional centers usually contain certain standard elements—royal lodgings, a "convent" for mamaconas, a sun temple, barracks, storehouses, kallankas, an ushnu, a main square, a water system—but it is difficult to identify which surviving ruin served which of these functions. Within the ruined buildings themselves, there are baffling details that defy explanation. Important sites such as Pisac and Machu Picchu were never mentioned by the Spanish chroniclers. All these unanswered questions add to the fascination of Inca architecture.

Two important structures that occur in most provincial centers are kallankas and ushnus. Garcilaso mentioned the kallankas he had known as a boy in Cuzco: "In many of the Inca's palaces there were large halls some two hundred paces long and fifty to sixty wide. They were not partitioned, and served as places of assembly for festivals and dances when the weather was too rainy to permit them to hold these in the open air." Such large buildings might have several doors, but these were placed symmetrically along their façades and did not relate to internal divisions.

In their first armed encounter with the Incas, in the provincial town of Cajamarca in November 1532, Pizarro's conquistadors made deadly use of kallankas. When the last paramount Inca, Huayna Capac, died of disease in Quito, a dynastic civil war broke out between two of his sons: Atahualpa, who was with the army in the north, and Huascar with the royal court in Cuzco. Atahualpa's generals won this civil war, and the victorious Inca was marching south to be crowned in the imperial capital. This was the moment when Pizarro's invasion force of some 200 men entered the north coast of Peru. Atahualpa sent officials to investigate the strangers, and then invited some of them to come to meet him during his march down the main highway, which ran through the mountains. When they arrived, Atahualpa billeted the 150 Spaniards in the kallankas that lined Cajamarca's great square. On the following afternoon, November 16, he himself was carried in a gilded litter in the midst of hundreds of his sumptuously liveried soldiers, courtiers, priests, and nobility, to meet the leader of the unusual visitors. Pizarro decided that, if conditions seemed favorable, he would attack and try to capture the semidivine emperor. It was one of the most reckless gambles in history. The conquistadors were hidden in the kallankas. As Pizarro's secretary recalled, each building had twenty openings "almost as if they had been built for that purpose." Pizarro's instructions were that "all were to charge out of their lodgings, with the horsemen [already] mounted on their horses." The resulting surprise attack was brutally effective. Atahualpa's courtiers and retainers were taken wholly unawares by cavalry and infantry charging into their ranks. Within a few hours 7,000 unarmed Peruvians were massacred and their Inca ruler was captured by the alien invaders.

Cieza de León described two kallankas on the square of Huamachuco, a couple of days' march south of Cajamarca, as being "twenty-two feet [7 meters] wide and about one hundred feet [30 meters] long, all of stone and trimmed with long, thick beams covered with straw, which they employ very skillfully." Further south, the undisturbed ruins of Huánuco contain two great kallankas, each about 70 meters (230 feet) long and standing in line along one side of an enormous plaza. There are remains of such halls moving south along the royal road, at Pumpu (now called Bombón) on Lake Junín, Tarma, and Vilcashuamán, and they doubtless existed at vanished sites such as Cajas, Tumibamba, and Quito. Chinchero, Topa Inca's royal estate northwest of Cuzco, has two well-preserved halls, and there was a huge open-ended one at his son Huayna Capac's Urubamba lodging.

The largest of all surviving kallankas is far away on the southeastern marches of the empire, at Incallacta, some 80 kilometers (50 miles) southeast of Cochabamba on the road to Santa Cruz. (Once known as Pocona, this outpost may have been sacked and burned in 1524 by Guarani raiders from what is now Paraguay. Accompanied—and perhaps encouraged—by a Portuguese adventurer called Aleixo Garcia, these warriors crossed the vast plains of what is now eastern Bolivia; and Garcia became the first European to glimpse part of the Inca empire.) The mighty kallanka measures 78 by 26 meters (256 by 85 feet) in plan. It has twelve narrow doors onto a square and, on the opposite wall, a long line of forty-four niches, with more niches surmounted by windows in the end walls. There may well have been three rows of pillars supporting the gigantic thatched roof, each sloping pitch of which was no less than 16 meters (52 feet) wide.

Francisco Pizarro's young cousin, Pedro Pizarro, wrote that "the Indians have these *galpones* [sheds] for their drinking celebrations," particularly when it was raining. One type of kallanka had an open end wall, the other "with the ends closed but with many doorways in one wall. These halls were very large and had no obstructions, but were level and clear." In provincial centers,

23 The ushnu administrative platform at Huánuco.

had stationed the gunner Pedro de Candia on this ushnu with his small cannon. Francisco de Jerez, another of Pizarro's secretaries, described it as "a stone fortress incorporated into the square, with a masonry staircase up which one climbs to it." Pizarro waited until the Inca and his followers filled the square. He decided that his reckless plan to kidnap Atahualpa might succeed and, according to one soldier, "signaled the artillery-man to fire the cannon into their midst." At this the Spaniards rode out of the kallankas, where they were hidden, and charged into the mass of unarmed Indians crowded into the square. In Pedro Pizarro's words: "The Indians were thrown into confusion and panicked. The Spaniards fell upon them and began to kill." It was thus a cannon on an ushnu that fired the opening shot of the Conquest.

kallankas also served to accommodate people who were moving along the roads on official service: soldiers, artisans, laborers, or colonists being transplanted to settle newly conquered regions. The young priest Cristóbal de Molina, who was in Peru soon after the Conquest, wrote that when travelers finished a day's journey, "they spent the night at the town they reached, in halls or large houses that had been made for this purpose. Some of these were over 150 paces long and very broad and spacious. A great quantity of people could be housed in each of them, and they were very well covered, clean and well appointed, with many doors so that they should be well lit and agreeable. Each person there was provided with a daily ration for him and his wife, each [waiting] in turn and without any bustle just as if they had been monks. For the common people of this land were the most obedient, humble and disciplined that I believe could be found anywhere on earth."

This same priest also noted that in every town along the main highways, the Incas had "a great royal plaza, in the middle of which was a tall rectangular platform [ushnu] with a high stairway leading up to it. The Inca and three lords would ascend this to address the people and to review the fighting men when they held parades or assemblies."

There was an ushnu in the square of Cajamarca. On the fateful November 16, 1532, when Pizarro's surprise attack captured the Inca Atahualpa, the Spaniards

The largest surviving ushnu is at Huánuco—an immense gray slab of masonry in the midst of a plaza over half a kilometer (550 yards) long. There was a less elaborate ushnu in the square of Pumpu, the next important town south along the royal highway. This site was excavated in the 1990s by the Peruvian archaeologist Ramiro Matos Mendieta. The most beautiful ushnu is that of Vilcashuamán. It is a stepped pyramid, all clad in the most perfect coursed masonry. Leading up to it is a flight of stone steps with a great trapezoidal portal at its foot. On top of the pyramid is a massive rectangular block of stone with two squared seats cut in its top. Cieza de León described it as "a bench where the Lord Inca sat to pray, all of a single [very large] stone...with two seats cut for the aforesaid purpose." But Vilcashuamán apparently had different ushnus for religious and for lay purposes. Cieza goes on to say: "In the middle of the great square was another bench, like that of a theater, where the Lord Inca sat to watch dances and lay feasts."

There are variations of the ushnu platform throughout Peru. On the main trunk road toward Cuzco there is a broad stepped ushnu platform at Curamba (Curapampa), in Chanca territory near Abancay. East of the Apurímac canyon is the platform of Limatambo at Tarahuasi, which was either a temple or ushnu, or both.

24 Manco Inca seated on an ushnu platform.

25 Holy women—mamaconas and acllas—making cloth for the state.

There are plenty of references to ushnus serving purely spiritual purposes—for sacrifices rather than as platforms for proclamations. Cabello de Balboa said that when Huayna Capac visited his new northern city of Tumibamba, he "had erected in the square a structure called usnu or chinquin-pillaca, where sacrifices might be offered to the sun and its different phases, with chicha [maize beer] poured out in its honor." The Indian artist-chronicler Felipe Guaman Poma de Ayala confirmed this use: "The Incas had in their empire special places to make their sacrifices, called usno. These consisted of a stone fixed in the ground that served as a seat from which they invoked their god." And he drew charming pictures of Atahualpa and of Manco seated on top of stepped ushnus when they presided over ceremonies. Cristóbal de Molina said that in the middle of the great square of Cuzco was "a golden usnu which was like a foun-

tain into which they poured a sacrifice of chicha." Bernabé Cobo mentioned another ushnu in Cuzco: a stone in the square where young men being enrolled into the Inca nobility made their first sacrifices. Many chroniclers marveled at this one, as "a pillar of gold where they drank to the sun on the plaza" with a massive stone basin at its foot to take the offerings. (Since it was made of gold, this ushnu pillar was immediately melted down by the conquerors.)

Archaeologists have no trouble finding kallankas or ushnus. But the identification of other standard buildings is far harder. Every provincial capital was thought to have been a microcosm of Cuzco itself. Each therefore had a replica of the sun temple, of the royal Inca palaces, and of the enclosure for mamaconas and acllas dedicated to the service of the Inca and the official religion. The Incas chose girls from all parts of the empire to be acllas. Guaman Poma said

26 In the finest coursed masonry, like this wall of the acllahuasi in Cuzco, the stones are perfectly rectangular, joints are slightly beveled, courses diminish in size as they rise, walls taper and incline inward, and corners are rounded.

that some "belonged to the Incas: they were beautiful and were like maidens destined for the Inca's service... Their sole occupation was to weave cloth for the Inca, of a quality superior to taffeta or silk; they prepared a special rich chicha which was matured for a month...and they also prepared very agreeable meals for the Inca." The most distinguished acllas, daughters of chiefs, sometimes slept with the ruler, or he awarded others as wives to chiefs or officials whom he wished to honor. Chroniclers give differing accounts of the relationship between mamaconas and acllas. The former seemed to Spaniards to correspond to their own nuns—dedicated to religious service for life, vowed to remain chaste, cloistered against the attentions of men, and ruled by a form of mother superior. The young acllas seem to have been entrusted to the care of the more senior and holier mamaconas.

We know which building in Cuzco was the acllahuasi, or house of the acllas. It is between the Jesuit Compañía and the cathedral. Its superb, austere wall of coursed masonry runs along one side of Loreto Street. Cobo was struck by its rows of expertly fitted ashlars, with each row progressively smaller than the one below, and the entire wall battered to slope inward. A curved, heavily rusticated end of this wall juts into the arcade at the side of the Plaza de Armas, and there is another beautiful corner on the opposite, southeastern edge of the complex. Manco Inca's men spared the acllahuasi when they burned the roofs of Cuzco in their attack in May 1536. Garcilaso saw its interior, with one end forbidden to all men, a narrow passage with the holy women's sleeping cells, workshops, and an elaborate series of bins to hold quantities of chicha and food. This acllahuasi was allotted to two conquistadors after the Conquest, but in 1605 it was acquired by the Dominicans and they made it a convent for their nuns of Santa Catalina. Much was leveled during this conversion. The rest reverted to its role as a retreat of holy women. Some of the building is still occupied by nuns and closed to visitors.

In the early days of the Conquest, when Pizarro's men were advancing down the northern coast of Peru, he sent his senior captain Hernando de Soto to lead a reconnaissance into the mountains. Soto's men entered the town of Cajas, on the main highway north of Cajamarca. "There were in that town three houses of cloistered women whom they called mamaconas. When we entered, the women were brought out onto the square and there were over five hundred of them. And the captain [Soto] gave many of these women to the Spaniards"— to the outrage and fury of Inca officials. A few weeks after this disgraceful mass rape of holy women, the Spaniards reached Cajamarca and kidnapped the Inca himself. When Atahualpa was in captivity he was closely attended by his female retainers. Pedro Pizarro and another soldier, Juan Ruiz de Arce, watched with amazement as the women dressed the Inca, held food for him to eat, removed any hairs from his person, and even held out their hands for him

27 The rock shrine of Quillarumi, near Anta, northwest of Cuzco.

to spit into. There are many reports of the dispersal of mamaconas and acllas during the turbulent years of the Conquest. Although we know that each town had such "convents," it is often hard to locate them. One enclosure at Huánuco was almost certainly its acllahuasi: this is enclosed by a high wall with only one entrance, and it was littered with containers for chicha and implements for weaving or cooking.

Other Inca buildings are equally difficult to identify from their ruins. The utensils, decorations, and wall hangings that distinguished important buildings vanished in the first Spanish onslaught. Fine masonry obviously indicates that a structure was for royal or religious use; but it is often hard to be more precise. At Huánuco—the best-preserved provincial town—there is a series of courtyards that clearly led to the quarters used by the Inca or

28 The ruins of Huchuy Cosco, a royal retreat high above Calca in the Yucay valley.

important officials. This enfilade of gates, courts, and buildings is described in chapter 17 about that great ruin.

The treatment of temples and shrines is more obvious. We know the religious importance of a few places from chronicle sources: the Viracocha temple at Raqchi, the coastal shrine Pachacamac, the oracle Saihuite beyond the Apurímac suspension bridge, pilgrimage destinations associated with the origin legend on the Island of the Sun in Lake Titicaca, and Cuzco's sun temple Coricancha. Most of these have chapters in this book. The Incas worshipped natural phenomena, and the most venerated of these might be enclosed in appropriate buildings. At Machu Picchu, for instance, there is no doubt about the religious significance of the rock outcrop surrounded by the curved wall of the torreón [ills. 107–116] or of the elegant inti-huatana ("hitching post of the sun"). The same applies to dozens of springs, caves, waterfalls, mountains, rock formations, and natural landmarks near Cuzco and throughout the empire.

29 The sacred spring of Tambo Machay, above Cuzco, was embellished with fine terraces and niches.

There is another category of Inca monumental site—in addition to Cuzco, administrative centers along the empire's highways, and holy shrines. Within a couple of days' walk from Cuzco is a series of sumptuous royal retreats or estates. As well as a palace in Cuzco, each Inca emperor built rural complexes for his recreation. These remind us of the country palaces of European kings or the dachas of the Soviet Russian elite. The significance of these estates has emerged only in recent decades, through research in chronicles and post-Conquest documents. Like palaces in Cuzco, these retreats were the private property of each Inca. One of their purposes was to supply food and produce (particularly luxuries) for an Inca's court. These estates therefore passed to his descendants, his ayllu or panaca, rather than to the next ruler. After the Conquest there were lawsuits when those clans tried to keep, contest, or regain ownership.

As far as is known, the eighth Inca, Viracocha, built Huchuy Cosco ("Little Cuzco," formerly called Caquia Jaquijahuana) beside the Anta plain north of Cuzco and high above the Vilcanota valley opposite Calca. Viracocha retreated to this crag when the Chanca seemed set to capture Cuzco in the 1440s. According to Cieza de León, he then "ordered palaces built for himself...where he could take his pleasure." It was here that his mummy was discovered by Spanish investigators a century later.

More certain is that the great Pachacuti (r. 1438–71) developed the concept of private estates. Early in his reign he conquered the fertile Vilcanota–Urubamba valley, which was agreeably lower than Cuzco. (This valley is often called Yucay, and to modern tour operators it is "The Sacred Valley." It is watered by the Vilcanota river, which changes its name to Urubamba as it flows northward. There are also towns called Yucay and Urubamba.) Pachacuti defeated a group called Cuyos and himself started a retreat at Pisac. He then conquered the Tampu (or Tambo)—named as one of the four founding tribes of Cuzco. Sarmiento de Gamboa tells us that "He went down the valley of Yucay to a place which is now called [Ollantay]Tambo, eight leagues [39 kilometers or 24 miles] from Cuzco, where he erected some magnificent buildings." Later, when an old man, Pachacuti "finished the edifices at Tambo, and constructed ponds and pleasure houses of Yucay. On a hill near Cuzco he erected some sumptuous houses at a place called Patallacta, and many others in the neighborhood of the capital. He made water channels for use and for pleasure; and he ordered governors of provinces under his rule to build pleasure houses on the most appropriate sites, to be ready for him should he visit their jurisdictions." Cobo said that Patallacta was a place that Pachacuti assigned for sacrifices and in which he died. His next move was to take the forested hills of Vilcabamba, and Machu Picchu was added to his property portfolio. Tambo Machay and Puca Pucará (shown to all visitors, just above Cuzco) were described by Cobo as a house "where he lodged when he went hunting." As we have seen, this great conqueror portrayed himself as a founder of laws and religious rituals and also as a passionate builder. He is said to have measured and planned buildings, working with clay models, and personally supervised their construction. This was in addition to remodeling Cuzco itself. Pachacuti's estates contain many temples, and their sacred areas are often protected by walls and gates, as at Pisac, Ollantaytambo, Machu Picchu, and Puca Pucará.

The tenth ruler, Topa Inca Yupanqui (who overlapped with his father and then reigned alone, 1471–95) created Chinchero 15 kilometers (9 miles) northwest of Cuzco. "He had very rich arrangements for his recreation and ordered extensive gardens to be constructed to supply his household." This was a lovely estate, with land that cascaded down superb terraces from the high plain to a river canyon and up the far side. One chronicler says that Topa Inca loved

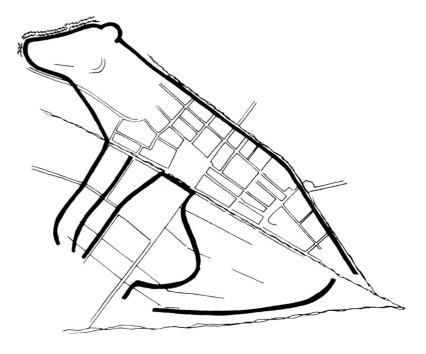

30 A sketch of how Cuzco's plan might have been shaped as a puma.

Chinchero so much that, at the end of his reign, he spent most of his time there with his favorite wife. He also developed the salt pans of Cache (which means "salt") near Maras [ill. 73] and estates at Urcos (at the southern end of the Yucay valley), and Calispuquio beyond the temple-fortress of Sacsahuaman.

The chronicler Juan de Betanzos (who was married to an Inca princess and well informed) tells us that the eleventh Inca Huayna Capac (1498–1527/28) employed 150,000 workers to create a huge estate in a meander of the Vilcanota. This workforce reclaimed swampland, rerouted and channeled the river, leveled hills, and moved a vast quantity of soil into terracing. The resulting palace was Quispihuanca outside Urubamba. Sixteenth-century documents say that this was surrounded by a park and lakes. Garcilaso recalled that its central hall was 6.5 square meters (70 square feet) in plan and open at either end. This was the building whose thatched roof was twelve times a man's height. But this palace complex differed from earlier Inca constructions in its extensive use of pirca and *tapia* (compacted clay) rather than laboriously fitted masonry—perhaps because Huayna Capac did not have the time or manpower for this. As a result, little remains apart from a monumental rectangular enclosing wall pierced by gate towers. This wall was plastered and vividly painted (some paint survives) and inside were huge open-ended kallankas, plazas, and smaller buildings.

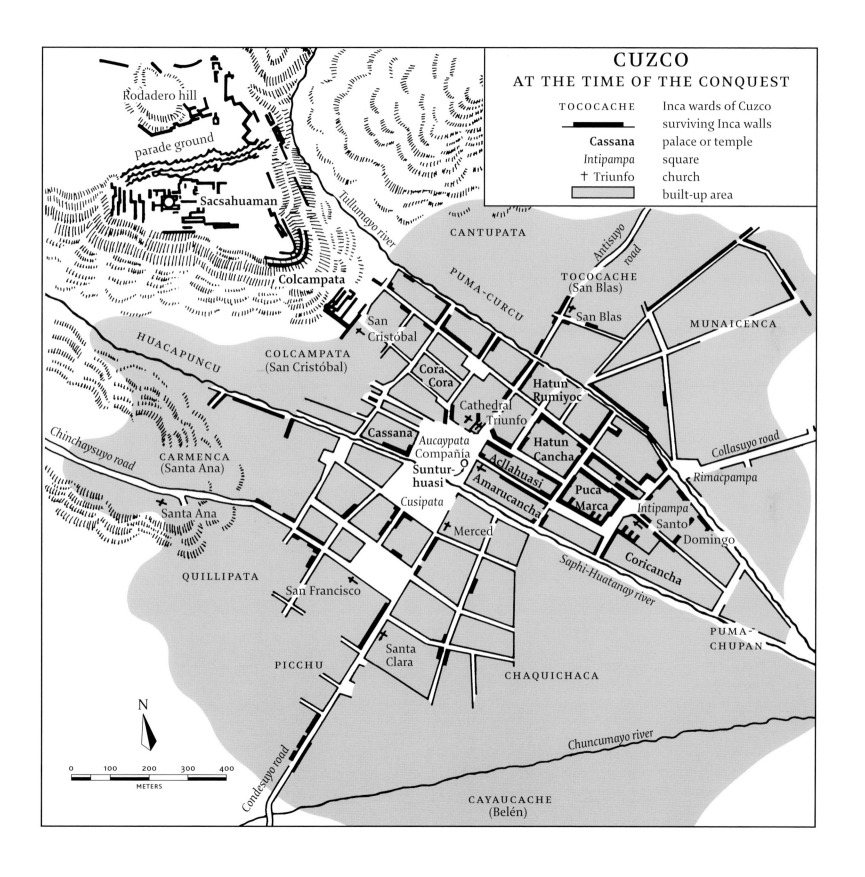

CUZCO
AT THE TIME OF THE CONQUEST

TOCOCACHE — Inca wards of Cuzco
■ — surviving Inca walls
Cassana — palace or temple
Intipampa — square
† Triunfo — church
▨ — built-up area

Rodadero hill

parade ground

Sacsahuaman

Colcampata

Tullumayo river

CANTUPATA

PUMA-CURCU

TOCOCACHE
(San Blas)

San Blas

MUNAICENCA

HUACAPUNCU

San
Cristóbal

COLCAMPATA
(San Cristóbal)

Cora
Cora

**Hatun
Rumiyoc**

Cathedral
Triunfo

Cassana

Aucaypata
Compañía

**Suntur-
huasi**

Cusipata

Acllahuasi

**Hatun
Cancha**

CARMENCA
(Santa Ana)

Chinchaysuyo road

Santa Ana

Amarucancha

**Puca
Marca**

Intipampa
Santo
Domingo

Collasuyo road

Rimacpampa

QUILLIPATA

Merced

Coricancha

Saphi-Huatanay river

San Francisco

PUMA-
CHUPAN

N

Santa
Clara

PICCHU

CHAQUICHACA

0 100 200 300 400
METERS

Condesuyo road

Chuncumayo river

CAYAUCACHE
(Belén)

Antisuyo road

The final Inca, Huascar (1527/28–32), complained that all the best land had been occupied by his predecessors. He did, however, start to build at Calca in the Yucay valley and a palace at Muina (near a lake on the road toward Lake Titicaca). We do not know which Inca constructed other notable sites near Cuzco—Choquequirao, Wiñay Wayna and other ruins along the Inca Trail, and Tipón. Huascar was soon defeated and executed by Atahualpa's generals. His half-brother Manco Inca was crowned by Pizarro in January 1534 but "rebelled" two years later. Manco added to the buildings and defensive wall of Ollantaytambo, partly because he used it as his headquarters during the siege of Cuzco in 1536–37. Manco then retreated to the forested hills of Vilcabamba. When his son Sayri Tupac was lured out of that neo-Inca state in 1557, he was awarded land near the estate of his grandfather, Huayna Capac. He started to build himself a palace there—before being poisoned by a Cañari chief who claimed that the land had been given to him. The tapia wall and gateway of Sayri Tupac's palace still flank the square of Yucay.

In the vision of the chronicler Martín de Murúa, an Inca's palace was as luxurious as the residence of an oriental potentate: "This great palace had two large main gates, one at the entrance to the vestibule and the other farther inside. From [the first] could be seen some of the finest of the celebrated stone masonry. There were two thousand Indian soldiers at this entrance gate, on guard with their captain... Between this gate and the other inner gate there was a vast, extensive courtyard, to which all who accompanied the Inca would enter; but only the Inca himself and his chief noble lords [the four members of his privy council] would enter the second gate. This second gate also had a guard, of Indians native to the city [of Cuzco] and related to the Inca...and near it was the armory and arrow store of the Inca's royal palace... Beyond was another great courtyard or patio for the palace officials and regular servants. They then entered further, to the rooms and chambers in which the Inca lived. All this was full of delights, for they had various arbors and gardens and the lodgings were very large and worked with marvelous skill." Garcilaso de la Vega confirmed that "all the royal palaces had gardens and orchards for the Inca's recreation. They were planted with all sorts of charming and beautiful trees, beds of flowers and...herbs found in Peru. They also made gold and silver replicas of many trees and lesser plants...done life-size, with all their leaves, blossoms and fruits," as well as models of maize fields, animals, birds, and reptiles. "The buildings of their palaces, temples, gardens and baths were extraordinarily uniform. They were of beautifully cut masonry, with each stone so perfectly fitted to its neighbors that there was no space for mortar."

Guaman Poma listed a variety of "royal courts, palaces, houses or lodgings that belonged to the Inca, as a dwelling place or for the functions and activities appropriate to his government." There was the *cuyus-manco*, the royal palace itself, within which were the private apartments, *quinco-huasi*. The suntur-huasi was "a round house, lodging of the Inca." Special buildings, each with its own name, served as reception for visitors, as a dormitory, for storage, for chicha preparation, for servants, and for the poor. The only rural estates that have ruins of residential palaces as we understand them were Pachacuti's Q'ellu Raqay at Ollantaytambo, possibly Topa Inca's at Chinchero, and Huayna Capac's Quispihuanca.

Almost all royal retreats have a great quantity of terracing, irrigation channels, and cascades of baths. The terraces were brilliantly engineered, with stout retaining walls and layers of different soils and gravel to maximize drainage. All this was to grow special crops, particularly maize for the mildly alcoholic chicha that was so important in Inca sacrifices, ceremonies, and celebrations. Terracing, of course, made steep land productive and tamed hillsides against erosion. But the terracing at royal estates is exceptionally elegant, beautifully fitted to the topography: it looks like the layers of a modern architect's model. The flights of terraces along the Urubamba demonstrated each Inca's power to marshal a great workforce to control nature. They often surpass mere utility, and become works of art.

The main square of Cuzco was surrounded by the palaces of the Inca rulers. Even Pizarro's pedantic secretary Pedro Sancho was impressed. He wrote that "the city of Cuzco...is large and beautiful enough to be remarkable, even in Spain. It is full of the palaces of nobles, for no poor people live there. Each ruler builds himself a palace and so do all the chiefs. The square is rectangular and is generally flat and paved with gravel. The palaces of four rulers lie around it and these are the most important buildings in the city, built of ashlars and painted. The finest is that of the former Inca Huayna-Capac. It has a gateway of red, white and multicolored marble, and has other flat-roofed structures that are also most remarkable." Pizarro's other secretary, Miguel de Estete, described this as "a rich gateway faced with pieces of silver and other metals." Pedro Pizarro recalled that "this Cassana had two towers, one at each side of the gate... These towers were of finely worked and very strong masonry. They were round and roofed in thatch that was laid very skillfully—the eaves of the thatch projected from the wall for an arm's length so that when it rained they sheltered horsemen... The Indian warriors set fire to these towers with burning arrows or stones when they besieged [Cuzco in 1536]. [They] contained so much thatch that they took eight days or more to burn—that is, until the timbers fell. Those towers were closed on top, with heavy beams placed above and earth on top of these, like *azoteas* [ornamental tiles]."

Garcilaso de la Vega remembered being awed by this palace when he was a boy in the 1540s: "The largest [hall in Cuzco] was that of Cassana, which was capable of holding three thousand people. It seems incredible that timber

PALACIOSREALES
INCAPVACICVTVSMA·

could have been found to cover such vast halls." The name Cassana meant "something to freeze." As Garcilaso explained, "The name was given to it out of wonder, implying that the buildings in it were so large and splendid that anyone who gazed on them attentively would be frozen with astonishment." It was so big that sixty mounted Spaniards could joust in it. Pedro Pizarro said that this "very large hall" had an open end-wall "from which the entire interior could be seen: its doorway is so wide that it extends from wall to wall and is open up to the roof."

When the conquerors partitioned Cuzco among themselves, Governor Francisco Pizarro took Cassana. Then in 1537, when Pizarro's former partner Diego de Almagro tried to claim the city, two Pizarro brothers were lodged there. Almagro had his men set fire to the hall's great roof, so that Hernando Pizarro had to flee as the flaming thatch fell. He then blocked the windows in one of Cassana's towers so that it could be a prison for Hernando and Gonzalo Pizarro and their young cousin Pedro. When the tide turned and Hernando won the ensuing civil war, he briefly imprisoned Almagro there in 1538 before executing him. A decade later, Garcilaso "saw the hall destroyed, and modern shops with doorways for merchants and craftsmen built in the Cassana." The Spaniards were turning half of the Inca's great central space into a Plaza de Armas surrounded by arcades. Such a square is the hallmark of a Spanish town—and it remains the hub of Cuzco to this day. The earthquake of May 1950 revealed stretches of Cassana's beautiful pale gray walls: these can be seen inside a restaurant and some shops.

Across the square from Cassana lay Amarucancha ("enclosure of the snake"), possibly the palace of Huascar, who reigned briefly before defeat by Atahualpa's generals. Garcilaso recalled a fine round tower that stood in front of Amarucancha, but "I saw no other remains of this palace: all the rest had been razed." The round tower's walls were four times the height of a man, "but its roof, made of the excellent timber they used for their royal palaces, was so high that I could say without exaggeration that it equaled in height any tower in Spain, apart from the [Giralda] in Seville. Its roof was rounded like the walls, and above it, in place of a weather vane..., it had a very tall, thick pole that enhanced its height and beauty. It was over sixty feet [18 meters] high inside and was known as Suntur-huasi, 'excellent house or lodging.'" This lovely isolated tower fell victim to a Spanish town planner, for it projected into the main square, and the Spaniards liked their plazas to be unobstructed. Garcilaso commented that with "its great beauty, it would have been well if the conquerors had preserved it." This palace also had a fine kallanka, though not as large as Cassana's. At the Conquest, the Amarucancha complex was awarded to Hernando de Soto and some other conquistadors. When Soto left Peru it passed to Hernando Pizarro, who later sold it to the Jesuits. This is why their lovely Compañía church is now on that side of the plaza; but behind it is a yard with stretches of superb Inca niches.

Other kallankas in Cuzco included Cora Cora (possibly on the site of the cathedral), a place fiercely fought over during Manco's siege. On the slope above was that of Colcampata, occupied by the post-Conquest puppet Paullu Inca. Paullu was christened as Cristóbal, and he turned his kallanka into a church of that name.

As we have seen, each Inca's palace in Cuzco and country estates did not pass to the next ruler. They were, instead, preserved as their builder's spiritual resting-place. As Cobo explained, "When the king died, the prince did not inherit his palace and fortune: it was left, together with the body of the deceased, to the clan he had founded. The entire estate was dedicated to the cult of his body and the support of his family. The clan embalmed the body of its royal father and preserved it together with all its belongings and ornaments." Each Inca also had houses and fields throughout the empire, and these were also kept intact after his death. The authors of a report on Inca government, written in Chincha in 1558, said that Inca emperors "considered it to be a point of honor not to take over or use a woman, field or servant or anything else that had belonged to their parents: instead, these had to be preserved in all the valleys [of the empire]. Had the Christians' [invasion of Peru] occurred later, all the fields and women and Indians would have belonged to the Sun [religion] and the Incas."

Pedro Pizarro tells us that when he reached Cuzco in 1533, it was full of people who "served these dead rulers. Every day they brought them all out onto the square, seated in a circle, each according to his antiquity. All the male and female attendants ate and drank there" with offerings to the dead Incas. This ancestor worship meant that every palace in Cuzco was intact when the Spaniards arrived. Nothing was hidden from grave-robbers: the Incas were too confident in the security of their empire and the honesty of its citizens. There is thus no hope of a discovery in Peru of a Tutankhamun's tomb.

Other Incas had other palaces in Cuzco. One of the early rulers, Inca Roca, built Cora Cora at the northern corner of the square. During Manco Inca's siege of Cuzco, Cora Cora was a strategic bastion captured by the Indians after a stiff resistance. Viracocha Inca may have used the Quishuar-cancha enclosure at the eastern end of the square; it later became a temple of the creator god, Viracocha, and was awarded to the Catholic Church after the Conquest as a site for the cathedral. One theory is that, unusually, Quishuar-cancha was a palace occupied by successive living Incas. Pachacuti's son, the great conqueror Topa Inca Yupanqui, may have had the Pucamarca palace, a short distance to the southeast of the square. Huascar probably improved Amarucancha, but he also built Colcampata on the hillside below Sacsahuaman. This palace

33 Qollqas (storehouses). Seated on the right is an administrator holding a quipu, the Inca abacus.

was later occupied by Paullu Inca, and something survives of its terrace and a short stretch of freestanding wall above. The Act of Foundation of Cuzco (as a Spanish town), which divided it among its conquerors, also mentioned a palace that young Manco Inca was building for himself on the terraces above the main square.

There was one type of building that was both functional and highly distinctive. Cobo noted that "great storehouses and granaries, which the Indians call qollqas, were built on the Inca's orders throughout the provinces of Peru. They stored and preserved the tribute and wealth of the crown and church in these... They generally built these depots or stores outside populated areas, in high, cool and airy locations, near the royal road. We see their ruins today around towns, on the crests and slopes of mountains. They consisted of many square buildings as small as ordinary rooms, set in a line like little towers, very neatly and symmetrically and spaced two or three yards [2–3 meters] apart from one another... The lines [of storehouses] sometimes consisted of twenty, thirty, fifty or more chambers. Since they were in high locations and arranged symmetrically they look admirable—for their walls are still visible today, and in some places they are standing in such perfect condition that only the roofs are missing." Cobo explained that the high, isolated locations were to protect stored goods from damp, and the spacing was to save a line of storehouses from burning if one caught fire.

These storehouses were the embodiment of the Incas' elaborate system of tribute; they were the key to their military triumphs; and they were the basis of a highly successful welfare state. Vast quantities of foodstuffs, weapons, cloth, and manufactured goods were produced by the empire's tribute payers. Some storehouses were reserved for the state religion, for sacrifices, offerings, and support of the temple attendants. Other stores held the Inca's personal tribute—cloth, precious objects, and fine chicha that the sovereign used to enhance the luxury of his estate or gave to deserving subjects—and there were also stores of food for distribution among the provinces and as insurance against bad harvests.

Bernabé Cobo explained that, apart from luxury goods, the Inca's storehouses "supported all the servants of the royal palace and of the mummies of the dead Incas. They provided food for the Inca and his relatives and attendant lords. They also supplied the garrisons, patrols and fighting men, who received no pay apart from food and clothing—each soldier was paid with two sets of clothing each year. The Inca would also grant chiefs permission to distribute part of the cloth and food in the stores in their districts to keep their subjects contented... Once a province had enough for its own needs [the Inca] provided for the requirements of other districts. Supplies were thus taken from one province to another—they often transported stores from the plains to the mountains and in the opposite direction. They took great care over this. It was done so systematically and efficiently that there was no lack in any area and none suffered want, even in lean years... Whatever was left over or not needed was kept in storehouses for a time of need. There was always quite enough when such times occurred: for they sometimes stored food for ten or twelve years." There was careful control of stocks in the storehouses, for although the Incas had no writing they had quipus. These highly efficient mnemonic devices consisted of knotted strings and functioned like abacuses to record units of measurement.

The complex of Inca storehouses may sound fanciful and utopian, but it was very real. Nothing had prepared the first Spaniards for the quantity of goods they found in Cuzco. Pedro Sancho described "storehouses full of cloaks, wool, weapons, metal, cloth and all the other goods that are grown or manufactured in this country. There are shields, leather bucklers, beams for roofing the houses, knives and other tools, sandals and breastplates to equip the soldiers. All was in such vast quantities that it is hard to imagine how the natives can ever have paid such immense tribute of so many items." The young Pedro Pizarro was equally amazed: "There was a great quantity of storehouses in Cuzco when we entered the city, filled with very delicate cloth and with other coarser cloths; and stores of tools, of foodstuffs, and of coca." But what struck him most were "deposits of iridescent feathers, some looking like fine gold and others of a shining golden-green color... Quantities of them were threaded together on fine thread and were skillfully attached to agave fibers to form pieces of cloth over a span in length. These were all stored in leather chests."

Guaman Poma recorded foodstuffs kept in other parts of the empire: "In the region of the Collas [around Lake Titicaca] they stored chuño frozen, dried potatoes; moraya cooked and dried potatoes; caya cooked and frozen oca [a sorrel tuber]; dried meat; and wool for weaving... In all parts of the kingdom they stored maize, sweet potatoes, chili peppers, cotton, maxno which was a fiber for dyeing wool, coca, and rumo which consisted of various foods specially treated for conservation and which could be eaten without prior cooking." Cobo spoke of jerked meat of llamas, vicuñas or deer, deposits of "different types of cloth—woolen, cotton and of plumage—sandals that they call ojotas, and weapons of the types used in each different province." Cieza de León often described qollqas full of weapons, cloth, and food, at such provincial cities as Tumibamba, Jauja, and at Vilcashuamán where there were 700 of them: "When the lord [Inca] was lodged in his dwellings and his soldiers garrisoned there, nothing, from the most important to the most trifling item, could not be provided."

The conquerors rapidly squandered these treasures, particularly in their succession of civil wars. Sixteen years after the first conquest, a royal army was

34 The northern half of Machu Picchu: Bingham's "industrial sector" and "prison group."

suppressing a rebellion by Pizarro's youngest brother, Gonzalo, and was quartered in the Jauja valley of central Peru. Cobo wrote: "Even though it waited there for seven months, supplies for the camp did not run out throughout this period. The reason was that there were many years' worth of produce stored in the depots: over 500,000 *hanegas* [800,000 bushels] of foodstuffs."

The chroniclers' accounts have been amply corroborated in archaeological remains. There are clusters of qollqa storehouses all over Peru. I recall seeing a particularly fine row of them on a bare hillside below the remote pre-Inca ruins of Tantamayo near the canyon of the upper Marañón, another set on a hill above Jauja, and six uniform rectangular huts on a steep hillside at Pisac, and others around Lake Titicaca. A sloping hillside near the flat expanse of ruins of Huánuco is covered in rows of huts that were clearly qollqas. Huánuco's American archaeologist Craig Morris in 1965 counted 497 storehouses and excavated 120 of them. He noted that they were divided into "functionally specialized sets devoted to the storage of various products." An isolated site called Cotapachi, near Cochabamba in Bolivia, has no fewer than 2,400 qollqas. Since there was no large town nearby, this was evidently a center for storage or redistribution of tribute produce. The qollqas at Cotapachi are all round and 3 meters (10 feet) in diameter, spaced 5.15 meters (17 feet) from one another in their rows, and with the rows themselves 9.5 meters (31 feet) apart. Such accurate measurements were an impressive example of Inca engineering skill; and the military precision of the qollqas' formation was typical of Inca administrative efficiency. Guaman Poma has a fine drawing of rectangular qollqas with conical thatched roofs. We shall see, in the chapter on Ollantaytambo, that these storehouses could have ingenious systems of ducting, under the floor and near the roof, to keep perishables like maize ventilated.

These tidy rows of storage huts are tangible evidence of the Incas' administrative brilliance. Hillsides neatly contoured with banks of agricultural terraces, stone-lined water culverts, and roads leading to all-important bridges all demonstrate the same engineering skill. The Inca empire was a network. A web of roads, *tambo* post-houses, and administrative centers radiated from Cuzco, the navel of the four quarters of Tawantinsuyu. Inca architecture responded to this pattern of expansion and imperial government. There were different requirements and different solutions in each zone of the empire: the imperial court at Cuzco and its adjacent rural estates; the surrounding Inca heartland; and great swathes of subject territory, ruled from provincial centers, and ranging from the Andes down to rich valleys of the coastal desert and endless tropical forests of the Amazon.

We know that the Incas mobilized vast squads of laborers to build so much in so short a time. We also know that the astonishing Inca masonry was simply the product of innumerable man-days of patient labor. What we do not know is the spirit in which the labor was performed, the relationship between the Inca state and its subjects. The attitude of Inca stonemasons doubtless ranged from pride inspired by adulation of the emperor-deity to the sullenness of forced labor based on fear. The chronicles and the behavior of Inca subjects during the collapse of Inca rule leave no doubt about the worship of the Inca ruler. Even the highest officials trembled and humbled themselves in the presence of the Inca; every pronouncement by the Inca was obeyed as the word of a divine oracle; and every aspect of the Inca's daily life was of the highest conceivable standard of excellence—his food, clothing, ornaments, servants, women, and of course his buildings.

In contrast to the obedience of the most loyal subjects was the unenthusiastic performance of conquered tribes recently coerced into the Inca empire. There were major revolts during the reigns of Pachacuti and all later Incas. Tribes that had been defeated by Inca armies were understandably the first to side with the Spanish conquerors—the Cañari of southern Ecuador, Chachapoya of northeastern Peru, Huanca and Chanca of central Peru, and Colla of Titicaca. The Incas dominated such rebellious regions by planting pockets of loyal settlers (called *mitimaes*) in their midst. A chief of Huancané on the north shore of Lake Titicaca testified, after the Conquest, that "the Inca Huayna Capac settled one thousand weavers...and one hundred potters...as mitimaes on our lands. Although their presence did us great damage, our ancestors did not dare resist the will of the Inca because they were so afraid of the tyrant."

Although we know that parts of the Inca empire were held down by force, there is remarkably little archaeological evidence of this. There were rudimentary defensive walls at Ollantaytambo and Pisac and a dry moat at Machu Picchu; but most Inca towns had no defenses of any sort. The great bastion of Sacsahuaman above Cuzco was built as a temple and storage area rather than a fortress and, surprisingly, it was not reproduced in other parts of the empire. Military control relied on the rapid movement of armies and their supply from the network of storage depots. During excavations of the important provincial center Huánuco, almost nothing was found to indicate a military presence.

It is difficult to determine the Incas' attitude to landscape. They were an agricultural people, with monthly festivals closely related to the farming seasons. Each age group of Inca subjects had appointed tasks closely related to the land and its produce. Inca religion was intimately based on nature: celestial phenomena—the sun, moon, stars, thunder, lightning, and rainbows—were all worshipped. Such humble natural features as rock outcrops, springs, caves, rivers, or mountains had powerful superstitious or spiritual significance. One infuriated Catholic priest explained that "this can be seen in the prayers they used to say when they knelt or prostrated themselves or stood still in some natural shrine. For they were not speaking to the hill, spring, river or cave, but to the great [creator god] Illa Tici Viracocha. They said that he existed in heaven and invisibly in that place. This was a very common practice among the Peruvians. They had different names for these natural shrines, calling passes *apachitas*, caves *huacas*, hills *urcos*, springs *pucyu*, and the heavens *hua-hua pacha*. They did not revere all hills and mountains, all springs and rivers, but only those which had some peculiarity worthy of special consideration, and these they held to be sacred places... The Peruvians frequently venerated such a natural shrine without building any edifice; but they often made a stone altar, called *usno*, in such places for their sacrifices."

Inca architects were therefore in close spiritual harmony with the land. Does this mean that they admired natural beauty? To modern visitors, much of the thrill of Inca architecture derives from its setting in spectacular land-scape. Chronicle sources give no clue as to whether the Incas themselves shared that aesthetic awareness—whether they chose locations because of their vistas or natural background. Pachacuti's palace near the river in Ollantaytambo has breathtaking views of the snows of Mount Verónica (Wakay Willka). Pilco Caima "palace" on the Island of the Sun has a lovely view across Lake Titicaca. And at Wiñay Wayna, the last site on the Inca Trail before Machu Picchu, a visitor reaches the end house of a group below its cascade of baths and is confronted by a window (quite rare in Inca buildings) through which is framed a Wagnerian waterfall! This was doubtless because water and falls were venerated. But Jean-Pierre Protzen is sure that it was also to delight in its beauty.

There may possibly have been a connection between the purpose of an Inca site and its topographical setting. The ruins of royal estates at Choquequirao, Pisac, Ollantaytambo, and Machu Picchu are on ridges projecting from slopes and with stunning views. Such dramatic locations probably had religious sig-nificance connected to sacred mountains. And we must remember that the Incas were mountain people, physically adapted to high altitude and unfazed by climb-ing giddy slopes. Some royal palaces—Vitcos or Huchuy Cosco—were on similar mountain spurs. Most provincial centers were, however, built in more familiar peasant locations: at the edges of fertile valleys. Quito, Tumibamba, Cajamarca, Huamachuco, Huánuco, Pumpu, Jauja, Chucuito, and Cuzco itself are all in or open onto valleys. This was the natural site for an agricultural community: close to its pastures and fields, but consuming as little flat land as possible.

It is just as difficult to tell whether the Incas appreciated aesthetic detail in their buildings as to sense their awareness of beautiful landscape. They wasted no time on decorative embellishments such as pilasters, carvings, cornices, and moldings. Pre-Inca civilizations on the Peruvian coast had covered their buildings with intricate frescoes, elaborate latticework, and sculpted ornaments, and often with painting. The Incas were too austere or too sophisticated for such obvious decoration—apart from some painting on plastered tapia or adobe walls. (The few Inca buildings in Cuzco that have snakes or pumas carved in relief on their stonework probably date from after the fall of the Inca empire, a time when masons could indulge their fancies free of official restriction.) As Humboldt noted, the Inca state imposed norms of simple, standardized plans and technology.

Unanswered questions remain. In an architecture so restrained in decora-tive elements, why was such attention lavished on the shaping and fitting of stones? Why incorporate huge blocks into terrace walls, or devote so much labor to achieving perfect interlocking of masonry joints? This was an official aesthetic, perhaps intended to proclaim the state's success in mobilizing great reserves of manpower. It was doubtless also the product of patriotic and pious devotion, a desire to build in the finest conceivable techniques for semidivine rulers and their official religion.

Whatever the motives, there is no question about the beauty of Inca architecture. It impressed sixteenth-century soldiers and ecclesiastics, and it delights modern observers more conditioned to appreciate simple and functional architecture. We are thrilled by countersunk joints, from delicate indentations on the walls of Coricancha to sharp rustication of the terracing of Colcampata or Tarahuasi. The pairs of projecting bosses, the subtle entasis on the curved wall of Coricancha, the perfectly graded coursing on the wall of the Cuzco acllahuasi, or the rounded ends of the ashlars where that wall reaches the main square, the angular sculpture of the holy caves, the "treas-ury" or the inti-huatana at Machu Picchu, crisp corners of buildings in Pisac or double-jambed gates and the "wall of the six monoliths" in Ollantaytambo, hillsides contoured with flights of terracing, the dramatic location of so many Inca buildings—these are just a few monumental features with beauty far beyond functional explanation. We can therefore enjoy the excellence of surviving Inca buildings, ponder the many questions they raise, and admire the vanished civilization that achieved so much in so short a time.

35 The shape of the "sacred rock," at the northern end of Machu Picchu, echoes that of Mount Yanantin beyond.

36 The precinct around the "sacred rock" on the Island of the Sun contained lodgings of priests and holy mamaconas, storehouses, and this avenue of niches that may have held sacred idols.

2. Island of the Sun

IN THE INCA CREATION LEGEND, there was a flood similar to that of the Old Testament. The creator god Viracocha flooded the land in order to destroy the first iniquitous race of men. "When the flood had passed and the land was dry, Viracocha decided to people it again. To make it more perfect, he decided to create luminaries to give it light. With this purpose, he went with his servants to a great lake in the Collao in which there is an island called Titicaca, which means 'Rock of Lead.' Viracocha went to this island and duly ordered that the sun, moon and stars should emerge and be set in the heavens to give light to the world; and so it was." It was said that after the darkness of the flood "the sun rose one morning with extraordinary brilliance from a rock on the island of Titicaca; and those who lived there believed that that spur of rock was the true house or lodging of the sun. They therefore built and dedicated a temple there that was sumptuous for that age." Juan de Betanzos commented on confusion in the creation legend: "Sometimes they hold the Sun up as the creator, and other times they say it is Viracocha. Generally, in all the land...the devil has them confused."

Manco Capac, the legendary founder of the Inca people, claimed this sacred Island of the Sun as his own birthplace. He invented the "fable that he and his wife were children of the Sun, and that their father had placed them on that island so that they should go about the land teaching the people." The mysterious island in Lake Titicaca thus emerges, in different legends, as the place of origin of the sun, of Viracocha, of all mankind, and of the Inca royal dynasty in particular.

The sky above Lake Titicaca has the intense blue of high altitude, for at 3,810 meters (12,500 feet) above sea level this is the highest navigable lake in the world. Boats and hydrofoils now ply its 171-kilometer (106-mile) length. The azure sky makes the water dark blue, and on a bright day the Island of the Sun looks Aegean, with its imported eucalyptuses and cypresses, and its swifts and dung beetles. But it is too high to maintain this illusion for long. Clouds race across from the surrounding Andes, and a chill wind whips the lake waters in a dangerous squall. The lake can suddenly become bleak and forbidding with choppy white-horse waves.

The Island of the Sun is almost 10 kilometers (6 miles) long, with its steep hills rising far above the waters of the lake. There is an Inca fountain at a wooded landing stage on the north shore, with a flight of steps and cascading water channels on the slope above. From the ridge along the bare spine of the island, a visitor looks down on fishing hamlets far below. There are llamas and alpacas on the terraced slopes, and Aymara shepherds play reed pipes. To the east, 5 kilometers (3 miles) across the water, rises Coati, the smaller Island of the Moon.

Cobo said that it was the tenth ruler, Topa Inca Yupanqui, who decided to build on the islands of Lake Titicaca. Local Indians told him about the divinity of their shrine, which commemorated both the appearance of the sun after the flood and the creation of the Inca tribe. The Inca was sufficiently impressed to take the shrine under his personal protection. "He was delighted to have found a place well suited to encourage worship and respect for the Sun among his subjects: for...the Incas greatly prided themselves on being descendants and worshippers of the Sun. Being well satisfied with the shrine, he determined to use all his energy, efforts and power to cause it to be venerated in all earnestness. He considered this an undertaking worthy of his great majesty." The Inca himself fasted and approached the holiest part, the "sacred rock," barefoot. All this was intended to enhance the sanctity of the shrine. "The Inca had many buildings built...to enlarge and add to the prestige of the shrine. He added magnificent new structures to the ancient temple, and ordered others built for other services: a nunnery of mamaconas, for instance; many splendid rooms and chambers for the lodgings of the priests and ministers; and a sumptuous tambo or hostel as accommodation for pilgrims, a quarter of a league before reaching the temple. He built great storehouses of food, clothing and other provisions for the pilgrims' route, around [the nearby peninsula of] Copacabana. The ruins of these survive today and I [Cobo] have seen them." (Father Cobo was at the Jesuit seminary on the edge of the lake at Juli, and visited the islands in 1615. The ruins were also described by Cieza de León, who was there in 1549, and by Alonso Ramos Gavilán, who lived in nearby Copacabana, in 1618.)

The incorporation of the Island of the Sun into Inca religion was a political masterstroke. The American archaeologists Charles Stanish and Brian Bauer made a very thorough survey of the island in the 1990s and confirmed that it had been a sacred place in the Tiahuanaco polity—which spread across the Andean highlands in the first millennium AD—and was further developed

37 The finest cloth covered the convex side of the "sacred rock."

38 The concave face of the "sacred rock" was plated in gold.

as a shrine during the "Altiplano period" from the collapse of Tiahuanaco in about 1100 to the rise of the Incas. That was a turbulent time, when the dominant Aymara-speaking peoples were contesting this region—the Lupaca on the southern shores of the lake, and the Colla to the north with a capital at Hatuncolla and mortuary complex at Sillustani (near Puno).

Stanish and Bauer admired how Topa Inca (or, according to some chroniclers, his father Pachacuti) achieved three objectives by enhancing this shrine. This merged the Viracocha creation legend with the origins of the Inca people, and also facilitated control of this prosperous region by adopting one of its holiest places. As they wrote, "Rather than simply explaining the origin of the heavenly bodies, the Lake Titicaca origin myth is transformed to explain how the first Inka (analogous to the sun) and his sister/wife (analogous to the moon) emerged from the island. In other words, Inka intellectuals successfully linked the ruling elite of Cusco with that of the principal shrine of one of their most important highland provinces... The Islands of the Sun and Moon became the ideological beachhead of Inka expansion to the south."

As Cobo and others explained, the Inca also made this sacred place a destination of state-controlled pilgrimage. It became on a par with two other great pilgrimage sites in the Inca empire: the sun temple Coricancha in Cuzco, and Pachacamac on the coastal desert south of modern Lima (another earlier shrine that the Incas astutely co-opted into their own creed). Pilgrims traveled to the Island of the Sun from all over the highland parts of the empire Tawantinsuyu.

The Copacabana peninsula, near the southwestern corner of Lake Titicaca, was barred at its narrowest neck, Yunguyo, by a wall and a gate at which guards checked pilgrims' credentials. (By coincidence, this is still a checkpoint in the frontier between Peru and Bolivia.) Cobo said that the pilgrims advanced along the peninsula to Copacabana, where they were made to give offerings and suffer penances before being allowed to sail to the island on reed boats. Excavations here revealed remains of extensive Inca buildings and pottery. (By another coincidence—or deliberate church policy—Copacabana remains one of South America's main Christian pilgrimage sites, attracting thousands of Aymara and Quechua worshippers.) The ancient pilgrims then crossed 2 kilometers (1.2 miles) of lake to the southeastern tip of the Island of the Sun.

Archaeologists (Bauer, Stanish, the Bolivian Carlos Ponce Sangines, Johan Reinhard and, long before them, Ernst Middendorf, Adolph Bandelier, and others) have identified the pilgrims' landing stage and all the other sites that chroniclers mentioned on the small island. They found a huge Inca presence. There were over sixty sites—villages, hamlets, agricultural terracing, small platforms that may have been for pilgrims' offerings, and of course the temple complex.

Close to the landing stage is the best-preserved building on the Island of the Sun: the "palace" of Pilco Caima. Curiously, none of the chroniclers mentioned Pilco Caima and its function is unknown. The structure is unusual in three respects: it is a freestanding complex of a dozen chambers and

39 A structure near the sun temple, possibly the base of a solar solstice marker.

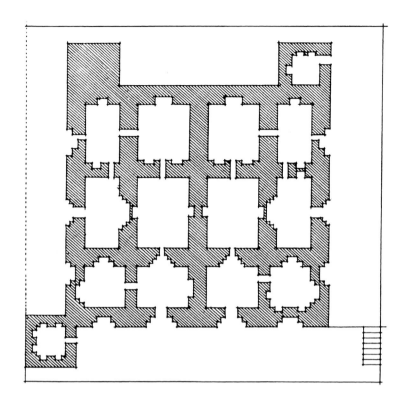

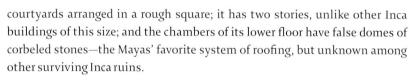

40 The diligent American traveler George Squier in 1877 made a passable plan of the "palace" of Pilco Caima at the southeastern end of the island.

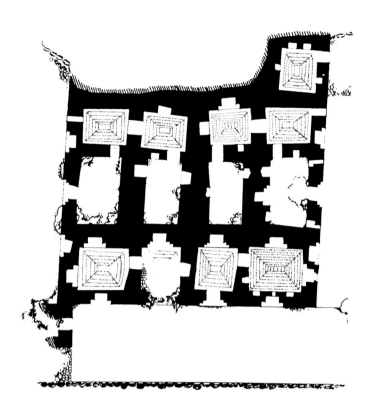

41 The true plan, as drawn by Bolivian architectural students a century later. Note the corbeled false domes.

courtyards arranged in a rough square; it has two stories, unlike other Inca buildings of this size; and the chambers of its lower floor have false domes of corbeled stones—the Mayas' favorite system of roofing, but unknown among other surviving Inca ruins.

Squier made a fine drawing of Pilco Caima, which shows that its upper floor has crumbled considerably during the century-and-a-half since his visit. He also produced tidy plans that made Pilco Caima look like a symmetrical Renaissance palace; Gasparini and Margolies published an exact plan, drawn by architectural students from La Paz, which shows that the chambers, passages, and niches of the Inca palace were not quite so regular or rectilinear. The American traveler noticed that some walls of Pilco Caima still retained patches of stucco and deduced that "the building was originally yellow, while the inner parts and moldings of the doorways and niches were of different shades of red."

What impressed Squier most was a terrace or esplanade facing the lake in the center of the second story. Its rear wall had traces of niches, arranged as

benches for anyone wishing to sit and admire the magnificent panorama. To Squier, this prospect is "one of the finest and most extensive in the world. The waves of the lake break at your very feet. To the right is the high and diversified peninsula of Copacabana, in the center of the view, the island of Coati, consecrated to the Moon...and to the left, the gleaming [mountain] Illampu, its white mantle reflected in the waters that spread out like a sea in front." This balcony, so clearly built to enjoy the view, convinced Squier that the Incas "were not deficient in taste or insensible to the grand and beautiful in nature."

Once on the island, pilgrims walked the 7 kilometers (4.3 miles) to the sacred area at the northwestern end. They could either take a lakeside road, past fishing and farming villages, or more probably climbed to a ridge that runs along the spine of the island. As they progressed, they passed various gates and places for offerings on the approach to the holy area. They could not advance beyond a gate known as Intipunku ("gate of the sun"), but observed the "sacred rock" from here. This final gate was covered in tiny, iridescent humming-bird feathers.

The "sacred rock," known as Titikala, is now just an outcrop of reddish sandstone; but it retains a powerful aura of sanctity. Squier was awed by its wild location: "At almost the very northern end of the island, at its most repulsive and unpromising part…where the soil is rocky and bare and the cliffs ragged and broken—high up, where the fret of the waves of the lake is scarcely heard and where the eye ranges over the broad blue waters from one mountain barrier to the other…is the spot most celebrated and most sacred of Peru. Here is the rock on which it was believed no bird would light or animal venture, on which no human being dared to place his foot; whence the sun rose to dispel the primal vapors and illume the world."

Two-and-a-half centuries before Squier, the Jesuit Father Cobo described the site in sufficient detail to guide modern visitors: "The rock that was so greatly venerated lay in the open… Its concave part, which is what was worshipped, is insignificant; but the altar to the sun was inside it. The convex portion is a rock outcrop whose sides fall to the water of an inlet that the lake makes there. The rock's decoration consisted of covering its convex face in a curtain of the finest and most delicate cumbi cloth ever seen; while the concave part was covered in plates of gold. A round basin-shaped stone can be seen in front of the rock. It is admirably cut, the size of an average millstone, with an orifice—which now holds the foot of a cross!—into which chicha was poured for the sun to drink.

"The temple was to the east, some forty yards [37 meters] from the rock. Images of thunder and of the other gods of the Incas were worshiped here together with that of the sun. Many idols were placed in windows, recesses and niches along its walls: some of these had human shapes, some were of llamas, others of birds or other animals, and all were made of copper, silver or gold, large and small in size. The ruins of the storehouses of the sun can still be seen near the temple, with chambers resembling the labyrinth of Crete. From the walls and remains still standing today, one is struck by the excellence of the whole of the building of this idolatrous shrine.

"To one side of the [Intipunku] gateway can be seen buildings which the Indians say were the lodgings of the ministers and servants of the temple. On the other side are traces of a large building which was the convent of the mamaconas, the women dedicated to the sun, who served it by making the beverages and curious cloths that were consumed in the ministry of the shrine. This house of the mamaconas was on the best location in the island."

The buildings around the "sacred rock" survive. The labyrinth of storehouses, called Chinkana, is on the southern slope of a gully that looks westward toward the Peruvian shore of Lake Titicaca. On the other side of the island is the compound of the mamaconas. Ramos Gavilán said that the last paramount Inca, Huayna Capac, sent two of his daughters to serve as holy women here. The path leading to the sacred promontory passes by another outcrop of rock. This contains eroded cavities, observed by Cobo, Squier, and Middendorf, that look like giant footprints. Ever since Inca times, treasure-seekers have hacked at this temple complex. The French oceanographer Jacques-Yves Cousteau sought the temple's treasure in a diving expedition below the promontory: this found thousands of frogs but no Inca gold. In 1991 the American archaeologist Johan Reinhard also dived into the lake, off an islet called Koa, and did discover remains of Inca and pre-Inca ceremonials. His finds are in a small museum at the site.

Elaborate rituals took place on the holy islands. Cobo told how in one ceremony the priests of the Island of the Sun saluted those of nearby Coati, the Island of the Moon: "A great many rafts were employed in this service, going back and forth between the islands. To make the representation more lifelike, the chief priest was prepared in one shrine to represent the person of the Sun, and an Indian girl in the other performed as the figure of the Moon. They drank to one another and the girl who represented the Moon caressed the man acting the Sun and begged him, with endearments, to shine out brightly and calmly every day, never hiding his rays, so that the crops should grow until the time when rain was needed." Ramos Gavilán said that pilgrims went to Coati island on their return journey from the "sacred rock."

Coati contains a remarkable ruin, Iñak Uyu, rarely visited because of difficult currents, the lack of an easy landing place, and because the island was once a Bolivian penal colony. These remains consist of a rectangular terrace roughly 53 by 25 meters (174 by 82 feet), opening onto the lake on one long face and surrounded on its other sides by a screen of chambers abutting against the hillside. It is very theatrical. Deeply recessed doorways and niches alternate along an ornamental façade. A striking feature of Coati is the frequent use of the Tiahuanacan step motif in an Inca building: local builders clearly drew their inspiration from the monumental pre-Inca ruin near the southern end of the lake. Doors and niches are all topped by stepped lintels, and there are some windows with the step pattern arranged in a diamond—just as at Tiahuanaco and on the monoliths built by Colla masons at Ollantaytambo. Coati is only partly restored, most of it covered in dry grasses and a few grazing alpaca; but, as on the neighboring Island of the Sun, a visitor senses how holy a place this was, five centuries ago.

42 The sculpted top of Puma Orco hill, 50 kilometers (30 miles) south of Cuzco. These and other ruins suggest that the Incas designated this site as Tambo-toqo, where the legendary Ayar brothers and sisters emerged from below ground.

3. Tambo-toqo and Huanacauri Hill

THE INCAS, WHO WERE RECENT ARRIVALS AMONG the powerful Andean peoples, adopted the places of origin of the Aymara of Lake Titicaca. But their tribe in fact flourished near Cuzco, some 300 kilometers (180 miles) to the northwest. Inca origin legends explain this discrepancy by describing an underground migration by the four founding Ayar brothers and their three sisters. The precursors of the Inca tribe probably did migrate from Titicaca, across the *puna* (high-altitude savanna) of the altiplano and down the Vilcanota river valley to Cuzco.

The legend said that the Ayar brothers and sisters emerged from a cave that had three mouths, which was known as either Tambo-toqo or Pacaritambo. Sarmiento de Gamboa explained these place names: "Six leagues from Cuzco, southeast along the Incas' road, is a place called Pacaritambo, which means 'House of Origin', in which is a hill called Tambotoco, which signifies 'House of Openings'. And, sure enough, in this hill there are three caves...of which the central one is called Capac-toco, which means 'Rich [or Chief] Opening'." A hill and a cave with these names still exist, 50 kilometers (30 miles) south of Cuzco.

One Ayar brother was trapped in the cave, but the others marched north to approach Cuzco. At the hill of Huanacauri, just southeast of the city, the brothers and sisters rested and tried to examine a rainbow. Climbing the hill, they saw a rock in human shape near the rainbow's end. The brother called Ayar Uchu volunteered to investigate. "When Ayar Uchu reached the statue or shrine, he sat upon it with great courage, and asked what it was doing there. At these words the rock deity turned its head to see who spoke, but it could not see him as he was pressing down upon it with his weight. Ayar Uchu then tried to depart but could not: for he found that the soles of his feet were fastened to the shoulders of the rock deity. His six brothers and sisters, realizing that he was trapped, ran up to help him. But Ayar Uchu, seeing that he himself was transformed and that his brothers were unable to free him, said to them: 'O brothers and sisters, you have done me an evil turn! It was for you that I came to this place where I shall remain, forever separated from your company. Go, my fortunate brothers; for I declare that you will become great lords! I beg you, however, to honor and venerate me in all your festivals and ceremonies, so that I shall be the first to whom you make offerings.'" Ayar Uchu was thus transformed into a stone effigy; and Huanacauri hill became one of the most sacred shrines of the Incas. Guaman Poma made a vivid drawing of a bareheaded Inca ruler and his queen kneeling to worship the triple cave of Tambo-toqo and the hill of Huanacauri with its human-shaped rock shrine.

When the legendary Ayar Uchu was turned to stone on Huanacauri, he promised that he would "bestow the gifts of valor, nobility and knighthood" on the young nobles of Cuzco. Henceforth, the initiation rites of Inca boys were based on Huanacauri. This initiation was an elaborate annual ceremony called Capac Raymi, which was held during the month of November. Cristóbal de Molina, a Spanish priest who was resident in Cuzco in the 1530s, left a detailed description of the Capac Raymi ritual. The boys to be initiated were equipped with special rush sandals, llama-gut slings, fine black woolen tunics, mantles and headbands, and black feather plumes. The initiates and their families observed a strict fast. There were special sacrifices of llamas, prayers to the idol Huanacauri, flagellation of the adolescents and their arming with special slings and battle-axes, and processions of maidens in festive dress attending the youths with jugs of chicha. The ceremonies lasted for many days. At one stage the young men slept at the foot of Huanacauri and then climbed it to worship at their ancestor's shrine. They made offerings of wool, performed a ritual dance, and were again flagellated and admonished by their elders to be brave.

Cobo described the final stage: "The boys then arranged themselves in many rows, behind one another. Behind each of these rows of boys was another of older men who acted as their patrons—each was responsible for one knight, whom he was to help if he grew tired. A magnificently dressed Indian stood in front of all the rows. When he shouted, all of them started to run furiously. Some would be seriously injured. When they reached the bottom the girls gave them drink, first to the patrons and then to the foster sons." The culmination of the month of ceremonial, sacrifice, and initiation-ordeals came when the young Inca nobles had their earlobes pierced to receive the golden disks that were the sign of their rank. During the Conquest the Spaniards easily recognized such officials and called them *orejones* ("large ears") because of these great ear plugs.

The Indian chronicler Joan de Santacruz Pachacuti Yamqui said that the shrine of Huanacauri contained a handsome stone idol shaped like a vulture.

43 The holy hill of Huanacauri, where the mythical Manco Capac paused after emerging from the caves of Tambo-toqo on his way to founding Cuzco.

44 An Inca and his coya queen worship at Huanacauri hill and the caves of Tambo-toqo.

45 Caves on the steep side of Puma Orco, and remains of buildings and ceremonial seats, seem to reflect Guaman Poma's drawing.

Cieza de León wrote that Huanacauri was the second most important holy place of the Inca empire: "In olden days there was a shrine on this hill, and around it was buried a great wealth of treasure." Guaman Poma wrote that "the shrine of Huanacauri, which was looted for the benefit of the Spaniards, contained incalculable quantities of gold and silver," and the great champion of the Indians Bishop Bartolomé de Las Casas (who never went to Peru himself, but knew many who had) said that the buildings of Huanacauri were still extant in his day. Now all is gone. Huanacauri hill is a beautiful bare slope on the Cuzco skyline. Closer investigation reveals nothing more than vestiges of building foundations on its rocky, eroded flanks.

46 The zigzags of Sacsahuaman's massive terraces, from the Rodadero, with the hill once crowned by three towers to the right, and the city of Cuzco in the distance.

4. Sacsahuaman

WHEN THE INCAS IMAGINED THEIR CAPITAL CITY, Cuzco, as a crouching puma, they conceived the hill that towers steeply above the city as the feline's head. This hill of Sacsahuaman* was a natural redoubt with cliffs falling toward the city below. All that was needed was to fortify the far side, to enclose the crown of the hill with zigzag ramparts that would be the teeth of the imaginary feline.

Sacsahuaman was far more than a fortress. It was primarily a shrine, an important temple of the sun to rival Coricancha in the city below. It was also the main storehouse for the ruling family and its army. Cieza de León attributed its construction to the great Pachacuti: "As the power of the Incas was increasing and Pachacuti had such great ambitions, ...he decided to build a temple of the sun which would surpass everything done until then. It should house everything imaginable such as gold and silver, precious stones, fine garments, arms of all the types they used, materials of war, sandals, shields, feathers, skins of animals and birds, coca, sacks of wool and a thousand kinds of jewels; in a word, everything anyone had ever heard of was in it."

Cieza considered the manpower needed for such a gigantic project: "The work was conceived on such a vast scale that even if the monarchy had lasted until now [1550] it would not have been completed. [Pachacuti] ordered that twenty thousand men be sent in from the provinces, and that the villages supply them with the necessary food." These great levies worked in relays so that the work was not too onerous. "Four thousand of them quarried and cut the stones; six thousand hauled these with great cables of leather and hemp; others dug the ditch and laid the foundations; while still others cut poles and beams for the timbers... The living rock was excavated for the foundations, and for this reason it was so strong that it will last for as long as the world exists." Sarmiento de Gamboa also noted that the Incas divided their laborers into parties, "each having its duties and officers: thus some brought stones, others worked them, others laid them." Garcilaso de la Vega actually named the four successive master masons who planned and directed this vast enterprise. He agreed with Cieza that the effort of dragging immense rocks from their quarries was prodigious: "Learned Indians...affirm that over twenty thousand Indians brought up [the largest] stone, dragging it with great cables. Their progress was very slow, for the road up which they came is rough and has many steep slopes to climb and descend. Half the laborers pulled at the ropes from in front, while the rest kept the rock steady with other cables attached behind lest it should roll downhill."

The temple-fortress of Sacsahuaman rests on a natural hill of sedimentary rock with intrusions of diorite, along the top of a cliff overlooking Cuzco. The Incas defended the far side with three mighty terrace walls. For 380 meters (415 yards) the hill is flanked by a magnificent zigzag of forty to fifty salient and re-entering angles. The three terraces or ramparts are clad with the finest Inca polygonal masonry, with gigantic boulders interlocking perfectly and rusticated with smoothly polished surfaces. Each stone bulges in the traditional Inca fashion. One huge block is calculated to weigh 90 metric tons; another, 128 metric tons. One single monolith is 4.9 meters high, 4.75 wide, and 2.6 thick (16 by 15½ by 8½ feet).

One of the first Spaniards to see this triumph of Inca masonry was Pizarro's secretary Pedro Sancho. He exclaimed that "these ramparts are the most beautiful thing to be seen among the buildings of that land. They are built of stones so large that anyone seeing them would say that they cannot have been placed there by human hands. They are as big as forest tree trunks. Some are 30 spans [6.5 meters or over 21 feet] high, others are equally long, and others twenty-five or fifteen spans—three carts could not carry even the smallest of them. They are not straight-sided stones, but are extremely well joined and interlocking with one another. Spaniards who see them say that neither the [aqueduct] of Segovia nor any other structure built by Hercules or the Romans is as impressive a sight as this!"

Garcilaso de la Vega echoed the wonder of every visitor who sees this triumph of Inca engineering: "The greatest and proudest work that [the Incas] ordered built to demonstrate their power and majesty was the fortress of Cuzco. To any who has not seen it, its dimensions sound incredible. But to any

---

* Sacsahuaman is the traditional Spanish spelling for the ruin; Saqsaywaman is the Quechua spelling. There are two interpretations of the Quechua name. One is "replete falcon," because *saqsay* means replete or full, and *huaman* is a falcon. The other is "garlanded head" (which tallies with the notion of a puma's head) because *sacsa* is mottled or garlanded, and *uma* means head.

who has seen and studied [its stones] with care, they make him imagine and even believe that they were made by some form of magic—built by demons rather than men!" What amazed Garcilaso and other conquistadors was the means by which stones of such size could have been dragged from a quarry and then assembled into the complicated jigsaw that has survived so perfectly to the present day. Garcilaso felt (correctly) that the Indians chose natural blocks rather than quarry them. He said that the rocks were quarried at Muina and Rumicolca, over 20 kilometers (12½ miles) southeast of Cuzco. Some geologists reckon that most of the limestone or green diorite in Sacsahuaman was quarried a few hundred meters north of the site or from the hill itself. But the American authority on the Incas, John Rowe, agreed with Garcilaso: much of the rock is andesite from quarries at Huacoto or Rumicolca.

Garcilaso pondered the effort of assembling stones of such size and getting them to interlock so perfectly: "It is indeed beyond the power of imagination to understand how these Indians, unacquainted with devices, engines or implements, could have cut, dressed, raised and lowered great rocks, more like lumps of mountains than building stones, and set them so exactly in their places." The Jesuit José de Acosta also marveled that "great masses of workers patiently toiled to lay one stone on another, a task that required many trials since most of them were not level or uniform."

The American architect Vincent Lee in 1987 suggested an alternative to Acosta's laborious technique: the Incas might have maneuvered a block onto the slope above the terrace wall and then copied the shapes of blocks with which it was going to fit, so that it could be cut before being lowered into place. This method, known as "scribing and coping," is used for shaping tree-trunks at the corners of log cabins in Lee's native Rocky Mountains. "It is the precise opposite of the 'trial and error' approach, in that it achieves the desired fit in one operation and thus requires only a single lowering of each stone, finally, into place." Lee further proposed systems of props and gantries—using logs slotted into the pairs of indentations seen on several blocks in Sacsahuaman—for the Inca masons to position their huge stones. The pragmatic architect tried to demonstrate his theories in practice, but failed partly because he could not begin to mobilize huge levies of manpower. Fellow architect Jean-Pierre Protzen doubted that the ingenious scribing-and-coping method could have been used for rocks of this magnitude. All authorities agree that the Incas heaved blocks into place using earth ramps, as observed by Cobo in the construction of Cuzco cathedral in the 1590s. The archaeologist Brian Bauer confirmed the use of contingents of laborers when he discovered a 5-hectare (12-acre) site called Muyu Cocha northwest of the ruins. This was a complex of humble houses full of domestic remains—including pottery from the Titicaca region, a source of expert masons. Cieza had seen these houses, still occupied in his day.

The zigzag arrangement of Sacsahuaman's three terrace walls may have represented the teeth of the head of Cuzco's puma, but they also provided obvious defensive strength. As Sancho remarked, "Anyone attacking them could not do so head-on, but would have to approach obliquely." Garcilaso said that gates in each rampart were closed by doors suspended from massive lintels. There is no evidence from surviving lintel stones here for such a system, but we know that it worked effectively against Spanish attacks during the siege of 1536. There are three gates and staircases in the lower rampart and a dozen in the upper ones. Far down at the eastern end of the walls was a great gate, unearthed and scrupulously restored by Peruvian archaeologists in 1968. Modern excavations of Sacsahuaman have also revealed an excellent system of drainage of the terrace ramparts. Thirty-six finely cut channels lead rainwater off the middle level rampart alone.

The original Sacsahuaman of the Incas consisted of far more than these three mighty terraces. Sancho, who saw it in all its glory, described it as "a very beautiful fortress of earth and stone. Its large windows overlooking the city make it appear even more beautiful." He wrote that "there are many buildings inside the fortress and one principal tower in the middle. This is square, of four or five terraces above one another. The rooms and chambers inside it are small. The stones of which it is built are excellently cut, so well fitted to one another that there is apparently no mortar, and so smooth that they look like polished slabs. The courses are regular, with the joins alternating as in Spain." Garcilaso said that there were three towers rising above the hill of Sacsahuaman. He named the largest as Muyuc Marca ("round tower"), and said that it contained a fount of water brought underground from a long distance. This was the Inca ruler's lodging, with its walls decorated with a tapestry of animals, birds, and plants sculpted in gold and silver. The other towers, called Sallac Marca and Paucar Marca, were square and contained many chambers for the soldiers of the garrison. "The towers went as far below ground as they did above it. There were tunnels between them so that one could pass from one to the others below ground as well as above it."

It was not until 1933, the fourth centenary of the Conquest, that there was a scientific excavation of the great ruin. Archaeologists led by Luis Valcárcel removed up to 4.5 meters (15 feet) of cover and revealed a series of fine chambers overlooking Cuzco. Their most thrilling achievement was to find the foundations of the three towers. Valcárcel wrote: "Only the bases of these magnificent monuments were discovered. The first tower [Muyuc Marca] was in the form of a cylinder, its base contained in a rectangle. The notable thing about it was that, in the central part, there was a deposit for water, from which the water was distributed by canals. The base of the tower has three concentric circumferences with the following diameters: [roughly] 9.5, 15 and 22 meters [30, 50

47 The foundation and water supply of Muyuc Marca, the "round tower."

and 75 feet]. The base of the tower of Sallac Marca is a rectangle of [some] 22 by 10 meters [75 by 33 feet]. There is evidence of several stories, and in the central part two platforms can still be seen. The tower of Paucar Marca has fallen into the worst ruin and only traces of it remain."

The hill was covered with a labyrinth of chambers. According to Sancho, "The fortress has too many rooms and towers for a person to visit them all in one day." Garcilaso de la Vega, who was born in Cuzco in 1539, used to play as a boy among the ruins of Sacsahuaman. He recalled years later

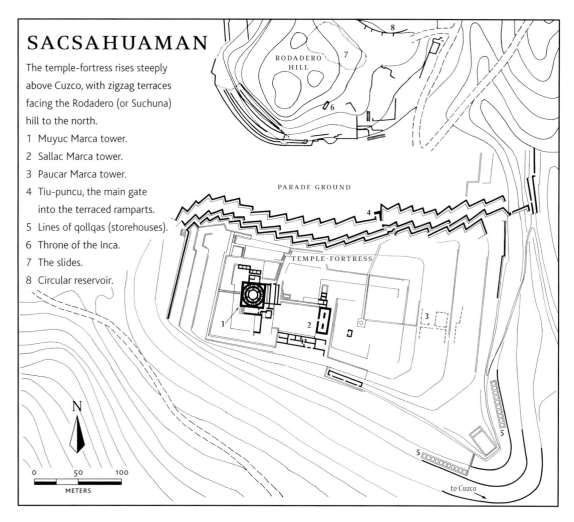

SACSAHUAMAN

The temple-fortress rises steeply above Cuzco, with zigzag terraces facing the Rodadero (or Suchuna) hill to the north.

1 Muyuc Marca tower.
2 Sallac Marca tower.
3 Paucar Marca tower.
4 Tiu-puncu, the main gate into the terraced ramparts.
5 Lines of qollqas (storehouses).
6 Throne of the Inca.
7 The slides.
8 Circular reservoir.

RODADERO HILL

PARADE GROUND

TEMPLE-FORTRESS

N

0   50   100
METERS

to Cuzco

be used against them; so they were happy to see Spaniards use it as a quarry, ruthlessly pillaging its tempting polished ashlars. Garcilaso said that they "pulled down all the smooth masonry in the walls, to save themselves the expense, effort and delay of having Indians work the stone. There is indeed not a house built by the Spaniards in the city that has not been made of this stone. The large slabs that formed the roofs of the underground passages were taken to serve as lintels and doorways. The smaller stones were used for foundations and walls. For the steps of staircases they sought slabs of stone of the size they needed, pulling down all the stones above the ones they wanted in the process... It was pulled down in such haste that all that was left, in my own time, was the few relics I have mentioned." Carolyn Dean noted that the pillaged stones came both from the three towers and attendant buildings and also from a parapet that once surmounted the great blocks of the zigzag terraces: in places, "we can yet see how the walls originally moved from uncoursed polygonally faced stones to roughly coursed rectangularly faced blocks."

To their credit, some contemporaries were appalled by this vandalism. Garcilaso accused his compatriots of doing it deliberately, out of envy of the achievements of the Incas: "In this way the majesty of the fortress was brought to the ground. [It was] a monument that deserved to be spared such devastation, which will cause everlasting regret to those who ponder what it was." Cieza de León, who reached Cuzco at the end of the 1540s, exploded with fury over the wanton destruction: "The Spaniards have already done so much damage and left it in such a state that I hate to think of the responsibility of those governors who allowed so extraordinary a thing to have been destroyed and cast down, without giving thought to the future... The remains of this fortress...should be preserved in memory of the greatness of this land!" Even the nationalistic Sarmiento de Gamboa admitted that "great regret is felt by those who see the ruins."

Below the mighty terraces is a level "parade ground" that was well suited to ceremonial activities involving thousands of participants. Cieza and others

that "there were so many underground passages, large and small, twisting and turning in all directions, with so many doors, all of the same size but some opening to one side and some to the other, that anyone entering the maze soon lost his way... When I was a boy, I often went up to the fortress with others of my own age. Although the stone part of the building was already ruined—I mean the part above ground and even a good deal of the part below the surface—we never dared enter certain parts of the remaining vaults, except as far as the light of the sun penetrated, lest we should get lost inside." Excavations at the end of the twentieth century revealed a maze of these small rooms, west of the circular tower.

The beautiful buildings of Sacsahuaman did not long survive the Conquest. Colonial governors of Cuzco wanted to demolish a temple-fortress that might

49 Rodadero or Suchuna hill from the ramparts of Sacsahuaman. The carved "throne of the Inca" is visible near the summit of the outcrop. Temporary markings on the parade ground are for the re-enactment of the Inti Raymi sun festival in June each year.

said that Sacsahuaman was a sun temple. So it is appropriate that this level space is the scene of a spectacular re-enactment of the Inti Raymi sun festival each June. Beyond it is another hill: Suchuna, known to Spaniards as Rodadero ("slide"). This diorite outcrop's most famous feature is the "throne of the Inca" or Kusilluj Hinkinan ("monkey's lift"), a series of broad, low steps cut into its eastern slope to form a symmetrical sculpture of great beauty. Cobo reported that it was a shrine on a ceque line, at which important rituals took place. To the north of this altar-throne, part of the hill is covered with passages, stairways, and niches, some with the Tiahuanacan step motif. The excavators of 1934 called this area Warmi Kajchana (meaning "where a woman is raped") because they found objects involved in a phallic cult here. This is the site of the famous slides that have delighted generations of Cusqueño children. These slides look like glacial striations but are not: they were caused by an intrusion of igneous diorite into limestone, with some form of faulting before the igneous rocks had cooled. This part of the Rodadero has two tunnels, resulting from karst erosion of the limestone, and a spring that was carved by the Incas to form another of the many shrines radiating from Cuzco.

Below the slides is a circular reservoir surrounded by niches. This was first discovered during excavations started in 1968, but more fully revealed by archaeologists of the INC (National Institute of Culture) in the 1980s. There were channels to fill the reservoir and others to draw water off for irrigation. The Incas called this Calispuquio ("spring of good health"). Another surprise was a series of agricultural terraces and canals, all of fine Inca masonry, which rose to cover the entire western end of the Rodadero hill.

Two hundred meters [220 yards] north of the amphitheater is the so-called Piedra Cansada, the "tired stone," a great block of limestone that looks as though it never reached its intended destination [ill. 175]. Cieza de León and Garcilaso both wondered how a block of this size was moved. Their speculations were in fact misplaced, for the rock is a natural outcrop that had been squared off and embellished by the Incas. Beside it is yet another throne of the Inca, with niches of superb precision like the alcoves of a baroque retable.

Pedro Sancho viewed Sacsahuaman with a soldier's eye, and was impressed: "Many Spaniards who have visited it, and who have traveled in Lombardy and other foreign countries, say that they have never seen a building to compare with this fortress, nor a stronger castle. It could contain five thousand Spaniards. It could not be battered and it could not be mined, for it is situated at the top of a hill." He also observed that it was the Inca empire's main arsenal: "The whole fortress was a deposit of arms: clubs, lances, bows, axes, shields, doublets thickly padded with cotton, and other weapons of various forms, as well as clothing for the soldiers assembled here from all parts of the land subject to the lords of Cuzco."

Cuzco was captured twice in the year 1533: once by Atahualpa's general Quisquis in the civil war between Atahualpa and Huascar; and then by Pizarro himself on November 15, after Quisquis had abandoned the city. There was no resistance at Sacsahuaman on either occasion. Two and a half years later, the Incas realized the full horror of European invasion and rose in a valiant attempt to expel the Spaniards. Manco Inca, leader of this rebellion, made Sacsahuaman his advanced headquarters. Peruvian levies secretly occupied the great temple-fortress, which the Spaniards had failed to garrison. It was from here that the chief priest, Villac Umu, directed the siege of Hernando Pizarro's Spaniards trapped in the city below.

At first the siege went well. In May 1536 vast Peruvian contingents surrounded Cuzco on all sides. The attackers set fire to their city's thatched roofs. They advanced along its streets, with mobile defenses against the Spaniards' horses, and trapped the invaders in a couple of palace enclosures beside the main square. Manco Inca's son later exulted that the besieged "secretly feared that those were to be the last days of their lives. They could see no hope from any direction and did not know what to do." "The Spaniards were extremely frightened, because there were so many Indians and so few of them."

The beleaguered Spaniards now decided that their immediate survival depended on the recapture of Sacsahuaman on the cliff above them. It was determined that Juan Pizarro would lead fifty horsemen—the greater part of the Spaniards' cavalry—in a desperate attempt to break through the besiegers and attack their fortress. Observers from the Indian side remembered the scene as follows: "They spent the whole of that night on their knees and with their hands clasped [in prayer] at their mouths—for many Indians saw them... On the following morning, very early, they all emerged from the church [suntur-huasi] and mounted their horses as if they were going to fight. They started to look from side to side. While they were looking about in this way, they suddenly put spurs to their horses and at full gallop, despite the enemy, broke through the opening which had been sealed like a wall, and charged off up the hillside at breakneck speed."

Juan Pizarro's horsemen galloped up the Jauja road, climbing Carmenca hill. They somehow fought their way through the Peruvian barricades. Pedro Pizarro was in that contingent and later recalled the dangerous ride, zigzagging up the hillside under fire from above. Once on the plateau, the Spaniards pretended to be dashing down the road toward the coast; but at the village of Jicatica they left the road and wheeled around beyond the hills north of Sacsahuaman. Only by this flanking movement could they avoid the steep ascent and mass of obstacles between Cuzco and the fortress.

Manco's men had fortified the "parade ground" between Sacsahuaman and the Rodadero with earth barriers. It took repeated attacks and heavy fighting for the horsemen to force these barriers. The Spaniards then rode toward the mighty terraces. They were greeted with a withering fire of slingshots and javelins. It was late afternoon and the attackers were exhausted by the day's fierce fighting. But Juan Pizarro attempted one last charge, a frontal attack on the main gate into the fortress. This gate was defended by side walls projecting on either side, and the Peruvians had dug a defensive pit between them. The passage leading to the gate was crowded with Indians defending the entrance or attempting to retreat from the barbican into the main fortress. Juan Pizarro had been struck on the jaw during the previous day's fighting in Cuzco and was unable to wear his steel helmet. As he charged toward the gate in the

50 A masterpiece of sculpture: the "throne of the Inca" on Rodadero hill.

setting sun, he was struck on the head by a stone hurled from the salient walls. It was a mortal blow. The Governor's younger brother, a magistrate of Cuzco and one of the most dashing conquistadors, was carried down to Cuzco that night in great secrecy. Francisco de Pancorvo recalled that "they buried him by night so that the Indians should not know he was dead, for he was a very brave man and the Indians were very frightened of him. But although the death of Juan

Pizarro was [supposed to be] a secret, the Indians used to say 'Now that Juan Pizarro is dead' just as one would say 'Now that the brave are dead.' And he was indeed brave."

On the following day the Peruvians counterattacked repeatedly. Large numbers of warriors tried to dislodge Gonzalo Pizarro from the Rodadero. "There was terrible confusion. Everyone was shouting and they were all entangled together, fighting for the hilltop the Spaniards had won. It looked as though the whole world was up there grappling in close combat." Hernando Pizarro sent twelve of his remaining horsemen up to join the critical battle—to the dismay of the few Spaniards left in Cuzco. Manco Inca sent five thousand reinforcements, and "the Spaniards were in a very tight situation with their arrival, for the Indians were fresh and attacked with determination."

But the Spaniards were about to apply European methods of siege warfare: throughout the day they had been making scaling ladders. As night fell, Hernando Pizarro himself led an infantry force to the top of the hill. Using the scaling ladders in a night assault, the Spaniards succeeded in taking the mighty terrace walls of the fortress. The Peruvians retreated into the complex of buildings and the three towers.

There were two individual acts of great bravery during this final stage of the assault. On the Spanish side Hernán Sánchez from Badajoz performed feats of prodigious panache worthy of a silent-screen hero. He climbed one of the scaling ladders under a hail of stones, which he parried with his buckler, and squeezed into a window of one of the buildings. He hurled himself at the Indians inside and sent them retreating up some stairs toward the roof. He now found himself at the foot of the highest tower. Fighting around its base, Sánchez came upon a thick rope that had been left dangling from the top. Commending himself to God, he sheathed his sword and started clambering up, heaving up the rope with his hands and stepping off from the smooth Inca ashlars with his feet. Halfway up the Indians threw a stone "as big as a wine jar" down on him, but it simply glanced off the buckler he was wearing on his back. He threw himself into one of the higher levels of the tower, suddenly appearing in the midst of its startled defenders, showed himself to the other Spaniards, and encouraged them to assault the other tower.

The battle for the terraces and buildings of Sacsahuaman was hard fought. "When dawn came, we spent the whole of that day and the next fighting the Indians who had retreated into the two tall towers. These could only be taken through thirst, when their water supply became exhausted." Besieged Spaniards recalled: "When the following day dawned, the Indians on the inside began to weaken, for they had used up their entire store of stones and arrows." The Peruvian commanders decided that there were too many defenders in Sacsahuaman, whose water supply was running out. Villac Umu broke through the Spanish lines with half his men and went to seek reinforcements. He left the defense of Sacsahuaman to an Inca noble, an *orejón* who had sworn to fight to the death against the Spaniards. This officer now rallied the defenders almost single-handed, performing feats of bravery that Pedro Pizarro

described as worthy of any Roman: "The orejón strode about like a lion from side to side of the tower on its topmost level. He repulsed any Spaniards who tried to mount with scaling ladders. And he killed any Indians who tried to surrender. He smashed their heads with the battle-ax he was carrying and hurled them from the top of the tower." Among the defenders, he alone possessed European steel weapons that made him the match of the attackers in hand-to-hand fighting. "He carried a buckler on his arm, a sword in one hand and a battle ax in the shield hand, and wore a Spanish morrión helmet on his head." "Whenever his men told him that a Spaniard was climbing up somewhere, he rushed upon him like a lion with the sword in his hand and the shield on his arm." "He received two arrow wounds but ignored them as if he had not been touched." Hernando Pizarro arranged for the towers to be attacked simultaneously by three or four scaling ladders. But he ordered that the brave orejón should be captured alive. The Spaniards pressed home their attack, assisted by large contingents of indigenous auxiliaries. Manco's son wrote that the battle was a bloody affair for both sides. As the Peruvian resistance crumbled, the orejón hurled his weapons down onto the attackers in a frenzy of despair. He grabbed handfuls of earth, stuffed them into his mouth and scoured his face in anguish, then covered his head with his cloak and leaped to his death from the top of the fortress, in fulfillment of his pledge to the Inca.

"With his death the remainder of the Indians gave way, so that Hernando Pizarro and all his men were able to enter. They put all those inside the fortress to the sword—there were fifteen hundred of them." Many others hurled themselves from the walls. "Since these were high the men who fell first died. But some of those who fell later survived because they landed on top of a great heap of dead men." The mass of corpses lay unburied, prey for vultures and giant condors. The coat of arms of the city of Cuzco, granted in 1540, had "an orle of eight condors, which are great birds like vultures that exist in the province of Peru, in memory of the fact that when the castle was taken these birds descended to eat the natives who had died in it."

Hernando Pizarro immediately garrisoned Sacsahuaman with a force of fifty foot soldiers supported by auxiliaries. Pots of water and food were hurried up from the city. The high priest, Villac Umu, returned with reinforcements, just too late to save the citadel. He counterattacked vigorously, and the battle for Sacsahuaman continued fiercely for three more days, but the Spaniards were not dislodged, and the battle was won by the end of May 1536. This was the only record of fighting on the great temple-fortress of Sacsahuaman. Its recapture by the Spaniards proved to be the turning point of Manco's long rebellion. So it was the battle that confirmed Spanish rule of Peru.

51 Partially restored retaining walls on the southwestern side of Rodadero hill.

52 Coricancha's curved wall as photographed by Martín Chambi
in 1925, before the church of Santo Domingo collapsed in an
earthquake and was rebuilt with a different west end.

5. Coricancha

WHEN THE SPANIARDS KIDNAPPED the Inca Atahualpa in northern Peru, they kept hearing about the fabulous wealth of Cuzco and its sun temple, Coricancha. Atahualpa had offered to buy his freedom with a huge ransom of gold and silver, and he callously urged his captors to secure the treasures of the empire's holiest temple (which he himself may never have seen). Pizarro therefore sent three envoys for hundreds of kilometers into the unknown heart of the Inca empire, to the legendary Cuzco itself. He dispatched the three men in February 1533, "commending them to God. They took many natives to carry them in litters, and they were very well served." But when they finally reached Cuzco, the foreign envoys were given a frosty reception by Atahualpa's general Quisquis, the recent conqueror of the Inca capital. "He liked the Christians very little, although he marveled greatly at them."

The three Spaniards went straight to Coricancha. They found, as they had hoped, that it was still intact. "These buildings were sheathed in gold, in large plates, on the side where the sun rises; but the more [their walls] were shaded from the sun, the baser the gold they had on them." Pizarro's men had to desecrate the temple by themselves. "The Christians decided to strip the ornament with some copper crowbars, without any help from the Indians—these refused to help because it was a sun temple and they said they would die if they did." The vandals sent this gold in litters, each carried by four men, on the long journey north. Pizarro's secretary Francisco de Jerez reported that the treasure from Cuzco finally reached Cajamarca in June: 200 loads of gold and 25 of silver, followed by a further 60 loads of poorer-quality gold taken from another temple. The plates from the temple averaged four spans (*palmos*) long (almost 90 centimeters or 3 feet) and weighed 2 kilos (4½ pounds) of gold each when melted down. There were seven hundred of these plates, looking "like boards from chests; they had been stripped from the temple's walls and had holes where they had evidently been secured." Other treasures from Coricancha included a footstool-shaped golden seat, and a fountain of pure gold that Pizarro's other secretary, Pedro Sancho, described as "very subtly worked, well worth seeing both for the quality of its workmanship and its shape."

When Pizarro's invaders finally entered Cuzco in November 1533, five months after their cruel execution of Atahualpa, they immediately advanced on the sun temple even though much of its gold had been removed earlier that year. The soldier Diego de Trujillo recalled the scene: "We entered the houses of the Sun, and Villac Umu—who was a form of priest in their canon—said to us: 'How dare you enter here! Anyone who wishes to enter here must first fast for a year, and must enter carrying a symbolic load and barefoot!' But, paying no attention to what he said, we went in." Inside, another of them reported: "We found many gold [figurines of] sheep [llamas] and women and jars and other objects. We found a lot in the chambers of the monastery."

Cobo called Coricancha "the richest, most sumptuous and most important temple in the empire." He could compare it only to Rome: "It was considered the head and metropolitan temple of their false religion, and was the holiest sanctuary of these Indians. All the people of the Inca empire frequented it, coming on pilgrimages out of piety. It was called Coricancha, which means 'Enclosure of Gold,' because of the incomparable wealth of this metal that was buried among its chapels and on its walls, vaults and altars. It was dedicated to the Sun, although statues of Viracocha, the Thunder, Moon and other leading idols were placed in it, for it served the same purpose as the Pantheon in Rome." The modern archaeologist Brian Bauer said that the importance of this temple cannot be exaggerated. In his masterly study of the archaeology of Cuzco, Bauer wrote that "for the Inca, the Coricancha marked the central and most sacred spot in the universe." The four quarters of the Inca empire, Tawantinsuyu, met at this point; it was the nucleus from which the lines of shrines around Cuzco radiated; and it was the junction of the *hanan* and *hurin* (upper and lower) wards of the city. Coricancha lay in the lower part of central Cuzco, in the district known as pumachupan, "the puma's tail," because it was in a triangle of land where the two streams joined and thus at the tail-end of the imaginary feline whose head was Sacsahuaman. Recent excavations in the temple yielded much fine pottery of the Killke period, the time between the eclipse of the Huari culture and the arrival of the Incas. So this had clearly long been a holy place.

Chroniclers made it clear that Coricancha had two types of gold cladding. In addition to walls entirely covered in the plates that were taken to Cajamarca, there was also a band of gold. Topa Inca Yupanqui ordered that this band be fixed just below the thatched roofs of its chambers. Two eyewitnesses wrote that this band was a span (22 centimeters or 9 inches) wide and of thinly beaten metal. Intriguingly, an earthquake in 1950 exposed regular grooves on the top of the masonry of some chambers, and these could well have been to secure this band. Some accounts also described the main gate and inner doors as clad in gold. Garcilaso said that the chapels dedicated to the Moon, Thunder, and Stars were coated in silver.

The temple buildings were deceptively simple. They stood on a platform enclosed by retaining walls of the finest masonry. There were six single-story rectangular chambers opening onto a square courtyard (or possibly seven, if there were two buildings where the church of Santo Domingo was superimposed). As so often with the Incas, the temple's beauty derived from excellence of workmanship and simplicity of plan. "The building of this great temple was of the finest craftsmanship to be found among these Indians. Inside and out it was made of amazing ashlars, extremely skillfully set, without mortar, and so finely adjusted that it would be impossible to improve on them." Cieza de León compared Coricancha to some of the most famous buildings in Spain, but acknowledged that it was "finer in terms of its walls and the cutting and laying of its stones; and its retaining wall was plumb and very well laid. The stone seems to me blackish and tough and of excellent quality." Most chroniclers agree that it was the great Inca Pachacuti who decided to rebuild Coricancha, on the site of a primitive earlier temple. Its stone is now known to have been brought from a quarry at Rumicolca, 35 kilometers (22 miles) to the southeast.

The daily ritual at Coricancha revolved around an image of the sun. Juan de Betanzos said that this idol was of solid gold and shaped like a naked, year-old baby. It was dressed in a tunic of the finest brocade and wore a royal fringe, a gold paten on its head, and golden sandals. Pedro Pizarro, who actually saw one such idol, described it as "a small covered statue which they said was the sun." When the conquistadors melted down tons of Atahualpa's ransom, even those tough desperados spared a few pieces of outstanding merit. These masterpieces of Inca metalwork were taken to Spain by Pizarro's brother Hernando. Among them was "a golden effigy, the size of a four-year-old boy," which may possibly have been the sun idol from Coricancha. Hernando Pizarro reached Seville in February 1534 and the Council of the Indies suggested that the King-Emperor Charles V would want to see the remarkable treasures he had brought. But the King (who is famous today as a patron of the arts) was callously indifferent: he wrote from Toledo ordering his officials to melt the objects down into coins. They reiterated their view that the King might enjoy seeing them; so he said that they should be put on public display for a few weeks in Seville, and then melted down. One boy who saw this exhibition and was thrilled by its "magnificent specimens" was the future chronicler Pedro de Cieza de León. This inspired Cieza to go to the New World. Albrecht Dürer had witnessed similar treasures from Aztec Mexico, exhibited in Antwerp a few years earlier.

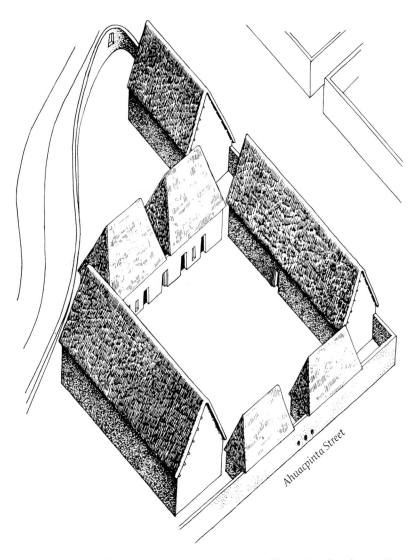

53 A reconstruction of Coricancha by Graziano Gasparini and Luise Margolies, showing its high thatched roofs and the simplicity of its temple chambers.

The artist exclaimed: "Never in all my life have I seen things that delighted my heart as much as these. For I saw among them amazing artistic objects, and I marveled at the subtle ingenuity of the people of those distant lands."

Coricancha may have had another sun idol in addition to the image of a boy: a golden disk called Punchao. (Representations of the sun were called Punchao. Some sources described these as figurines, others as disks. They were probably both; but we will never know since all were melted down for their gold content.) The Spanish horseman Mancio Sierra de Leguízamo boasted that he had received this sun disk as part of the Inca's ransom at Cajamarca, but had lost it in a night of gambling. This story gave rise to a Spanish expression, "To gamble the sun before it rises"; but the story is improbable since, apart from the objects sent to King Charles, the ransom treasures were all crushed and melted down so that their bullion could be divided among Pizarro's men. After the failure of Manco Inca's rebellion, he retreated to Vitcos in Vilcabamba. In July 1537 the dashing conquistador Rodrigo de Orgóñez pursued, very nearly caught Manco, and returned with massive booty—including a golden image of the sun. This cannot, however, have been the important disk or figure from Coricancha because the Spaniards became convinced that they had never found the main sun image. Cristóbal de Molina wrote in about 1550 that "the Indians hid this sun so well that it could never be found up to the present day." Cieza imagined the missing Punchao as "an image of the sun of great size, made of gold, beautifully wrought and set with many precious stones." After Manco Inca's assassination by renegade Spaniards in 1545, his sons ruled his enclave in Vilcabamba for a further thirty-six years. Sun-worship was the main religion of this neo-Inca state. When in 1572 a Spanish expedition pursued Manco's son Tupac Amaru into his Vilcabamba retreat, it captured a Punchao figure. Sarmiento de Gamboa, who was on that expedition, described this as the size of a man. The Viceroy, Francisco de Toledo, said that it was made of cast gold and had "a golden chalice inside the body of the idol" that contained a dough made from the hearts of dead Incas. "It is surrounded by a form of golden medallions in order that, when struck by the sun, these should shine in such a way that one could never see the idol itself, but only the reflected brilliance of these medallions." After Tupac Amaru's execution, Viceroy Toledo sent this image to King Philip of Spain, but its whereabouts is now unknown.

Despite the sacrilegious insult of Spaniards in 1533 barging into his holy of holies, the high priest Villac Umu continued to perform his rituals for some months after the conquerors' arrival. Pedro Pizarro described the daily ceremonial. The mummies of dead Incas were brought out to the main square and food and drink were offered to them. A magnificently robed Villac Umu then carried the sun image from Coricancha to the square. The sun idol was placed on a bench covered in a bright feather mantle. Mace-bearers who processed behind the High Priest fed the Punchao by burning food before it and pouring chicha into a ceremonial font. "While they were burning the food, an Indian arose and cried out so that all could hear; and when they heard his voice, everyone who was in the square and outside it crouched down and fell silent, without speaking, coughing or moving until the food was consumed." After the ceremony, the sun idol was returned to Coricancha, where it rested during daylight on a gold-plated platform along one side of the courtyard. At night it was placed in a small chamber that was also clad in gold plates. Cobo said that "many mamaconas slept in its company. These were daughters of the nobility and claimed to be the wives of the sun, pretending that the sun made love to them." Pedro Pizarro added, cynically, that "they pretended to live chastely, but they lied, for they involved themselves with the male servants and guardians of the Sun, who were many."

Coricancha was the hub from which the ceque lines of shrines radiated in all directions of the compass. Cobo listed these lines of holy places, almost certainly from a lost document of 1559 by Cuzco's then *corregidor* Juan Polo de Ondegardo. In brilliant fieldwork, Brian Bauer has actually located many of the shrines listed by Cobo. One was a stone brazier called Nina, next to Coricancha. The temple's mamaconas were responsible for tending the fire in this brazier. They used only a carved and painted red wood specially brought up from the Pacific coast (perhaps from the *algarroba* carob tree). A cook prepared sacrificial food each morning. "As the sun appeared on the horizon and struck with its rays at the Punchao, which was a golden image of the sun, placed so that, as the sun rose, its light would bathe the image... The women offered the sun [the] food that they had prepared, burning it with special solemnity and songs."

These mamaconas were also responsible for tending a famous garden of maize, which was almost certainly on terraces below the western wall of the temple and attached to it. "They irrigated [the garden] by hand with water that they carried up for the Sun. Whenever they celebrated their festivals—which was three times a year: when they sowed, when they harvested, and when orejones [Inca nobles] were initiated—they [also] filled this garden with stalks of maize made of gold, with life-sized ears and leaves all of fine gold, which they kept stored in order to place them here on those occasions." These replicas may have been taken to Cajamarca for the ransom. One was sent to Spain, and the inventory of objects taken by Hernando Pizarro included: "A stalk of maize, of 24-carat gold, with three leaves and two cobs of gold, which weighed 10 marks [or] 6 *onzas de oro*, 4 *octavos*." The Ethnologisches Museum in Berlin and the Art Museum in Denver both have maize cobs made of precious metals, although neither is thought to have come from Coricancha's famous "Garden of the Sun."

Garcilaso said that Coricancha consisted of six chambers or chapels: two large, two medium-sized, and two small. The two large halls, which lay to the north and south of the courtyard, have been demolished, but all or part of the other four survive. The large halls were probably gabled, but the surviving smaller chambers have walls that are flat on all sides. John Rowe found that these walls taper, from 91 centimeters at the base to 81 at the top (36 to 32 inches), and lean inward slightly with the top overhanging its base by 4 centimeters (1½ inches). Because the chamber walls all have twelve courses of stones and their tops are perfectly level, Rowe concluded that the surviving masonry is complete and was never capped by adobes. Garcilaso said that these chapels were "covered in the form of a pyramid," evidently meaning a hipped roof of four pitches with the thatch tied to a wooden frame that rested on the flat walls.

The most famous surviving feature of Coricancha is the magnificent curving wall beneath the western end of the church of Santo Domingo. This is in the shape of a half parabola, a lovely arc of dark-gray stone. It is 6 meters (20 feet) high, of which about half is terrace wall. Its stones are particularly brilliantly finished and fitted, and there is even a slight entasis bulge halfway up, to correct any optical illusion about the wall's strength. The chronicles do not mention this famous wall, except to say that one of Cuzco's important shrines was "a stone called Subaraura, which was where the open gallery of Santo Domingo now stands: it was believed to have been the chief of the puru-raucas [the gods who helped the Incas defeat the Chanca and were later turned to stone]." This holy stone evidently occupied an elaborate niche above the curving wall, but it was removed by censorious Spanish priests.

Another interesting feature of Coricancha is the stone font in the center of its cloister. It is a sober porphyry basin, rectangular but with its corners angled to form an octagon. It could once have been clad in gold. The Dominican friar and chronicler Reginaldo de Lizárraga saw it in place in 1600 and said that there was a tradition that it had once been covered with a golden disk. He wondered whether this could have been the disk that the conquistadors thought was the image of the sun. There is, however, doubt over whether this font is truly Inca: its octagonal shape looks more colonial.

At the Conquest, Coricancha fell to Juan Pizarro, the Governor's brother who was killed in the attack on Sacsahuaman in 1536. He bequeathed the sun temple to the Dominicans, the powerful religious order that administered the Inquisition. Friar Vicente de Valverde, the chaplain of Pizarro's invading force and later first bishop of Cuzco, accepted the bequest and arranged for Dominican friars to come from Spain. The Dominicans have occupied the site ever since. They built a church where the great northern hall and main gate of Coricancha once stood. Fortunately, the temple's cancha (courtyard) plan could easily be adapted to form a monastic cloister: the Spanish friars built a fine two-storied baroque colonnade above and around four of the Inca chambers. The chambers themselves were used as rooms of the monastery, whose refectory and dormitories were (and still are) on the demolished southern part of the Inca temple. Thanks to this continued religious use, much of Coricancha has survived.

The Dominicans were well aware that their monastery occupied the holiest place in the Inca empire. Reginaldo de Lizárraga, for one, was proud of the Inca remains in his order's house. When in 1558 Manco Inca's son Sayri Tupac was lured back to Cuzco from his neo-Inca kingdom of Vilcabamba, he was instructed in the Christian faith and taken to Mass in Santo Domingo. He worshipped there with much devotion—although Garcilaso noted that "malicious observers said that he was doing it to worship his father the Sun and the bodies of his ancestors who had been kept in that place." When this Inca descendant died three years later, his will provided for a chapel to be built in the church of Santo Domingo and asked for him to be buried there. Various witnesses said that Sayri Tupac was indeed buried in this church and was later joined there by his wife-sister Cusi Huarcay and by his brother Tupac Amaru, who was executed by the Spaniards in 1572.

The first modern investigator to penetrate Coricancha was the tireless George Squier in 1865. He reported that "the few ignorant but amiable friars that remain of the once rich and renowned order of Santo Domingo in Cuzco admitted me as an honorary member of their brotherhood, gave me a cell to myself, and permitted me, during the week I spent with them, to ransack every portion of the church, and every nook and corner of the convent, and to measure and sketch and photograph to my fill. Here a long reach of massive wall, yonder a fragment, now a corner, next a doorway, and anon a terrace—through the aid of these I was able to make up a ground plan of the ancient edifice." The result was a commendable plan of what remained of the Inca walls, and a charming sketch of the friars in their cloister.

The German archaeologist Max Uhle was there in 1905 and reported that Inca walls lay beneath one of the side altars of Santo Domingo. By far the most important observation came in 1943, when the American archaeologist John Rowe was allowed to explore the monastery for several months and made brilliantly accurate measurements of its Inca remains. Rowe agreed with Uhle that the foundations of the original north wall and entrance gate could be revealed by excavation beneath the church and the triangular terrace in front of the monastery door.

A fateful date for Coricancha was May 21, 1950, when a severe earthquake destroyed much of the church (itself rebuilt after the other great earthquake of 1650) and its Churrigueresque late eighteenth-century bell tower. The following year, UNESCO sent a mission led by the Yale art historian George Kubler (an expert on Spanish colonial architecture) to recommend a program to restore Cuzco's ruined monuments. This team resisted pleas to demolish Santo Domingo to reveal what remained of Coricancha. It argued that "the church and cloister are not irreparably damaged, and these colonial buildings are of outstanding importance and beauty... It is unnecessary to dismantle any part of the Dominican establishment to get at foundations [of Inca walls beneath it]. They may be traced and exposed by a system of underground passages."

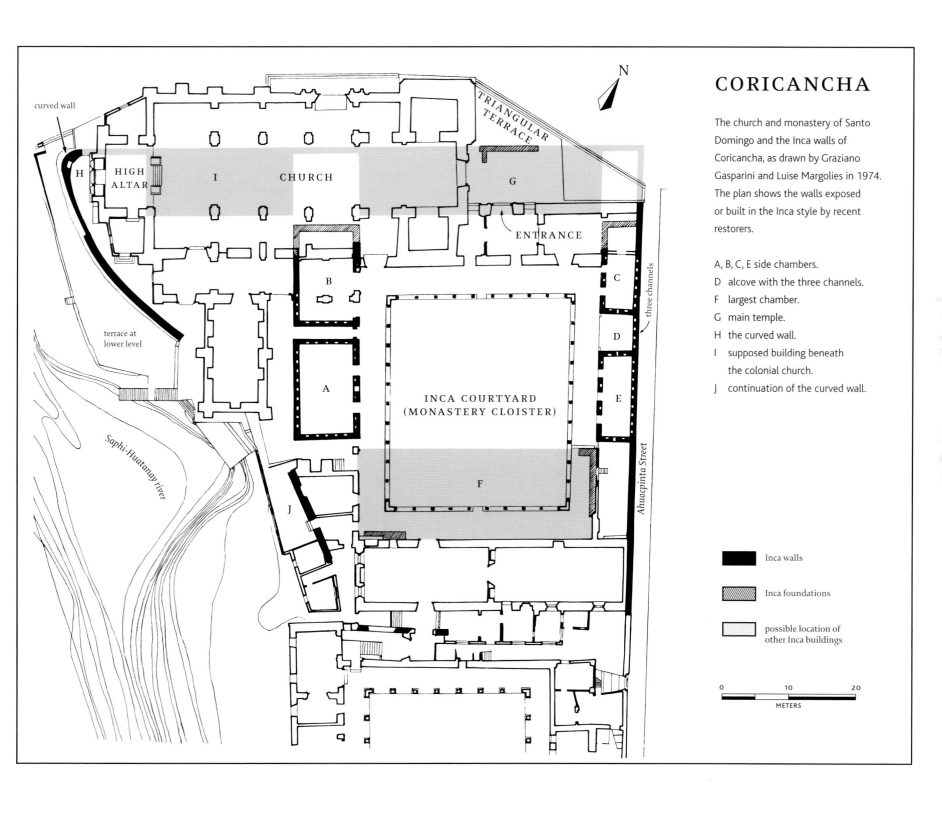

curved wall

N

CORICANCHA

The church and monastery of Santo Domingo and the Inca walls of Coricancha, as drawn by Graziano Gasparini and Luise Margolies in 1974. The plan shows the walls exposed or built in the Inca style by recent restorers.

A, B, C, E side chambers.
D alcove with the three channels.
F largest chamber.
G main temple.
H the curved wall.
I supposed building beneath the colonial church.
J continuation of the curved wall.

TRIANGULAR TERRACE

H HIGH ALTAR   I   CHURCH   G

ENTRANCE

C

terrace at lower level

three channels

D

Saphi-Huatanay river

B

A

E

Ahuacpinta Street

INCA COURTYARD
(MONASTERY CLOISTER)

J

F

■ Inca walls

▨ Inca foundations

░ possible location of other Inca buildings

0   10   20
METERS

During the 1960s and 1970s Coricancha/Santo Domingo was restored by a team led by the architect Oscar Ladrón de Guevara Avilés. These restorers faced the difficult task of reconciling a damaged colonial building with the remains of the Inca temple hidden within it. They decided to ignore the recommendation of the UNESCO team and to give precedence to anything Inca. The result was that many colonial additions were removed, and the baroque cloisters now rest uneasily above Inca walls. The four Inca chambers to the east and west of the cloister are fully revealed. Where their original dimensions were obvious, the restorers adopted the dubious practice of building walls in the Inca manner to replace those that were missing. Some art historians deplored the damage to the Dominican cloister; other purists objected to the pastiche rebuilding of Inca chambers. But I think that the restorers were right. Thousands of visitors get a good impression of the Incas' most important temple.

The Venezuelan architectural historians Graziano Gasparini and Luise Margolies compared Rowe's pre-earthquake plans of 1943 with the state of the structures three decades later. They generously allowed us to reproduce their plan and reconstruction sketch. Some foundations of the large north and south buildings had been revealed. A wall of the northern building, which Garcilaso described as the main temple, emerged where Rowe surmised that it would: beneath the triangular platform in front of the monastery door. This stretch of foundation is directly in line with the northern end of the curved wall, and between it and the temple would have run the enclosure wall whose foundation was seen beneath the church by Max Uhle.

Garcilaso wrote that beside the main temple chamber there was "a cloister with four sides, one of which was the wall of the temple... Around the cloister were five halls or large square rooms each built separately and not joined to one another...and forming the other three sides of the square." This description exactly fits the surviving chambers. The southern chamber (F on the plan), facing the temple, is gone, but excavations have revealed the foundations of its northeastern corner and part of its southern wall. (The friars have ceded their refectory here to be an attractive museum of their art.)

The two eastern chambers (C and E), to the left on entering, are smaller than those facing them on the west. They may have been dedicated to the thunder *illapa*, and to the rainbow *cuichu*. Garcilaso said that the chapel for the thunder, thunderbolts, and lightning was clad in gold, whereas that for the rainbow was decorated with a colored arc. The modern restorers rebuilt the northern end of the northern of these two rooms, adding an Inca door to match one in the other

chamber. Their work also revealed a fine Inca floor, cobbled with neat round pebbles. Rowe measured the magnificent stretch of 60 meters (197 feet) of wall that is intact on the northeast side overlooking Ahuacpinta Street. This wall is a masterpiece of Inca stoneworking. It rises 4.5 meters (15 feet), of which the lower third is the retaining wall for the temple platform and the upper 3 meters (10 feet) are the walls of the two chambers.

Between the eastern chambers is an open passage (D) from which three small channels run through the wall to emerge above Ahuacpinta Street. These channels are symmetrical, cut cleanly into the top of a single ashlar. There are various theories about them. One is that they were drains for sacrificial offerings or effluents; another that they were for water, either drinking water from the fountains inside the temple, or to carry off excess rainwater; lastly that they were for sound, either for instructions from priests inside the temple to assistants without, or for musical effect—when struck, the channels sound the notes re, la, and mi. Whatever their purpose, the three holes give elegant, satisfying relief to that superb stretch of Inca wall.

Across the courtyard were the two larger chambers (A and B). According to Garcilaso, chamber A was dedicated to the planet Venus, the Pleiades, and other constellations; chamber B to the moon. The restorers cleared colonial structures from chamber B, built its rear wall in Inca style, and extended it toward the church. They opened a passage that once existed between the two chambers, and rebuilt the northern wall of chamber A to complete this passage. The walls of chamber A, which used to be the monastery's chapter house, are decorated with twenty-five handsome, equidistant niches (of which the northern five are modern reconstructions). Garcilaso wrote that its roof was once embellished with figures representing the stars, and its walls were clad with silver plates. There is a large niche in the center of the eastern wall of this temple of the constellations: half of this was destroyed to open a colonial doorway but it is now restored. This niche is surrounded by stones, apparently perforated to take golden cladding. Garcilaso said that three of Coricancha's chambers were still standing in the 1560s, and he recalled four "tabernacles" hollowed out of their walls facing the courtyard: "They had moldings round the edges and in the hollows of the tabernacles. As these moldings were worked in the stone, they were inlaid with gold plates on the tops, sides and also the floors of the tabernacles." Betanzos imagined the Inca sitting in these niches, contemplating the temple that to the Incas was "the center of the center of the universe."

55 The three channels in the superb coursed masonry of Coricancha's eastern wall on Ahuacpinta Street.

56 A double-jambed trapezoidal door, between the two chambers on the west side of the courtyard.

57 Niches in the wall of the "chamber of Venus and other constellations" (chamber A on the site plan), during restoration, after being used as the monastery's chapter house.

58 The ruins of Pisac are perched on a spur above the Vilcanota valley: the inti-huatana group on the right, and Pisacllacta below to the left.

6. Pisac

THE GREAT MYSTERY ABOUT PISAC WAS ITS ANONYMITY. Here is a stupendous ruin of the finest Inca stonework, with many attendant buildings, baths and storehouses, exceptional flights of terracing and quantities of tombs, all well defended by walls, gates, and towers. It is a major site close to Cuzco, a mere 30 kilometers (19 miles) to the northeast and at the same altitude of 3,300 meters (10,800 feet). And yet, no chronicler mentions Pisac either in terms of Inca history, or as important in the Inca empire, or as the scene of any post-Conquest action. The mystery was finally mitigated when the historian María Rostworowski found a document in the Archive of the Indies in Seville which said that Pachacuti had royal estates at [Ollantay]Tambo and Pisac. Sarmiento de Gamboa had written that one of Pachacuti's first conquests was of the Cuyos, in the valley of Pisac, and that this Inca used to go "for greater pleasure and enjoyment...to the town of the Cuyos." So Pisac was a royal estate of that great ruler.

Garcilaso wrote that the sun temple Coricancha was imitated throughout the Inca empire. The central group of buildings in Pisac could well have been such a replica: a sun temple with five rectangular chapels nearby. These hip-roofed chambers are preserved to their original roof line, as are those that survive in Cuzco, and are built of the most magnificent coursed masonry. This central group at Pisac, displayed theatrically on three artificially leveled terraces and perched on the saddle of a mountain spur far above the Yucay valley, is one of the most spectacular achievements of Inca architecture.

The central, dominant feature of Pisac's temple group is an outcrop of rock jutting above two levels of platform and surrounded by a 19-meter (62-foot) D-shaped wall of the finest masonry. A tall trapezoidal gateway, with its lintel still in place, leads up to this shrine. The rock has two stone bosses or gnomons rising from its top surface, and there is another projecting horizontally from its wall; there are four more such projections in other buildings of the temple group. The first modern visitor to record his impressions of Pisac was George Squier. His Indian guides told him that the central group at Pisac was called inti-huatana, and he knew that Garcilaso had explained that this means "hitching place of the sun." The gnomons were clearly intended for astronomical observation or worship. Squier was also told that the central boss had once been clad in a copper sheath. He recalled seeing similar bosses near Huaitará

in the central Andes, overlooking Ollantaytambo, on the Tullumayo stream beside Colcampata in Cuzco, and in front of the original temple of the sun on the Island of the Sun, in Lake Titicaca. His visit was long before the discovery of Machu Picchu, which has the most famous of all inti-huatanas [ill. 128]. These bosses also reminded the American traveler of pillars near Cuzco by which the Incas observed the sun's passage. They were "inti huatanas or sun-fingers, where the sun might appear to be stopped, or tied up for a moment in his course; and on which, in his passage through the zenith, he might sit down in all his glory."

Beside the Pisac inti-huatana is a magnificent two-door rectangular building. It has the lintel in place on each of its doors and is closely associated with a series of liturgical baths and watercourses. This may have been the temple of the moon. Or it may have been linked to the water itself, for such engineering is a feature of all royal estates. As Jean-Pierre Protzen wrote: "Beautifully crafted fountains fed cascading waters through exquisitely carved channels, from one to the next. The purling sound of water must have delighted the site's residents. Whatever rituals were performed at these fountains, they must have been very important, because most of the waterworks were conspicuously located along major pathways or staircases." At Pisac there is another set of fountains unrelated to buildings, in a saddle below the uppermost Kalla Qasa ("parrot's pass") residential group.

On the terrace above the "temple of the moon," the northernmost of the five temple chambers has sharply cut stone pegs projecting from ashlars between its internal niches—a triumph of virtuoso masonry. These pegs may have had a dual purpose, for tying down the roof and also for hanging belongings. Above the entire group is a great platform, presumably an ushnu, with a low stone throne facing west toward the sunset. Immediately above the inti-huatana is a group of houses around a courtyard. This contains a rock sculpted with back and arms like a sofa, for two people to sit facing the sunrise.

A path from here climbs the mountain on its western flank. Squier described this route as "steep and devious...skirting the faces of cliffs a thousand feet [300 meters] sheer down on one side, and five hundred feet straight up on the other; where the brain grows dizzy, and where it is impossible for two men to pass abreast. Along such narrow pathways, where the condor sails level

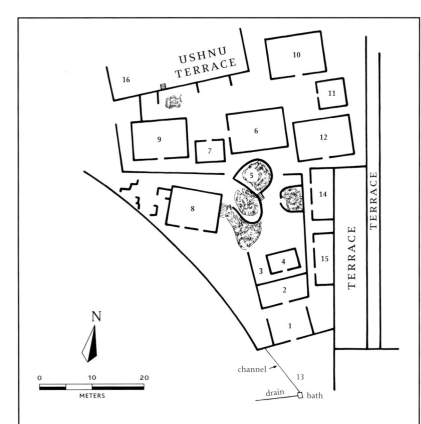

The inti-huatana group of Pisac occupies a triangular terrace. The main sacred outcrop (5) is surrounded by a D-shaped wall. Some rectangular buildings (6–12) may have been chapels of a temple similar to Coricancha. To the south is a liturgical bath (13) fed by a water channel. An ushnu platform (16) overlooks the site. Buildings 1–4 and 14–15 may have housed priests or mamaconas.

60 The uppermost gnomon of the sun temple.

with you above the abyss below, and where you lean inwards till your shoulder grazes the rock, along such paths as these…the visitor to Pisac must make his perilous way." Beyond the frightening cliff is a flight of steps and a tower, with a cluster of buildings perched recklessly on the mountainside. One path descends, through a 16-meter (52-foot) tunnel in a rock fault, to the perfectly preserved foundations of an Inca bridge on either side of the Kitamayu ravine. On the far side is a hillside full of rows of rock tombs, the largest highland Inca cemetery in Peru. The cliff of Tanqanamarca above the tombs may have been a place of execution, for persons sentenced to death in Inca law were thrown from such mountain precipices.

The ruins of Pisac are, unusually, spread out in clusters that do not observe one another. Another path climbs and, passing a short and low tunnel, reaches

Kalla Qasa, the largest group of buildings in Pisac. Here, on the crest of the ridge, is a mass of chambers and towers protected by a magnificent limestone wall reminiscent of Sacsahuaman. Squier imagined this as a frontier outpost of the Inca army, protecting the Yucay valley from the wild Amazonian tribes to the east: "There are inner walls and fortified barracks with outlooks and portholes, all admirably situated for defence, with covered parades and granaries, abodes for servants, and the material protection for a garrison of two thousand men. Quaint symbols cut on the rocks, needless stairways built up against them, *dilettante* elaboration of doorways, and a hundred other evidences exist here for an idle and *ennuyé* garrison. On the eastern side of the mountain every approach road is guarded by at least two stone gates and stretches of defensive wall. All the gates have stone pegs sunk into the inner sides of their jambs to secure their doors." Pisac's defenses may have been to provide seclusion, privacy, and a degree of protection for the Inca and his court.

This slope of Pisac (below the visitors' car park) has one of the most spectacular views in the Inca empire. The entire mountainside is disciplined with great flights of terracing that undulate majestically to fit its curving contours. Central irrigation channels plunge down the hill and fan out into each terrace. There are long flights of stairs, and flying steps projecting diagonally from the terrace walls. Modern archaeological authorities have made great efforts to clear and restore these terraces. They would like to see them farmed by the local community; but Inca terraces were designed to be worked labor-intensively

61 A trapezoidal gateway leads to the "sacred rock" of the sun temple.

with foot-plows, whereas farmers now prefer to use oxen whose weight is too great for the old retaining walls. Below, Pachacuti's laborers moved quantities of earth to create 70 hectares (173 acres) of level ground, and they even diverted the river into 3.3 kilometers (2 miles) of straight, stone-lined channel. Pisac's agricultural terraces far exceed the needs of its dwellings: they were clearly designed to grow surpluses for the court in Cuzco. Paradoxically, there are

few obvious qollqa storehouses: only one line of six rectangular huts, built of adobe, on a steep slope 300 meters (1,000 feet) from the inti-huatana group.

There are interesting structures on the mountain spur above the modern town of Pisac. One is a fine two-story building at a hub of paths below the inti-huatana. Víctor Angles Vargas, a modern interpreter of Pisac, regarded this as an administrative center, since it is such an important building,

62 The chamber with two doors, seen from the sun temple.

63 The inti-huatana group, with the sacred outcrop (right center).

on the narrowest part of the saddle with views to east and west over the enclosing ravines.

Nearby is Pisacllacta or Pisaqa, an artificial platform skillfully leveled to contain a curving group of thirty independent but uniform enclosures. Some walls in this section are of the finest coursed masonry. But others are of adobe, a building material well regarded by the Incas and much used in Pisac. The Inca builders used flat, rectangular adobe bricks, well packed with ichu grass for added strength. They laid their bricks in an "English" bond, alternating the long stretchers with the shorter ends or headers at the corners of buildings. Doors and niches had wooden or stone lintels and there were often wooden braces to strengthen corners of adobe houses. The clays of the adobes varied from yellow to brown and there was mud plaster over many walls. Inca architects were always skillful in adapting their buildings to the steep terrain of the Andes. One device was to have gables sloping at different angles or with a longer pitch on the valley side of a roof. Close to the Pisacllacta group is a solitary building that John Rowe called the *mirador* ("lookout") because its southern wall has large openings onto a panoramic view of the valley below. This is the finest adobe house in Pisac, with good bricks and bonding, niches, and braces.

A final feature of Pisac is its towers, of which there are remains of some twenty throughout the ruins. The finest are on the steep slope, the snout of Pisac's spur, above the modern town. These towers are of distinct types. There are massive watchtowers with solid bases, equidistant from one another for shouted messages and admirably sited to repel attack from below. Other towers are more conical, with sharply tapering walls. These appear to have been water cisterns: their bases are chambers carefully sealed with plaster, and they are connected to irrigation channels.

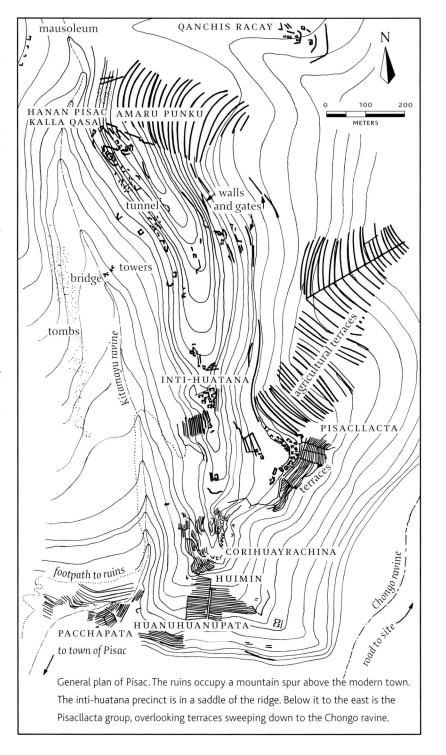

General plan of Pisac. The ruins occupy a mountain spur above the modern town. The inti-huatana precinct is in a saddle of the ridge. Below it to the east is the Pisacllacta group, overlooking terraces sweeping down to the Chongo ravine.

65 A magnificent flight of terraces covers the entire eastern slope of Pisac. Above it lies the Pisacllacta group; below, the Chongo ravine.

66 The terrace that flanks Chinchero's plaza has twelve superb niches, but their unusual width and rectangular shape may indicate post-Conquest masonry.

7. Chinchero

WHEN THE SECOND GREAT CONQUERING INCA, Topa Yupanqui, was an old man, in roughly 1500 of the Christian era, he decided to build a town on the plateau north of Cuzco. This was at Chinchero, 30 kilometers (19 miles) by road from the capital, near a large lake at the eastern edge of the Anta plain, where one Inca road dropped steeply down to the Yucay valley, another climbed to Huchuy Cosco (probably the estate of the Inca's grandfather, Viracocha), and a third went northwestward to Moray and the salt pans.

Juan de Betanzos wrote that Topa Inca Yupanqui built this town to house the growing population of Cuzco, as a retreat for Inca nobility, and above all for his personal recreation. The Inca himself drew the plan of his new town, took the lords of Cuzco there, and told them which sectors each was to build. "After seeing the plan that the Inca prepared...the master builders took their cords and measured the town...with the houses and streets outlined." Twenty thousand men were said to have been employed in the construction, which took five years. The Inca loved Chinchero and spent most of the last three years of his life there; but, aged about seventy and ill, he finally returned to Cuzco to die.

The monumental heart of Chinchero crowns a low hill above the town. There was a magnificent great hall, measuring 12.7 by 44 meters (42 by 144 feet), now the church. This hall had an innovation in Inca architecture: its northern end was largely open—a feature that was later developed, to expose almost the entire end wall at Huayna Capac's Quispihuanca palace near Yucay and in the Cassana palace in Cuzco. That opening is clearly visible in the polygonal Inca masonry on the end of the church: at 7 meters (23 feet) it exposed well over half that wall. In colonial times the opening was filled in to leave only a small side door to the church. The church's atrium porch was built on one of Inca Chinchero's two plazas, resting on several filled-in Inca houses. There is also a theory that there was a second great hall, at right angles to the one occupied by the church: its wall may form part of the handsome bell tower.

The upper square was then divided by a terrace, with a retaining wall that is the town's most striking feature. This terrace has twelve great niches, of which two toward the center are wider than the others. Its line of sentry-box niches reminds us of Tarahuasi and other sites, but it may have been built after the Conquest at the same time as the church. This later attribution would be because the niches are more rectangular than trapezoidal, its cornice of fifty-eight capstones looks Spanish, and some blocks do not fit together to the highest Inca standard. Parts of the terrace may, however, have been walls of filled-in Inca houses, with their doors blocked to become niches.

Chinchero's other plaza is a great platform to the north of the town, known as Capellan-pampa, with a lovely view across a valley ravine to distant snow-capped mountains. This is where the Inca doubtless conducted his ceremonies and reviewed his army. A line of three kallanka-like halls overlooks the plaza, but these are on a terrace so that the openings in their northern walls were windows rather than doors—access to the parade ground was by a broad stepped passage between two of the buildings and below the great hall. Only the foundations and lower walls of these buildings survive, but they were impressive structures. The easternmost is narrow and rectangular, 48 meters (157 feet) long, with six double-jambed windows over the plaza, many small niches in its southern wall, and curious entry atria at either end. The middle building is smaller, squarish, with eight great niches on the inner wall and a single broad, double-jambed window to the plaza. It is easy to imagine this being the Inca's personal viewing pavilion. The western building is a more conventional kallanka hall, 42 meters (138 feet) long and with seven great openings toward the parade ground.

A glory of Chinchero is the terracing of the hillside below the monumental center and the parade-ground plaza. These terraces follow the shape of the hill but are straight and with right angles, unlike the curving contours of Pisac's terracing: Gasparini and Margolies wrote that they "form great angular amphitheatres." With high walls and stonework of fine quality, these are what Susan Niles called "high-prestige" terracing. But the Spanish archaeologist José Alcina Franch pointed out that Chinchero is at the edge of a broad, fertile plain that is still famous for its potatoes and quinoa, so that the purpose of these beautiful terraces was ritual, aesthetic, or as a demonstration of human mastery over nature, rather than purely agricultural. The spiritual dimension is emphasized by a series of rock-outcrop shrines imbedded amid the terracing. There is a sculpted complex known as Titicaca, immediately below the plaza; Antasaca outcrop on the hill southeast of the church; a prominent stone called Pumacaca just east of the three kallankas; and Chingana down

67 Chinchero's church was built in the great hall of Topa Inca's royal retreat. Its largely open end wall, an innovation of late-Inca architecture, was filled in by the church builders.

the hill to the northeast of the terraces. The Titicaca outcrop is notable for its carved, curving staircases and a stepped tunnel entrance [ill. 7], shelves and niches, a groove like a vertical drainpipe, and a grotto further down the hill. An anthropologist resident in Chinchero told the archaeologist John Hyslop that local people still revered—and feared—these outcrops, and that their ancestors had been made by their priests to chip the carving off Antasaca. The Pumacaca stone has worked surfaces and possible animal carvings; it is so prominent that Alcina felt that it may have been the reason for the buildings beside it. Chingana and the smaller stones at its base are covered in worked shelves, frets, and a watercourse.

Betanzos wrote that Topa Inca Yupanqui himself designed the town of Chinchero, and much of his plan survives. On the slope south of the upper

68 The view westward from the Pumacaca shrine (left foreground) to the ruins of three kallanka-like halls which overlook the Capellan-pampa parade ground. Photograph by Susan Niles.

plaza and monumental center is a grid of streets: six in one direction and five at right angles to them. This orthogonal pattern is reminiscent of the town of Ollantaytambo, but the layout is less regular because it is on a steep curving slope. Both complexes were evidently built to house the ayllu of the Inca aristocracy, as Betanzos said. Work at Chinchero, however, appears to have continued after the Spanish Conquest. The architectural historian Stella Nair studied houses on this grid of streets whose stone walls were topped by adobe bricks, just like those of the residential sectors of Inca Cuzco. "However, on closer examination, one notices that many of the blocks have been worked with metal hammer tools introduced by European immigrants." The pattern left by metal chisels differed from that of chipping by Inca stone tools. Nair also found one section of Chinchero where houses had classic Inca

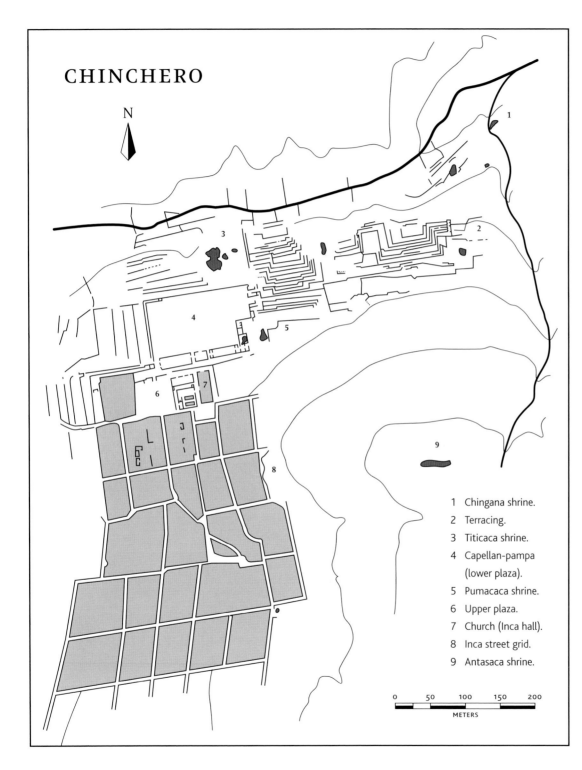

CHINCHERO

N

1 Chingana shrine.
2 Terracing.
3 Titicaca shrine.
4 Capellan-pampa (lower plaza).
5 Pumacaca shrine.
6 Upper plaza.
7 Church (Inca hall).
8 Inca street grid.
9 Antasaca shrine.

0   50   100   150   200
METERS

plans—freestanding, single-room, single-story, rectangular structures with few connecting doors or passages—but their adobe bricks were made in Spanish-style molds, and some old houses even had arches and entrance halls.

Chinchero was one of the hated "reductions" into which the Viceroy Francisco de Toledo in the 1570s forced scattered Peruvian peasants to congregate. It was Toledo who founded the church dedicated to Our Lady of Montserrat in the great hall of Topa Inca Yupanqui's palace. The town seems to have prospered in the seventeenth century, but with an indigenous population: a famous painting of 1693 in the church shows the native elite wearing a blend of Spanish and Inca dress, the same fusion demonstrated in their domestic architecture.

A fine Spanish archaeological mission, led by José Alcina Franch, excavated and restored Chinchero between 1966 and 1971. It reported that the Inca site was extensive, occupying the entire area of the modern town. Evidence of burned roofs appeared frequently in the excavations. This confirmed a report that in 1545 Manco Inca's commander Pumasupa had attempted an attack on Cuzco—currently under-defended because of civil wars—and had a skirmish with Spaniards at Chinchero. Many late-Inca ceramics were also excavated, since Chinchero was probably a center of pottery-making. The town declined, like so much of highland Peru, during the later colonial and republican periods. It was a backwater, away from the main road west from Cuzco. This isolation changed recently, when the road to Chinchero was paved and became a favorite route for tourists going to (or returning from) the "Sacred Valley" of Yucay and the Vilcanota. The National Institute of Culture continued the restoration of the town's monuments and superb terraces, so that Chinchero is now one of the most attractive places to visit near Cuzco, with a colorful and unspoiled weekly market.

70 There are three rock shrines in a terraced valley below Chinchero. The largest (center), known locally as Titicaca rock, has two carved stairways: one on its surface, visible here, and the other in the dark cleft to the right. Another, the Chingana stone, is further down the valley, and the third is pictured on page 189.

71 Agricultural terraces of Moray follow the contours of depressions in the limestone plateau.

8. Moray

IN THE VERTICAL WORLD OF THE ANDES, flat agricultural land is scarce and landslides are a constant threat. The Incas solved both these problems by building agricultural terraces.

A typical Inca agricultural terrace (*pata*) would be between 1.5 and 4 meters (5 to 13 feet) high, contained by a stone wall of fieldstones roughly shaped to fit one another. Such containing walls might be 60 to 75 centimeters (2 to 2½ feet) thick, and, as Garcilaso observed, "they slope back slightly so as to withstand the weight of earth with which they are filled." The inward lean of a terrace wall was fifteen to twenty degrees. Within this containing wall, Indian farmers carefully filled the cavity with larger stones at the base for drainage and good soil at the surface.

Effective irrigation was essential for terraced agriculture, and the Incas used admirable ingenuity and engineering skill—as well as the customary prodigious labor—to channel water to their terraces. Banks of terraces were linked by a web of long flights of stairs, but individual terraces could also be climbed by occasional projecting steps—stone slabs protruding in diagonal flights from the face of the terrace wall.

The most enigmatic Inca terraces are at the Inca site of Moray, near Maras, on the limestone plateau 38 kilometers (24 miles) northwest of Cuzco. Here, three large circular depressions were carefully terraced, as if to form the seating for a giant circular arena—although the terraces are purely agricultural and far too high for seating. Slopes near the depressions were similarly terraced. The limestone may have subsided into sinkholes typical of karst topography, or deep gullies may have opened into dolines. But the Incas clearly expended much energy to sculpt these depressions into perfect circles and to fill the land between them. The lowest tier of terraces in the three depressions is between 40 and 45 meters (131 to 148 feet) in diameter, and the surface of each terrace is between 4 and 10 meters (13 to 33 feet) wide. The three depressions have six or seven layers of terracing around their sides, and these terraces were once level and filled with earth of good quality.

The natural cavities of Moray are near no large settlement: so the Incas used them as a shrine and a place for special agriculture. One crop highly prized by the Inca court was the shrub coca, whose leaf looks like a bay leaf but is a mild narcotic when chewed and mixed with lime. Coca chewing is now widespread among Andean Indians, but it was once a privilege reserved for the ruling caste. Hernando de Santillán, a Spanish administrator who was particularly well informed about Peruvian ways, wrote about coca: "They considered it something very precious and of great nourishment and sustenance, because they say that someone taking it feels no hunger, thirst or fatigue. This coca grows in all the valleys and lowlands, and in very deep gullies in many parts of the mountains—anywhere that the wind does not disturb the land, where the sun shines intensely and the climate is hot and humid." The terraced depressions of Moray would admirably fulfill these requirements for growing coca, but they could equally well have grown fine maize.

A more ingenious interpretation has come from anthropologist John Earls. He discovered vertical stones in the Moray terraces that mark the limits of afternoon shadow at the equinoxes and solstices. Local people told him that these stones were called *ñustas* ("princesses") and that they themselves used similar stones to mark shadow limits in their own fields. Earls concluded, by additional experiment, that each terrace at Moray reproduced climatic conditions in different ecological zones of the Inca empire. Because of their sheltered position, each of these terraces represented roughly 1,000 meters (3,300 feet) of altitude in normal farming conditions, so that the entire complex contained in miniature twenty or more ecological zones. The Moray site would thus have helped Inca officials to calculate yields from different parts of the empire in each year.

72 The Moray terraces may have been used for agricultural experiment or ceremonial purposes.

73 A natural flow of salt near Maras has been channeled since Inca times into a crystalline labyrinth of evaporating pans.

74 The plateau at Maras, overlooking the Urubamba valley, with the Lares hills in the distance and a hedge of *maguey* (agave) in the foreground.

9. Ollantaytambo

FIFTY KILOMETERS (30 MILES) down the Vilcanota–Urubamba river northwest from Pisac, the mighty fortified temple of Ollantaytambo towers above the Yucay valley. The Spaniards first became aware of this town during Manco Inca's great rebellion of 1536–37. The siege of Cuzco lapsed into stalemate after Pizarro's men recaptured Sacsahuaman. Most of Manco's levies returned to their harvests; but he planned to mobilize them again the following year. The besieged Spaniards learned that the Inca had his headquarters at Ollantaytambo. They decided on a bold, desperate attack at this very center of Peruvian resistance. Hernando Pizarro took all his best men for this strike: seventy horse, thirty foot, and a large contingent of indigenous auxiliaries.

The march down the Vilcanota–Urubamba was difficult. A horseman wrote that the river "had to be crossed five or six times, and each ford was defended." One such garrison-fort is Chocana, 2 kilometers (1¼ miles) upriver from Ollantaytambo on the left bank. Its houses, stores, irrigation system, and narrow streets are remarkably well preserved. Some walls even retain original red frescoes. There is a massive terrace wall, and another fort blocking the opposite side of the river. Nineteenth-century travelers—the Austrian Charles Wiener, the German Middendorf, and the American Squier—left drawings of these handsome parapets crouching beneath the cliffs of the valley wall. There is another small fort, Choquekilla, also on the left bank not far upstream. To Squier, this was "confined between heavy artificial walls, …a long building of two stories, with turrets and loopholes, hanging against the mountain… It more resembles the castles of the Rhine…than anything we have yet seen." Inca engineers channeled a meander of the Urubamba here. Their road on the left bank is still intact, enclosed by walls; and there are remains of a suspension bridge where this enters the town and joins another road on the right bank. The bridge's abutments are visible on either bank, and its central pier on a rock outcrop is protected against the river's current by stone breakwaters.

Pedro Pizarro recalled that "when we reached [Ollantay]Tambo we found it so well fortified that it was a horrifying sight. For Tambo's location is naturally very strong with very high terraces, and fortified with great masses of masonry… Its gate was tall, with great walls on either side made from compacted stone and clay: a very thick rampart, with only one small opening in it through which an Indian could pass on all fours." The Spaniards attacked from a plain beside the river, but they gradually realized that they were in a trap. "The Indians were fighting them from three sides: some from the hillside, others from the far bank of the river, and the rest from the town… The Inca was in the fortress itself with many well-armed warriors." "They amassed such a quantity of men against us that they could not crowd onto the hillsides and plains." Jean-Pierre Protzen (who worked for years in Ollantaytambo and published a definitive work on its architecture) has convinced me that the battle occurred *outside* Ollantaytambo, where the modern road climbs a zigzag toward the gate. This is because an anonymous account of the siege of Cuzco speaks of *eleven* terraces, and that is precisely the number beneath the town's southeastern wall.

Two of the older conquistadors bravely rode their horses up against the terraces. They were repulsed and "it was amazing to see the arrows that rained down on them as they returned, and to hear the shouting." Another group of horsemen tried to attack the wall and terraces, but the defenders "hurled down so many boulders and fired so many slingshots that, even had we been many more Spaniards than we were, we would all have been killed." A missile broke the haunch of the lead horse. The animal rolled over, kicking, rearing, and falling down the terraces, so that it dispersed horsemen trying to follow. Hernando Pizarro sent a party of foot soldiers to try to seize the heights above the wall, but these men were driven back by a hail of rocks.

As the Spaniards wavered, the Incas attacked. They charged out onto the plain "with such a tremendous shout that it seemed as if the mountain were crashing down. So many men suddenly appeared on every side that every visible stretch of wall was covered with Indians. The enemy locked [Pizarro's men] in a fierce struggle, more savage than had ever been seen by either side." The Indians had acquired some Spanish weapons and were learning to employ them. They attempted to fire captured culverins and arquebuses, with powder prepared by Spanish prisoners. "It was impressive to see some of them emerge ferociously with Castilian swords, bucklers and morrión helmets. There was one Indian who, armed in this manner, dared to attack a horse: he prided himself on death from a lance to win fame as a hero. The Inca [Manco] himself appeared among his men, on horseback with a lance in his hand, keeping control of his army."

Manco's secret weapon was starting to take effect. Unobserved by the Spaniards, Peruvian engineers dammed the Urubamba river and diverted it along prepared channels to flood the plain. Spanish horsemen soon found themselves trying to maneuver in rising water that eventually reached the horses' girths. "The ground became so sodden that the horses could not skirmish." Hernando Pizarro saw that his position was untenable, and ordered a retreat to Cuzco. His men tried to slip away under cover of darkness, abandoning their tents below Ollantaytambo's unbreached wall. But the column of retreating horsemen was observed "and the Indians came down upon them with a great cry...grabbing the horses' tails." Pedro Pizarro praised his adversaries: "They attacked us with great fury at a river crossing, carrying burning torches... There is one thing about these Indians: when they are victorious they are demons in pressing it home, whereas when fleeing they are like wet hens. Since they were now following up a victory, seeing us retire, they pursued with great spirit." Manco's son Titu Cusi recalled how delighted his people had been by the defeat of this powerful force. A few of the attackers were killed, but "the Inca was extremely sad that Hernando Pizarro had gone, for he was sure that had he delayed another day no single Spaniard would have escaped. In truth, anyone who saw the appearance of the fortress could have believed nothing else."

Ollantaytambo was the scene of a very different assembly in the following year, 1537. The arrival of Spanish reinforcements had broken the siege of Cuzco. The Spaniards were regaining control of all Peru and Manco Inca decided that he was too exposed, even in the fortress-temple of Ollantaytambo. He determined to retreat into the fastnesses of the Vilcabamba hills, leaving the mass of his countrymen under foreign domination. "Before leaving they armed themselves and, in a great square near their camp in which an idol

75 Ollantaytambo from across the Urubamba river. A defensive wall rises above the spur containing the temple complex, with diagonal ramps below for hauling blocks to the site. Beyond the Patacancha ravine is the steep flank of Pinkuylluna hill, with groups of storage buildings.

76 The "avenue of the hundred niches." In Inca times the roadbed was a meter lower, and it may have been flanked by a similar niched wall on its other side.

stood, they begged and prayed [for] it not to desert them, with many tears, sobbing and sighs. Near this idol were others with insignia of the Sun and the Moon. In the presence of these, which they regarded as gods, they offered sacrifices by killing many animals on their shrines and altars." Manco Inca then retreated to the northwest, never to return to the Yucay valley so beloved by his royal forebears.

Where the modern road enters Ollantaytambo, you can see Tiyupunku, a gate of two double-jambed entrances flanked by guardhouses and a parapet walkway as in a European castle. This marks the start of the long "avenue of the hundred niches." George Squier wrote in 1877 that "past [the gate] the road continued between a high niched wall, on the one hand, and the cliff with its gurgling *azequia* [water channel], on the other. Thus shut in betwixt wall and

77 Seventeen superb terraces contour the 45-degree slope from the square of Mañay Raqay to the sun temple.

78 Terrace stairway to the sun temple.

mountain side, and our view circumscribed, we jog on for half a mile. Then the wall ends." Squier included a drawing of the splendid wall of niches; and this shows that since his day most of it has been buried by the roadbed, sometimes up to the sills of the niches. Since such small niches are usual only in internal walls, I wondered whether this had been one wall of a couple of long kallankas, or even that the Inca road might once have been roofed. Protzen allowed that the kallankas were a distinct possibility, and decided that the road might once have had a wall on either side but no roof.

Beyond the "avenue of the hundred niches," the hills open for the ravine of the Patacancha stream. The town of Ollantaytambo lies at its mouth. Straight ahead is the hill of the sun temple. It is a majestic sight, with the rocky spur buttressed to the east by a monumental flight of seventeen straight, broad terraces. They climb at a smooth angle of 45 degrees, and both embellish and protect the sanctuary above. With side terracing, this cascade forms a magnificent amphitheater. To the south, overlooking the river, the outcrop is flanked by tiers of undulating terraces. The temple must have looked inspiring when more intact, with its spur converted into a gigantic stepped pyramid crowned by the gleaming enclosures of its sacred buildings.

Access to the temple is by a stairway that starts in the center of the terraces and continues up their left edge. Near the top, another stair turns left up a flight of five superbly cut, subtly curving, tall terraces that protect the northern side of the spur. The fourth of these terraces has the same fine polygonal masonry as the others for the first 20 meters (66 feet). Some of these blocks have unusual pointed bases that Harth-Terré called "scutiform" because they reminded him of heraldic shields. At this terrace's western end was once a roofed chamber or entrance passage. The terrace wall here slopes inward to the chamber and contains ten

79 The portal to the sun temple area, with pairs of bosses.

80 The trapezoidal gate at the far end of the wall of niches.

81 Two of the niches. Bosses may have been left for aesthetic effect.

82 Detail, the wall of niches.

83 The sun temple was approached from the upper terraces by either the double-jambed gate to the right or through the "enclosure of the ten niches" whose outer wall has collapsed.

84 Six great monoliths flank the eastern wall of the sun temple.

elegant niches. The outer wall of this "enclosure of the ten niches" has gone, but its far end has a trapezoidal gate with its lintel in place. The terrace starts with the foundations of one of the finest of all Inca niches or portals. It is double-jambed, fitted with supreme skill, and surrounded by enigmatic pairs of bosses protruding from otherwise smooth stones. But it appears never to have been finished. Both gates lead up to the main Temple Sector.

Ollantaytambo's sun temple is unfinished and now sadly mined and fragmented. Protzen lamented that fragments of surviving walls are a provocative sketch of what might have been: "It is nearly impossible to imagine what the overall plan would have been like, if the Inca architects had had the opportunity to complete the project." It was clearly planned on a majestic scale. Its terraces alone provide "a glimpse of the splendor of the masterpiece that will never be." Spanish zealots may have started to destroy it because they feared its religious significance and its potential as a fortress. Seekers of building blocks contributed to the sack. Ashlars were used to build the Spanish town below: we see stones of the temple's pale-pink porphyry in the foundations of the church and flanking the door of the curate's house.

The visitor now clambers to the jewel of Ollantaytambo: the magnificent "wall of the six monoliths." This monolithic screen stands to a height of 4 meters (13 feet) at the right-hand stone, but it is impossible to say what form of structure it once supported. The German artist Johann Moritz Rugendas sketched the monoliths in the 1840s and showed stones above them that have since disappeared. The narrow fillet stones between the monoliths are a bond found nowhere else in the Inca empire. Protzen wondered why the main temple has only this one superbly cut wall. The answer may have been that these temples were being built or modified in phases by different generations of architects. There is a mysterious passage running for almost 8 meters (26 feet) behind the frieze of monoliths. The thinner monoliths have been shored up with niched walls of Inca masonry to form the corridor. One can imagine priests using this passage during some now-forgotten ritual.

Behind and above the sun temple is the so-called Middle Sector, excavated by Luis Llanos in 1934. Its buildings are generally of fieldstone in clay. One is long and narrow, possibly a storage passage, with twenty-six niches staggered diagonally in two rows. Another square building has a floor plan of 53 square meters (570 square feet): it may have been a kallanka-type hall for indoor celebrations. This sector also has remains of water channels and "fountains."

The temple platform is littered with blocks. Some may remain because they were too large to remove. Others appear never to have been used—either because parts of the temple were being built when the Conquest occurred, or because earlier construction phases had never been completed. To Protzen, "it seems evident that the site was undergoing a major remodeling at the time it

85 Detail of a monolith's stepped motif and unique fillet bonds.

was abandoned." Some loose blocks were apparently torn off walls; others had been used previously and reworked.

There is a row of twelve green ashlars cut with outstanding precision. These have smooth surfaces and sharp angles, with no hint of the pillowed faces or sunken joints seen on most Inca blocks. Their masonry is just like that in the great pre-Inca ruin Tiahuanaco near Lake Titicaca. Another striking Tiahuanacan similarity is T-shaped grooves on some blocks—these were clearly to join one block to another with H-shaped copper clamps. We have seen how, in 1567, an aged chief from Acora on Lake Titicaca recalled that his people had sent many Indians to work on the Inca's constructions, as well as copper bars for his buildings. All these blocks with T-grooves had been removed from some earlier building. The sun temple's six monoliths also have Tiahuanacan traits, in both the vertical fillet bonds and three stepped motifs on the central block. The fillets are strongly reminiscent of monoliths separated by smaller blocks in the sides of the Calasasaya platform at Tiahuanaco. Step symbols are one hallmark of Tiahuanacan design that is found in only a few Inca ruins. Those at Ollantaytambo are now sadly weathered, but they were sharper in Squier's day in the 1870s. Another monolith has a projection that has been crudely chipped. Could it once have had an effigy of the sun or a feline, both of which were central to Tiahuanacan worship?

There is remarkable written confirmation of the link between Ollantaytambo and Tiahuanaco in the chronicle of Pedro Sarmiento de Gamboa. This historian conducted official interrogations of aged Peruvians during the 1570s, in an attempt to discredit Inca rule for propaganda purposes. The inquiries did reveal surprisingly bitter hostility to the Incas, even among subject tribes close to Cuzco itself. Some informants told of how the conqueror Pachacuti demanded that their Tampu ancestors pay homage. When the ancestors refused, the Inca subdued them with a large army and destroyed their town. Pachacuti then "took as his own the valley of Tambo which was not his." (It is clear from this that "tampu" or "tambo" in Ollantaytambo did not mean post-house but referred to the tribe of that name.)

Having taken Ollantaytambo as his personal fief, Pachacuti erected the magnificent buildings we now see. For this he and his son used tribute labor from the Collao, the area near Lake Titicaca and Tiahuanaco. Sarmiento revealed that "the sons of Chuchi Capac, the great chief of the Colla, had to labor as captives at masonry and other work [in Ollantaytambo]. Their father in the Collao had been conquered and killed by the Inca. These sons of Chuchi Capac felt that they were being treated basely. Proud to be the sons of so great a father, and also seeing that the Inca had disbanded his army, they determined to risk their lives to gain their freedom. One night they fled with all the people who were there." These Colla nobles—the first recorded strikers in

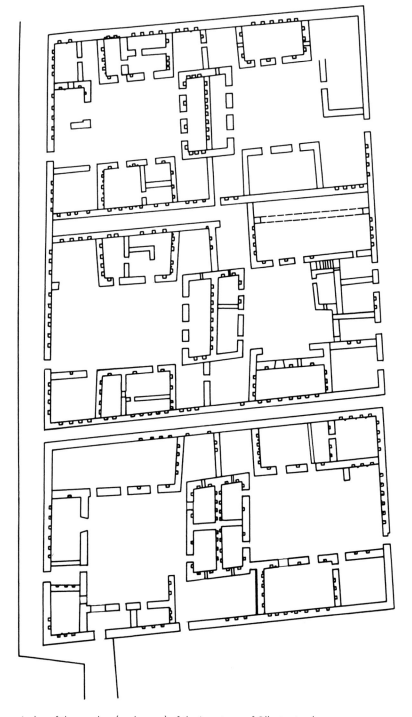

86 A plan of the canchas (enclosures) of the Inca town of Ollantaytambo.

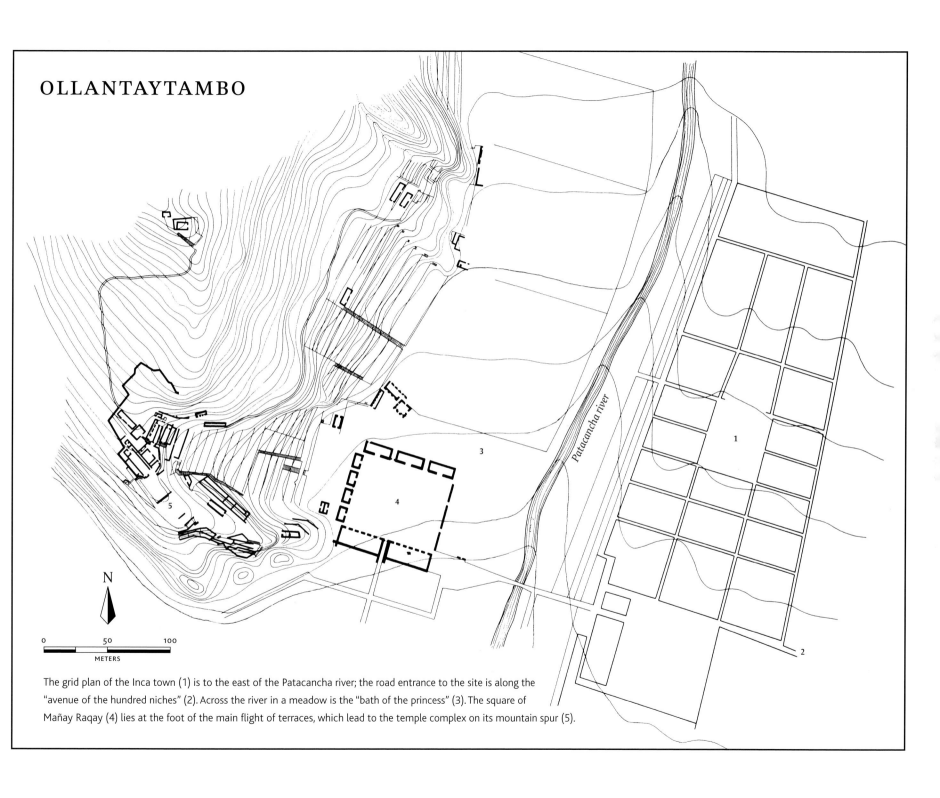

OLLANTAYTAMBO

N

0   50   100
METERS

The grid plan of the Inca town (1) is to the east of the Patacancha river; the road entrance to the site is along the "avenue of the hundred niches" (2). Across the river in a meadow is the "bath of the princess" (3). The square of Mañay Raqay (4) lies at the foot of the main flight of terraces, which lead to the temple complex on its mountain spur (5).

88 A stone footbridge at the edge of Mañay Raqay square.

Peru—hurried back to their homeland, raising tribes in revolt as they went. The result was a great uprising of the Colla and other southern tribes, a rebellion that Pachacuti suppressed only with much fighting and bloodshed. The workers' abrupt departure might explain some of the unfinished building blocks at Ollantaytambo. This use of Colla forced labor would also explain why Tiahuanacan building techniques recur at Ollantaytambo—they had been kept alive around the lake, particularly in the chullpa tower-tombs of Sillustani.

At the foot of the seventeen terraces is a plaza surrounded by monumental buildings. This sector is called Mañay Raqay (or Manyaraki), which means "hall of petitions" in Quechua. A handsome two-storied building of masonry and adobe at the edge of this square may at some time have served as a court for hearing petitions, and the plaza was clearly a public space with formal functions. All this could have been built after Pachacuti's reign, because its buildings are of a slightly different style, and because there are vestiges of

89 The ceremonial pool known as the "bath of the ñusta" (princess). Its fountain is carved with the Tiahuanacan stepped motif.

foundations of earlier structures with another plan. Mañay Raqay's buildings are tall, of adobe or tapia on a base of semicut stones in mortar, and with unusually large portals—like the last paramount Inca Huayna Capac's palace at Urubamba. Guaman Poma wrote that Huayna Capac's son Manco Inca erected many buildings at Ollantaytambo during the year 1536–37 when it was his headquarters.

East of the square, up the Patacancha valley, is a series of elaborate Inca shrines and watercourses topped by excellent terracing. One irrigation channel pours over a lovely stone font, now hidden in a private meadow between Mañay Raqay and Ollantaytambo town. This elegant stone has a carved façade that rises in a stepped pattern, and its spout is of a stone so hard that it has not weathered. This is known, romantically, as the "bath of the ñusta" (Inca princess).

The surroundings of Ollantaytambo are almost as interesting as the temple complex. The village at the foot of the hill is the most perfect example of Inca town planning still in use. The town is arranged in a grid, with streets intersecting at right angles. Four long streets that run parallel to the Patacancha contain magnificent portals, each leading to a cancha enclosure. There are no cancha doors on the six lateral streets. This was no ordinary peasant town: it was evidently built for royal or religious dignitaries, perhaps court officials or visiting nobility. Cobo stressed that only Cuzco and the most important towns were built on regular plans. He also pointed out that only the houses of chiefs had courtyards, in which people could gather for drinking ceremonies or other meetings.

Each of the village's blocks contains two canchas. These are independent of one another, back to back, with gates on opposite sides of their blocks. Inside the monumental double-jambed portals, the canchas are all alike. There is a gatehouse of open-sided masma design facing the main, three-doored house across the courtyard.

90 Entrances to cancha enclosures and a water channel in the Inca town of Ollantaytambo.

91 One of the alleys or transversal streets.

700-meter (770-yard) depression—probably a former course of the Patacancha—has been shaped to form a sunken avenue, known in Spanish as the Callejón. This is flanked by an impressive row of alcoves and full-height niches, built of rough fieldstone in mortar once covered by clay plaster. These elaborate alcoves may once have had lean-to roofs, and their strange design is unique to Ollantaytambo: they must once have housed attendants in some forgotten ritual. The Callejón has a remarkable microclimate, two or three degrees warmer than the surroundings; so it may have grown maize or even coca. There is no obvious road down the Callejón—visitors have to scramble through fields, over walls, and down terraces.

The goal is the palace of Q'ellu Raqay, a purely domestic building whose courtyards and stuccoed chambers remind one of a Moroccan riad. The indefatigable George Squier made a fine plan of this palace and said that "its remains are still distinct, and some parts of it almost entire. It was elaborate in plan...and shows that Inca architecture...did not balk at the task of raising buildings of more than a single storey." He demonstrated this with a charming sketch of an Indian couple chatting below a two-storied square building that has plenty of windows and an external stone staircase.

The main house of one cancha backs onto that of another cancha, so that each house has its roof pitched down from the dividing wall. The thatched roofs were tied down to pegs. A pair of identical buildings also faces inward on either side of the patio. The four houses in each cancha are arranged with open spaces in the corners of the walled compound, probably for use as corrals for domestic llamas. The elegance of Ollantaytambo's residential area is enhanced by stone-channeled culverts that bring mountain water pouring along its straight cobbled streets. By Andean Indian standards, the village compounds were small palaces. All their buildings are liberally provided with storage niches, and some have ring-stones high on walls that may have secured back-looms. But internal partition walls are recent additions, by the families who live there with their dogs, chickens, and scurrying guinea pigs.

The residential grid is next to the modern town's Plaza de Armas. On the far side of this, strange and fascinating ruins slope down toward the Urubamba. A Q'ellu Raqay palace has deteriorated badly since the 1870s. It was examined by John Rowe, who was sure that this was where Pachacuti relaxed amid gardens of flowers and ornamental plants. Karen Chávez and Alan Sawyer made some excavations and clearance in 1978, but it has become more ruined and overgrown since then. However, with its interconnecting and overlapping chambers, Protzen found that it "is not merely unusual; there is no known Inca structure like it." Its setting is lovely. To Squier, the palace stood "on a series of charming terraces overlooking the smiling valley," and Protzen noted a magnificent view of the snowcapped shoulder of Mount Verónica.

The hills that tower over Ollantaytambo have a number of fascinating Inca remains on their steep slopes. Immediately overlooking the main flight of terraces, two-story houses cling giddily to the mountain. Behind and above runs a wall of quarried stone set in yellowish clay mortar. The wall climbs steeply up the mountain and, in places, seems superfluous for defensive purposes.

It could have been built by Manco, but was otherwise more for symbolic, religious seclusion than to repel attackers—in the manner of token defenses from Pachacuti's reign, around central Pisac and Machu Picchu and the Viracocha temple at Raqchi. The paths on this mountain are narrow, and the slopes precipitous. It is a place better suited to surefooted Indians impervious to vertigo than to foreign visitors. Above the enclosure wall to the west is a complex now known as Inca-huatana or "hitching place of the Inca." This consists of a wall with tall niches whose sides have securing holes some 80 centimeters (2½ feet) above the ground; in front is a towerlike structure that overhangs the precipice. We know that Inca punishments included beatings and cord tortures and, for capital crimes, death by being hurled from cliffs. In popular imagination, therefore, this Inca-huatana was a place of execution; but it could just as well have been an observatory or signal station.

Opposite Ollantaytambo's sun temple, on the far side of the stream and town, is a steep hill that projects into the angle between the Patacancha and Vilcanota–Urubamba valleys. This hill is Pinkuylluna, "where the pinkuyllu flute is played." Two enigmatic groups of buildings perch on this rocky slope. Modern guides with lively imaginations describe these as universities, nunneries, or prisons; the archaeologist Víctor Angles Vargas argued that they were places where people who lived on these hills assembled for communal tasks or entertainments; or they could have been barracks for the soldiers who appeared on this hill when Hernando Pizarro attacked Manco. However, careful research by Gasparini and Margolies, Protzen, and others showed that they were qollqa storehouses.

Cobo wrote that the Incas often placed their storehouses in high places that were cool and windy, to reduce humidity and decay. This is true of those at Ollantaytambo, and they also had subtle ventilation systems. There are two types of qollqa here. Eleven are tall buildings of fieldstone in clay mortar coated in yellow plaster. These contain a total of thirty-two rectangular chambers, two to four per store: small, squarish chambers with channels in their floors for drainage or ventilation. Ledges show that these buildings had upper floors or attics for further storage. Similar qollqas at Huánuco probably stored fresh potatoes, which were at risk of germinating, growing fungi, or being eaten by vermin; but Protzen felt that Ollantaytambo was too warm for potato storage and that maize was more likely. The second type of storehouses are long, narrow structures with steep gabled roofs and many tall windows. These are 3 meters (10 feet) wide and between 10 and 38 meters (33 to 125 feet) long. Each has six windows over the valley, ten on the upper side, and a window and door at each end. Their split-level floors also have drainage or ventilation channels. Professor Protzen made models of these huts in a wind-tunnel, filled them from a smoke-generator, and tested wind velocity with an anemometer.

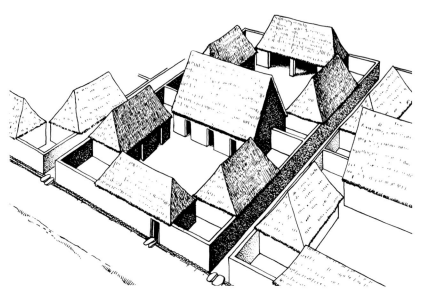

92 A reconstruction of two canchas.

This showed that they "proved to be quite aerodynamic and to shed winds most effectively." They had gentle air currents, which improved when they were full of produce, and they shed driving rain most effectively. But there are still unanswered questions: "How the stored goods were used and for what purposes are not known."

Anyone visiting Ollantaytambo must ponder the prodigious human effort expended in quarrying and cutting these vast blocks and dragging them down to the valley and up to the temple. One "tired stone" that never completed the journey lies half buried on an inclined plane below the promontory. Squier measured it and found that it was over 21 feet long by 15 broad, and with 5 feet projecting above ground (6.55 by 4.6 by 1.5 meters). Characteristically, Squier crossed the Urubamba and climbed up to the quarries in which these blocks originated. This is a stiff walk, some 5 kilometers (3 miles) from the town, and rising to quarries that are between 400 and 900 meters (1,300 to almost 3,000 feet) above the valley. Protzen did some of his finest research in these Cachicata (Kachiqhata) quarries. It was here (and in ones near Cuzco) that he taught himself Inca masonry skills. He found that these were not quarries in the modern sense, since the Incas did not cut blocks from bedrock. Instead, they found places where cliffs of the unstable Andes had crumbled in massive rock falls, and then shaped the tumbled boulders. Protzen's discoveries about stone-chipping techniques are described in this book's introduction on Inca architecture (see page 24). The infrastructure of these quarries was impressive: huts for the workers, barracks and irrigation channels to accommodate

93 The canchas are still in use as farmyards.

them, and an elaborate network of some 8.8 kilometers (5.5 miles) of roads and ramps that involved moving 40,000 cubic meters (1.4 million cubic feet) of dirt and rocks. One of the two quarries covers 52 hectares (128 acres) and contains seventeen half-finished large blocks. These stones are mostly of igneous rhyolite, which splits fairly easily when expertly pounded, but there was no magic formula such as acids or freezing water for this (Ollantaytambo is too warm)—just patient labor.

Protzen pondered how the ancient builders moved the stones from the quarries, down to the river, across it, and then up to Ollantaytambo's temple mount. That journey started with a 40-degree-steep chute, shaped by sliding blocks rather than by stream water. Squier had peeked over "the brow of the headland, over which [the stones] were toppled, sliding down two thousand feet [610 meters] into the valley. The plane worn in their descent is distinct, and lying around us are blocks more or less shaped artificially... How these

94 A carved outcrop north of Mañay Raqay square.

blocks were got across the swift and turbulent river, in the bed of which some still remain, I do not attempt to explain." Once down the slides, the blocks were hauled over flatter ground—their undersides have striations from this hauling. Protzen presumed that they were pulled across the river when it was at its lowest, but there are now no signs of fords or jetties on its banks. There are four abandoned blocks on the left bank of the Urubamba and twenty on the right, and some of these weigh over 100 metric tons. Pedro Gutiérrez de Santa Clara, like his contemporary Garcilaso de la Vega, wrote that "these Indians used to move very large stones with muscle power, pulling them with many long ropes of lianas and leaf fibers," and Cieza de León said that for 4,000 men in the quarries there were 6,000 employed in this hauling. We know that the Incas made massive cables of ichu grass and

95 Pinkuylluna hill from the sun temple.

hides for their suspension bridges. Protzen reckoned that they surrounded the largest blocks with a net or harness and had about 1,800 men pulling on four great ropes. This train would have stretched for 190 meters (620 feet) along the roadway or ramp. Rollers, sledges, or lubricants may have been used, but there is of course no surviving evidence of these. Protzen found, however, that a bed of loose stones or pebbles was a better surface than compacted earth. The ramp for the climb to Ollantaytambo's temple spur is plain for all to see. But the American professor had no answer for at least one question: How did the Incas negotiate turns with huge rocks hurtling down mountain chutes?

96 Machu Picchu lies on a saddle dominated by the granite pinnacle of Huayna Picchu.

10. Machu Picchu

IT WAS ON JULY 24, 1911, that the young American Hiram Bingham discovered the ruins of Machu Picchu. He had had his first glimpse of Inca ruins (at Choquequirao) on a trip to Peru two years earlier. Returning home, he fired his classmates at a Yale reunion with his own excitement. The result was the Yale Peruvian Expedition of 1911. Bingham had all the necessary qualities for finding Inca ruins: he was full of enthusiasm and curiosity, he was brave and tough, he had a doctorate in Latin American history, he was rich from his Tiffany-heiress wife, and he was something of a mountaineer and explorer. He was also phenomenally lucky. His expedition was the first to use a new mule trail blasted through the mighty granite gorges of the Urubamba below Ollantaytambo. This rough trail had been cut with great effort by government engineers to provide an outlet for coca and sugar-based *aguardiente* from plantations on the lower river. It opened a stretch of river that had been bypassed by all previous conquistadors and travelers. Ever since Inca times, the only route to the Vilcabamba region was by the Amaibamba pass behind Mount Verónica, north of Ollantaytambo. A road through this pass rejoined the Urubamba river some 40 kilometers (25 miles) downstream from Machu Picchu. The gorge beneath the magnificent ruin had thus been untraveled for centuries.

When Bingham's mule train moved down this new trail, it passed from the open highlands of the Incas into the edge of the Amazon rain forests. Below Ollantaytambo, trees seize the land and cover it without interruption as far as the Atlantic Ocean, thousands of kilometers to the east. Bingham was struck by the soaring beauty and savage contrasts of the region he was penetrating. The seething water of the mountain rivers, the granite cliffs, and the sparkling snowy peaks reminded him of the grandeur of the Rockies. But the tropical vegetation that clings to the steep hillsides or cascades over the rocky outcrops, and the mists that shroud the sugarloaf hills were like the most stupendous views of Hawaii (where he had grown up with missionary parents). "Not only has it great snow peaks looming above the clouds more than two miles overhead; gigantic precipices of many-colored granite rising sheer for thousands of feet above the foaming, glistening, roaring rapids; it has also, in striking contrast, orchids and tree ferns, the delectable beauty of luxurious vegetation, and the mysterious witchery of the jungle. One is drawn irresistibly onward by ever-recurring surprises through a deep, winding gorge, turning and twisting past overhanging cliffs of incredible height."

Bingham had been directed toward Vilcabamba by the Peruvian historian Carlos Romero. An important chronicle had recently been discovered: an autobiographical report by Manco Inca's son Titu Cusi Yupanqui, who had ruled the neo-Inca state of Vilcabamba for twelve years before the Spaniards finally conquered the area in 1572. This chronicle and other contemporary documents mentioned various places in this last refuge of the Incas. Bingham hoped to find their ruins. He wrote that he had heard the name Machu Picchu, both from someone in Cuzco who told him that it had ruins finer than Choquequirao, and also from a travel book by Charles Wiener. When Wiener was at Ollantaytambo in 1875, he said that local people "spoke to me of other towns, of Huaina-Picchu and of Matcho-Picchu towards the east." Wiener did not reach the ruins; but he located them on a map in his book (albeit on the wrong side of the Urubamba). (We now know, from research by Paolo Greer and Dan Buck, that Wiener got the names from a mineral prospector called Augusto Berns, who bought a large tract of land opposite the ruins in the 1860s, lived there for four years, and drew a sketch map of the area with his saw mill and a "gold mine" marked on the site of the ugly modern town Aguas Calientes. The Peruvian government sent the German mining engineer Herman Göhring to investigate the mine, which proved non-existent; but in 1874 Göhring drew a fine map that located Machu Picchu and Huayna Picchu mountains, and his report of 1877 mentioned a fortress called Picchu (among others). In 1887 Berns registered a limited company in Lima called Huagas del Inga ("Inca Ruins" or "Tombs") which proposed to loot the site. His prospectus said that he had seen "important gentile and subterranean constructions" sealed by cut stones and clearly containing Inca treasures. But there is no record or sign of this company doing any grave-robbing.)

Bingham was only two days out of Ollantaytambo, along the new trail, when his party camped by the edge of the Urubamba. A local muleteer called Melchor Arteaga asked their purpose. When they told him it was to find Inca ruins, he said that there were excellent ones called Machu Picchu and Huayna Picchu on top of the opposite precipice. Bingham recalled the reference in Wiener and decided that he must investigate.

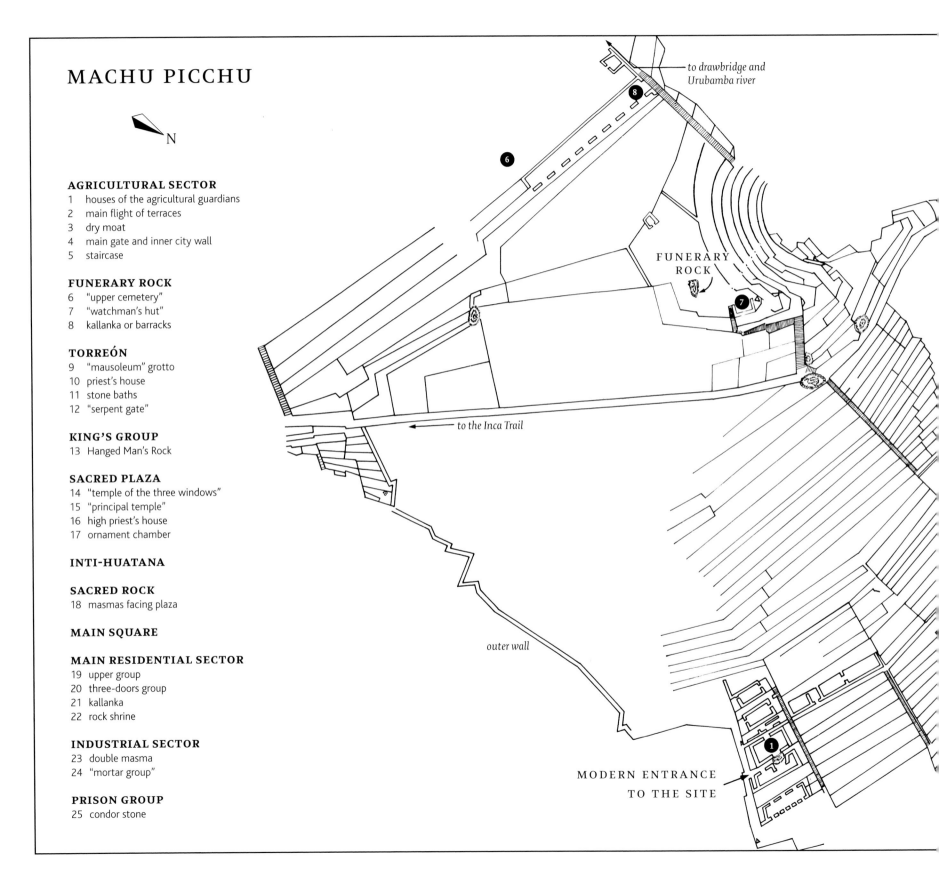

MACHU PICCHU

N

AGRICULTURAL SECTOR

1 houses of the agricultural guardians
2 main flight of terraces
3 dry moat
4 main gate and inner city wall
5 staircase

FUNERARY ROCK

6 "upper cemetery"
7 "watchman's hut"
8 kallanka or barracks

TORREÓN

9 "mausoleum" grotto
10 priest's house
11 stone baths
12 "serpent gate"

KING'S GROUP

13 Hanged Man's Rock

SACRED PLAZA

14 "temple of the three windows"
15 "principal temple"
16 high priest's house
17 ornament chamber

INTI-HUATANA

SACRED ROCK

18 masmas facing plaza

MAIN SQUARE

MAIN RESIDENTIAL SECTOR

19 upper group
20 three-doors group
21 kallanka
22 rock shrine

INDUSTRIAL SECTOR

23 double masma
24 "mortar group"

PRISON GROUP

25 condor stone

to drawbridge and Urubamba river

FUNERARY ROCK

to the Inca Trail

outer wall

MODERN ENTRANCE
TO THE SITE

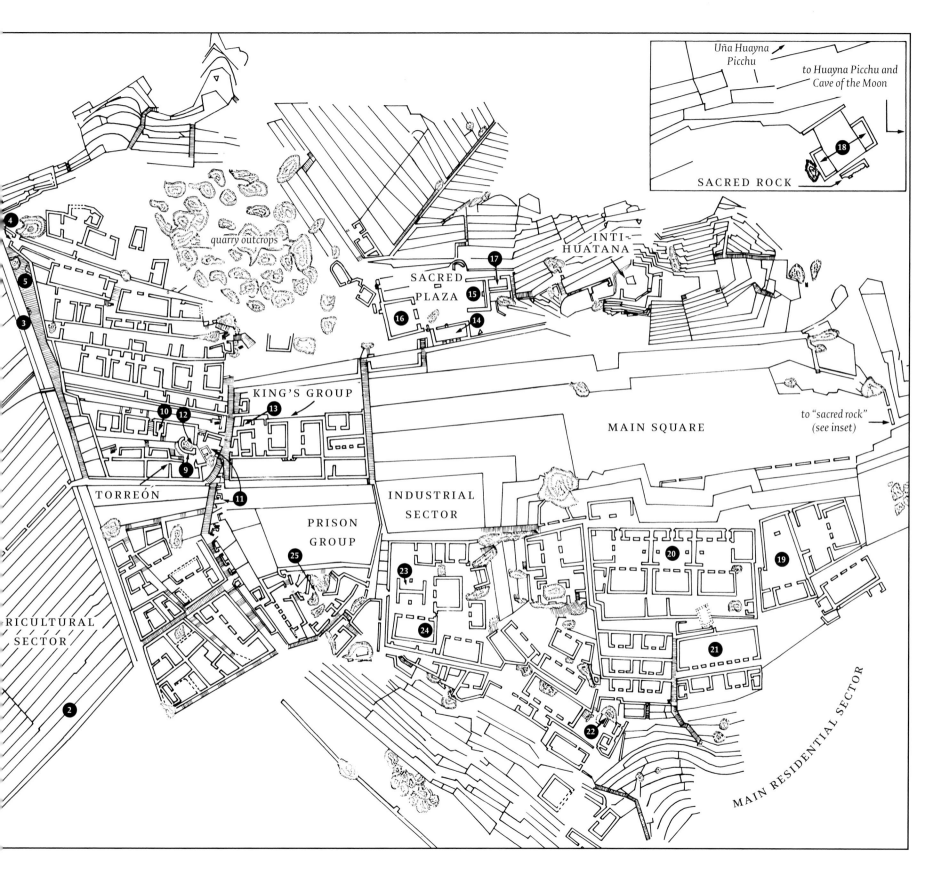

Uña Huayna
Picchu

to Huayna Picchu and
Cave of the Moon

18

SACRED ROCK

quarry outcrops

4

5

3

17

INTI-
HUATANA

SACRED
PLAZA

15

16

14

KING'S GROUP

10 12

13

9

MAIN SQUARE

to "sacred rock"
(see inset)

TORREÓN

11

INDUSTRIAL
SECTOR

PRISON
GROUP

25

23

20

19

RICULTURAL
SECTOR

24

21

2

22

MAIN RESIDENTIAL SECTOR

98 When Hiram Bingham discovered Machu Picchu, it was choked by vegetation. In his photograph of 1915, the torreón (right foreground) and the "principal temple" (center left) are visible.

99 Machu Picchu, 1971: wall, dry moat, and staircase in the foreground.

He set out on that misty morning of July 24, 1911, with Arteaga and a Peruvian sergeant. They crept across plunging rapids of the Urubamba on a spindly bridge of logs fastened to boulders, and then "had a fearfully hard climb… A good part of the distance I went on all-fours." They paused for lunch (of cooked sweet-potatoes and a gourd of cool water) with "several good-natured Indians" who had made themselves a farm on ancient agricultural terraces some 2,000 feet (600 meters) above the river. After lunch, Bingham left their hut, unenthusiastic at the prospect of more climbing in the humid afternoon heat. But just around a promontory he came upon his first thrilling sight: a magnificent flight of stone terraces, a hundred of them, climbing for almost a thousand feet up the hillside. These terraces had been roughly cleared by the Indians. However, it was in the deep jungle above that Bingham made his breathtaking discoveries. There, amid dark trees and undergrowth, he saw building after building, a sacred cave, and a three-sided temple whose granite ashlars were cut with all the beauty and precision of the finest masonry in Cuzco. Bingham left an unforgettable account of his excitement that afternoon, of the dreamlike experience of entering the untouched forest and seeing archaeological wonders, of finding each successive treasure of the lost city on that sharp forested ridge: "I suddenly found myself in a maze of beautiful granite houses! They were covered with trees and mosses and the growth of centuries, but in the dense shadow, hiding in bamboo thickets and tangled vines, could be seen, here and there, walls of white granite ashlars most carefully cut and exquisitely fitted together… Surprise followed surprise until there came the realization that we were in the midst of as wonderful ruins as any ever found in Peru." On his first attempt, he had discovered the most famous ruin in the Americas.

On that historic afternoon, Bingham merely noted the spectacular discovery and made a quick sketch plan of a central plaza. The Yale Expedition pressed on into Vilcabamba where its amazing luck continued, when locals steered them to Vitcos and Espíritu Pampa, the two other most important sites in the region. The National Geographic Society appreciated the tremendous impact of the ruin Bingham had glimpsed. It sent him back the following year, 1912, well endowed to clear and excavate the site. Bingham described this as a discouraging task. The ruins were deeply overgrown. His reluctant Quechua workers toiled from July to November to cut down hardwood forest and thick undergrowth. In places he found "massive trees, two feet thick, perched on the gable ends of small, beautifully constructed houses." Machu Picchu is now well trodden by the daily influx of visitors, and the site is continually being restored and maintained. It is only by looking at Bingham's early photographs that we can appreciate how choked it had been by centuries of invading vegetation. Bingham led a third expedition to this part of Peru in 1915. In addition to work at Machu Picchu, this explored the Inca approach road high in the hills above the Urubamba and located a number of other ruins along what is now known as the Inca Trail.

It has been said that Hiram Bingham was not the first to discover Machu Picchu. He himself acknowledged that people in Cuzco told him vague reports of ruins in that area; he knew that Wiener had heard the name forty years earlier; the Indians who gave him lunch had lived there for four years, and one Anacleto Alvárez had farmed the terraces for a decade; and when Bingham reached the ruins he learned "from some rude scrawls on the stones of a temple" that it had been visited in 1902 by one Agustín Lizárraga, a local muleteer. After 1911 other claimants emerged to declare primacy—British missionaries called Payne and McNairn, and American, Scottish, and German mining engineers named Franklin, Stapleton, Haenel, and Von Hassel. None of this matters. I feel that an explorer must find something unknown to his society, and must then return and tell the world about his discovery. By this definition, Bingham was unquestionably the discoverer of the magnificent ruin. This is gracefully acknowledged by the Peruvians, in a plaque at the modern entrance and the naming of the zigzag approach road as the Carretera Hiram Bingham. Bingham also looked the part. The 35-year-old was tall (6 feet 4 inches; 1.93 meters), ruggedly handsome, fit, and energetic. This adventurer who pushed through snake-infested tropical vegetation to glimpse mysterious temples was the inspiration for the Indiana Jones movies. The actor Harrison Ford resembled Bingham, who wore an early-explorer outfit of jodhpur-like trousers, safari jacket, jaunty kerchief, high boots, puttees, and a slouch hat.

Machu Picchu is full of enigmas, mysteries that cannot be fully resolved. Like many Inca sites, it was built on previously unoccupied land, so that excavation would reveal little that cannot now be seen. The first question is its purpose. Why did the Incas expend so much effort to build such an elaborate place in such a strange location?

To me, the most plausible explanation for Machu Picchu is that it was one of the royal estates in the Cuzco region. As such, it would have been used by the Inca and his court as a country palace, where they could rest, relax, and worship. In 1987 John Rowe published a sixteenth-century document from the Cuzco archives that mentioned "Picho" as a royal estate of Inca Pachacuti—that Inca's ayllu or descendants were claiming the area as their property. Another legal action in 1568 spelled out that "the Incas, former rulers of this kingdom, had a usage and custom to make estates and royal dwellings in distinct and separate places, during the time they reigned, and in the said places they established hereditary estates, livestock pastures, gold and silver mines, woodlands and other properties." We know that one of the conqueror Pachacuti's first campaigns, in the 1440s, was to occupy Vilcabamba as a buffer against the Chanca. Cobo and other chroniclers confirmed that Pachacuti "started his conquests with the provinces of Vitcos and Vilcabamba, a difficult country to subdue because of its wildness and extensive undergrowth and dense jungles." Machu

Picchu's architecture is very uniform, and hardly any building shows signs of alteration. The style is late imperial Inca, from the half-century after Pachacuti started his headlong expansion.

Most (but not all) modern authorities regard Machu Picchu as Pachacuti's personal retreat. It has the necessary attributes. It is full of the finest masonry, which was available only to royalty; there are abundant temples, for the Inca's worship; there are excellent watercourses and cascades, also for religious purpose; there is a small but excellent enclosure that Bingham identified as the royal lodging (and all later observers agree with him); other residential compounds could have housed the Inca priesthood and elite; and the surrounding slopes are lavishly terraced for agriculture. Conversely, Machu Picchu has few requirements of other types of Inca settlement. It was not a replica of the capital, Cuzco; nor did it have the features (ushnu, acllahuasi, copious storage facilities, large kallankas) of a provincial center. It was far too elaborate to be either a tambo way-station, frontier fortress, agricultural village, or town of non-Inca subjects.

The Peruvian archaeologist Federico Kauffmann Doig does not agree that Machu Picchu was an Inca's personal estate. He feels that sixteenth-century Spanish lawyers were wrong to try to equate Inca usage with Spanish feudal law. To him, this site and nearby Wiñay Wayna and Intipata (both on the Inca Trail and with hillsides of magnificent terracing) were administrative centers, to produce food for Cuzco's growing population, as well as being "seats of propitiation rituals." Other authorities have stressed this quantity of agricultural terracing, as well as the strategic location at the northern edge of the Inca heartland. Six complexes of terraces on the slopes below Machu Picchu yield 1.5 hectares (3.7 acres) of level surfaces; those beside and above the city add a similar area. All this terracing would have produced an impressive annual harvest of some 4.5 tons of shelled maize.

Machu Picchu does have some defenses. The approach road from the south (the Inca Trail) passes through tunnels that could easily be closed, and it is blocked by an outer gate as it comes in sight of the city. Another road, from Vilcabamba to the northwest, runs along the face of a sheer cliff and is broken by a stronger defense: a deliberate void spanned by a log drawbridge, 2 kilometers (1¼ miles) from the city. The inner city is on a mountain saddle that drops precipitously to river gorges to the east and west. To the north the spur of land ends in the granite sugarloaf of Huayna Picchu, which rises like the horn of a rhinoceros, with the Urubamba roaring around a hairpin bend below its sheer walls. The only vulnerable flank was thus the south. On this there were two defensive walls. One crosses the ridge south of the agricultural terraces. The inner city is further protected by a dry moat between it and these terraces, with buildings inside this moat forming the second defensive wall.

100 The canyon of the Urubamba, seen from the Inca Trail. The railway runs close to the river, along the trail that had been opened shortly before Bingham's expedition in 1911.

The old Inca road enters the city at the top of this steeply sloping bulwark. It passes through a massive trapezoidal gate whose outer face is flanked by a defensive platform. Inside this stone gate are reminders of its long-vanished door: a stone ring (eye-bonder) in the stone immediately above the lintel, from which the wooden door was doubtless suspended, and vertical stone cylinders, "barholds," sunk into the jambs to hold a horizontal locking beam. A final defensive feature of Machu Picchu is a web of lookouts to warn of any approaching enemy. The pinnacle of Huayna Picchu has the remains of Inca structures that could have served as such.

Machu Picchu's defenses were useful, but not formidable enough to define a fortress. The modern archaeologist Lucy Salazar imagines the Inca and his court moving to Machu Picchu during the cooler and less rainy months from May to September. The gates and walls would have protected them from a surprise attack, by forest tribes or even the restless Chanca. Bingham had a high regard for these defenses. But the Hungarian Paul Fejos, who led an American-funded expedition in 1939–40, was less impressed by their military value. He noted that most of the chain of ruins farther up the valley were undefended and concluded that none of them had been built primarily for defense.

The bulwarks also served for religious seclusion. They are reminiscent of the enclosure walls that surround the temple of Viracocha at Raqchi, the sacred end of the Island of the Sun in Lake Titicaca, and the temple areas of Pisac and Ollantaytambo. This segregation of a holy area is compatible with Machu Picchu's use as a royal estate of Pachacuti, since that Napoleon-like figure organized every aspect of Inca life, including rituals for its different strands of worship.

Machu Picchu is an intensely spiritual place. It is full of temples and sacred outcrops, and its breathtaking location inspires every visitor with reverence for the natural world. This was no accident. Johan Reinhard—the American archaeologist-mountaineer who discovered the famous "Ice Maiden," the frozen mummy of a child sacrificed high on a Peruvian mountain—is sure that Machu Picchu is related to veneration of surrounding mountains. The site's water flows from a spring on a hill called Machu Picchu, which is a spur of the snow-clad peak Salcantay (6,271 meters; 20,574 feet), 13 kilometers (8 miles) to the south. Various chronicles said that Salcantay was highly revered by the Incas. From Machu Picchu, the Southern Cross constellation (of five bright stars) rises east of Salcantay, is immediately above the peak at its zenith, and sets to the west of it. The Southern Cross and the Milky Way were significant in Inca thought. Another snowy peak, Pumasillo ("puma's claw") (6,075 meters; 19,931 feet), is due west of Machu Picchu, so that the sun sets behind it at the December solstice—another important event in the Inca calendar. The beautiful mountain Verónica or Wakay Willka (5,750 meters; 18,865 feet) is visible

to the east. In one aspect of their religion, the Incas worshipped all natural phenomena and, in their vertical world of the Andes, mountains were literally the pinnacle of such veneration. In the late sixteenth century, the Christian church realized that Inca beliefs were still widespread. Diligent priests were assigned to the "extirpation of idolatry" and they destroyed tens of thousands of small idols and sacred objects. But the Indians told them that they could never obliterate the largest shrines of all—the caves and mountains.

Modern visitors to Machu Picchu generally descend the Urubamba on a narrow-gauge railway built along the path blasted in 1909, and climb to the site on a zigzag road built during Luis Valcárcel's cleaning operation in 1934. The ruins are entered near the modern tourist hotel. This entrance leads to a group of buildings near the foot of the main flight of terraces. Bingham called them the "houses of the agricultural guardians." These five rectangular houses are on different levels, but are larger and taller as they descend. The lowest and tallest has three doors on its upper side and a series of six openings from which to admire the canyon below. One house has been restored with a thatched hip roof resting on four level-topped walls.

From this group, visitors walk along a terrace to reach the dry moat, the inner city wall, and one of the longest of Machu Picchu's scores of staircases. The hillside above and below is contoured in a magnificent flight of over forty terraces. Quite apart from their agricultural value, these terraces were the Incas' way of taming the unstable mountain against erosion. Such is the steepness of the slope that most of the terraces require retaining walls 3.5 meters (11½ feet) high to provide only 3 meters (10 feet) of horizontal platform. This main group of terraces faces north to enjoy the longest possible exposure to the subequatorial sun. Curved terraces to the west of the inner city, below the inti-huatana group, are far steeper—virtuoso feats of engineering that seem to have been largely an aesthetic frame for the site.

Excavations at the end of the twentieth century made fascinating discoveries. The American civil engineer Kenneth Wright and Peruvian archaeologist Alfredo Valencia surveyed every aspect of Machu Picchu and learned about its foundations. Parts of it are on outcrops of granite bedrock; but much of the ridge was originally very irregular, poised between two fault lines. Pachacuti's levies of laborers had transformed the saddle, leveling some areas and landfilling others. They created a level and well-drained surface by adding a deep layer of loose rock stabilized by hidden underground walls. It is calculated that the man-days expended in this earthmoving represented 60 percent of all the work of building Machu Picchu! This artificial base has admirably withstood the weight of massive buildings, the (much lighter) footfall of thousands of tourists, and centuries of heavy rain. But it is the reason why a few buildings—notably the great temple on the north side of the Sacred Plaza—are subsiding,

101 The southern end of Machu Picchu, overlooking the Sacred Plaza and quarry. Beyond, terraces lead up to the "watchman's hut," the Inca Trail, and Mount Machu Picchu.

102 The modern road that zigzags up the slope climbed by Bingham in 1911.

with serious cracks in their masonry. Engineers are at a loss about how to reinforce that ruin's foundations.

Before entering the inner city, it is worth climbing to the top of the agricultural sector between the two defensive walls. The staircase between the moat and the inner wall ascends to the inner city's main gate. From here the visitor walks back along the old Inca road, on a terrace, and then climbs other staircases to an area that is known as the "upper cemetery." Bingham gave it this name because his men excavated a number of skeletons here, from a cave and

103 The shrine that Bingham called "funerary rock," near his "watchman's hut," with the kallanka barracks hall beyond.

from the narrow plateau above the terraces. The cave was only one of some fifty burial caves found at Machu Picchu, most of them on the slopes below the city. Bingham offered rewards to any of his men who could find a cave. By the end of his explorations he was sure that his men had scoured every accessible part of Huayna Picchu and Machu Picchu mountains and the ridge between. He said that practically every square rod of the ridge had been explored.

The "upper cemetery" was guarded by the "watchman's hut," a masma whose steeply pitched roof has been restored [ill. 1]. The hut now provides welcome shelter for visitors on the many days of heavy rain at Machu Picchu. The trapezoidal windows in its end walls give a famous view over the legendary city. The "watchman's hut" faces an open space containing one of the many worked rock outcrops that abound here or in any Inca site. This sculpted

104 The Urubamba from the "watchman's hut." The "prison group" and lower liturgical baths (still overgrown) are to the left.

105 In Martín Chambi's photograph of 1928, much of Machu Picchu had been cleared but not yet restored, and the "prison group" (on the slope to the right) was still overgrown.

rock, with its flattened surface, molded protuberances, and tiny access steps, was obviously a shrine. It may have served for sacrifices of llamas or as a funerary altar, a place for displaying mummified bodies of important people, and Bingham therefore called it the "funerary rock." It was in a prominent, public place, overlooked by another terrace and plaza that might have held the spectators of such rites. On the far side of this upper plaza is the so-called tambo (post-house barracks): a small kallanka with eight large doorways in its façade and one in either end. The tambo stood at the junction of two Inca

107 The curved wall of the torreón, with the probable priest's lodging to the right and the enigmatic "serpent gate" to the left. Photograph by Martín Chambi, 1928.

106 The inner city was entered by a single gateway, which is seen at the lower left in the opposite photograph.

roads to the city: the Cuzco road (the Inca Trail), which came down the slopes of Machu Picchu mountain from the southeast; and another which climbed from Vilcabamba to the west—this is the trail with the cliff-hanging drawbridge. The archaeologist Alfredo Valencia in the 1990s excavated the overgrown terraces below the ruins and discovered another, handsomely paved Inca road that ran diagonally down them all the way to the Urubamba river.

Looking down from the vantage point of the cemetery lookout, the dual nature of Machu Picchu becomes evident. The inner town is very obviously divided by the line of grassy central squares. In this it was the mirror of Cuzco, which was split into Hanan-Cuzco and Hurin-Cuzco. As Bernabé Cobo explained, the Incas "divided every town or chiefdom into two sections or groups known as hanan-saya and hurin-saya, which mean the upper ward and the lower ward." Cobo stressed that the two ranked equally. The Inca rulers made the distinction so that their subjects' loyalties would be divided—an insurance against sedition—and to facilitate tribute and labor levies. It was also done to "give their subjects an incentive for competition and emulation in any craft or task they undertook on royal orders... The two divisions always performed on their own; the men of one never interfered with those of the other. At festivals and public celebrations each group did its utmost to excel, to gain an edge over its competitor in the innovations or entertainment they devised."

Manuel Chávez Ballón, for many years custodian of the ruins, propounded this dual interpretation: that Machu Picchu had two moieties or sayas east and west of the central plazas. He argued that each contained the essential elements of an Inca ceremonial center: royal lodging, temples to the sun and to Viracocha, storage areas, and accommodation for court officials and soldiery. Luis Millones felt that in the upper hanan sector the sacred and agricultural zones were above one another, while in the hurin they were side-by-side. Not everyone agreed with this theory of duality. It would not apply if Machu Picchu was a royal estate, a sacred retreat, rather than a residential town. Bingham, George Kubler, Victor Angles, and others noted a different character in each cluster of buildings and therefore assigned a different function to each part of the city. They saw the central squares as fortuitous. The buildings that rise on either side of these plazas are grouped around them only for convenience and to exploit the topography; they do not mirror one another in hanan and hurin wards. Kubler described the city's design as "a patterned blanket thrown over a great rock: the pattern falls in many folds."

Entering through the main gate at the top of the dry moat and broad staircase, visitors pass above a sector of buildings arranged on seven terraces. These houses are of pirca, fieldstones roughly shaped and set in clay mortar. The doors of each row of buildings face inward toward the terrace wall of the tier above. It is an apparent labyrinth of enclosures and courtyards, but there is a pattern, a plan adapted to the slope of the hill. Some of these structures were habitations—notably a fine house with four doors onto the street just inside the main gate—but others may have been for storage or for housing servants.

Staircases at the northern end of this upper group lead down to the famous torreón ("bastion"), so called because its curved wall recalls a tower in a medieval fortification. There was, of course, nothing military about the torreón: its purpose was entirely religious. It contains masonry as fine as anywhere in the Inca empire. The beautiful curving wall is of regular courses of tightly fitting ashlars, leaning slightly inward. The inner walls of the curve and its attendant rectangular temple are equally perfect, with niches and stone bosses of impeccable precision.

The curved wall surrounds a sacred outcrop of rock, and this has inspired many interpretations. Hiram Bingham called the torreón the sun temple of Machu Picchu, partly because its curving wall recalls those of the sun temples of Coricancha in Cuzco and at Pisac. This definition was confirmed in the 1980s in an exciting collaboration between archaeologists and the astronomer David Dearborn and archaeologist Katharina Schreiber. They found that one window in the curved wall observes the sun at the June solstice or Inti Raymi ("sun festival," a very important event in the Inca calendar), while another window points to the December solstice or Capac Raymi ("chief festival," also the time when noble Inca boys passed their initiation rites). Inca priests may have used cords and plumb bobs (several of which were found nearby) on the window to project a precise shadow; lines on the outcrop altar apparently recorded this

108 Steps cut into bedrock lead to the two-story priest's house and the torreón.

in a form of sundial; and a bronze mirror was found that could have reflected the sun. Reinhard noted that the Pleiades (seven bright stars in the constellation Taurus) rise close to the sun at the June solstice, to the north immediately above Huayna Picchu when viewed from this temple. The Incas associated the Pleiades with crop fertility and weather forecasting. Another archaeologist

109 The rock altar inside the torreón, possibly an astronomical observatory.

110 Trapezoidal niches and stone pegs inside the "royal mausoleum."

111 Coursed masonry and stepped rock at the grotto entrance.

112 The carved steps leading to the priest's house.

113 A gnomon carved within the grotto.

high priest, or chapels dedicated to lesser celestial deities such as the thunder, moon, or rainbow. Whatever its purpose, the building demonstrates triumphs of Inca masonry: coursed ashlars fixed with stunning virtuosity; courses diminishing in size as they rise; walls tapering and leaning inward; blocks cut to turn at the corners and bonded for exceptional strength; perfect trapezoidal doors and a window looking out over the Urubamba. The sacred nature of this temple is confirmed by the remains of a defensive gate—with lintel ring and horseshoe-shaped grooves and barholds in either jamb—in an unroofed entry passage alongside the "house of the ñusta" [ill. 18].

The curved temple's "altar" is the top of a mighty granite boulder that thrusts upward from the slope of the hillside. Below this, Inca masons skillfully converted the rock's overhang into a grotto, sealing part of its entrance with a coursed wall rising out of a stepped outcrop. The stepped pattern may have symbolized a mountain; and the cave it created was a shrine in its own right. The bedrock within the cave blends smoothly with Inca walls that contain niches large enough to hold royal mummy bundles. Bingham therefore dubbed this the "royal mausoleum." Had Pachacuti died here, this vault might have held his mummy before it was transferred to Cuzco. Otherwise it could have served for ancestor worship, in the Incas' cult of their divine lineage. The angles of this chamber are cut sharply (a difficult feat), but they are asymmetrical. Such stoneworking is sufficiently surprising to constitute a hollow sculpture of great beauty, three-dimensional and plastic, with strange shadows and a deep sense of religious mystery.

Pachacuti's actual mausoleum may have been a tomblike vault at the top of the steps cut into bedrock, beside the upper story of the probable high priest's residence. This rectangular vault, of the finest masonry, was found to be empty by Bingham's team and was reopened in 2008 by the director of Machu Picchu, Fernando Astete. Juan de Betanzos, the chronicler married to a senior Inca princess, wrote that Pachacuti had an effigy made of his fingernails, hair, and other body parts, and ordered that this and a golden image of himself be placed beside his body, which was to be buried in a large pottery urn. "After he was dead, he was taken to a town named Patallacta, where he had ordered some houses built in which his body was to be entombed." Patallacta just means a high town, and it could well have referred to Picchu (the old name for the place that Bingham and his contemporaries called Machu ("Old") Picchu).

There are two striking features about the torreón and its mausoleum. One is the curved wall, a rarity in the rectangular world of Inca architecture. Such curves surround sacred outcrops, generally associated with sun worship—as at Pisac, Coricancha in Cuzco, and Ingapirca in Ecuador. The other beautiful element is the fitting of coursed ashlars into bedrock. The art historian Carolyn Dean wrote that the Incas' "practice of integrating rock outcrops into their

114 The "mausoleum" beneath the torreón outcrop. Photograph by Martín Chambi, 1928.

associated the curve of the torreón with the rainbow, which appeared on the Inca's personal banner and was part of his claim to be descended from the sun.

The southern part of the temple complex is a lovely two-storied structure of the finest masonry. As usual in Inca building, there is no internal staircase: the upper story opens toward the temple courtyard, while the lower faces west onto the terrace below. This building is known, for no good reason, as the "house of the ñusta" (princess). It was more probably the residence of a

115 The sculpted grotto, known as the "royal mausoleum," below the torreón.

structures suggests a strategy akin to grafting, wherein Inka walls appear to grow from the earth's stony skeleton, rather than being set on it... Grafting structures onto rock outcrops served to interweave the built environment and the natural environment, creating a stunning amalgamation of nature and architecture." The Inca regarded both architecture and agriculture (particularly terracing) as a means of celebrating their union with Pachamama, Mother Earth, and also of bringing order to untamed areas, and planting their imprint on conquered peoples. Machu Picchu has many examples of masonry springing from natural rock—notably the flamboyant outcrop in the midst of the "prison group," temples around the Sacred Plaza, and the inti-huatana pinnacle. Masonry imbedded into rock and curved walls are both features of places built by Pachacuti, as was the choice of sites on moun-

116 The principal liturgical bath, seen from the "king's group," with the hanging gate of the torreón beyond.

117 The principal liturgical bath is close to the Inca's residence or "king's group."

tain spurs with magnificent views. He formalized Inca worship of the sun and of natural features.

The opening to the north of the sun temple is a curious full-length trapezoidal doorway that opens onto the void. Its base is carefully stepped, with a narrower opening at the center, and surrounded by strange holes that pierce the surrounding stones. One theory was that sacrificial effluents might have poured from these holes or, more fancifully, that snakes were made to glide through them. Bingham later surmised that the holes were used to attach a Punchao, the golden image of the sun. The opening looks north and could have reflected the sun at midday (this is the southern hemisphere); and with its surrounding holes, it is reminiscent of the niche in Coricancha that possibly also held a sun image.

This strange gateway looks down onto another of Machu Picchu's enigmatic features: the cascade of stone baths. There are sixteen of these cisterns, with

118 The water channel leading to the principal bath. It is not known how Inca masons cut the rectangular concave angle with such consummate skill.

internal niches. The channels that fill and drain each tank are obvious but perplexing, for they are too low to permit much water to accumulate. It would have been difficult to use these tanks as either human baths or cisterns. Bingham imagined a biblical scene with Inca women filling water jars at these spouts, which would have been feasible. But the baths of Machu Picchu are so beautiful that they must primarily have been liturgical fonts for some form of ceremonial. There are sacred springs and cascades of baths in many Inca ruins, such as Tambo Machay [ill. 29], Choquequirao, Pisac, Ollantaytambo [ill. 89], the Island of the Sun in Lake Titicaca, and at Wiñay Wayna and Choquesuysuy (both near Machu Picchu). But none of these can compare with the flight of cisterns at the heart of the famous ruin.

In the late 1990s Valencia and the water-engineer Wright studied Machu Picchu's amazing hydraulics, and cleared and restored the channels and cisterns. They got the water to flow again, thus giving the town a delightful splashing counterpoint to the thundering of the Urubamba in its canyon far below. The water comes from a perennial spring 750 meters (2,460 feet) from the baths. It flows along a skillfully engineered gravity canal, at first with a gradient of between 2.5 and almost 5 percent, but then at a gentle 1 percent along a terrace into Machu Picchu. When Valencia excavated terraces on the eastern slope—far below the main ruins, to the north of the zigzag motor road—he discovered two more fountains of excellent workmanship. When he finished clearing these and their channels, the water "burst into operation after being buried for some 450 years."

Just above the central flight of basins is a lovely three-sided shelter, with a stone bench looking down on this ceremonial center. The shelter must surely have been the scene of rituals connected with the sacred sites nearby. As one looks out from it, to the right is the torreón sun temple with its strange "serpent gate" and the "royal mausoleum" below; looking down are the basins and a stupendous view across the Urubamba valley; and to the left, the city's finest residential group of buildings.

Hiram Bingham called the residence beyond the first bath the "king's group," because of the great strength and beauty of its masonry and the steep pitch of its roofs. He reasoned that "no one but a king could have insisted on having the lintels of his doorways made of solid blocks of granite each weighing three tons." Once through the mighty entrance, whose "artistic workmanship defies description," a visitor passes below a ring, 2 meters (6½ feet) from the ground, cut into a boss projecting from the rock above. This doubtless held some lamp or image; but to popular imagination it is the Hanged Man's Rock. Beyond is a central, service courtyard with two fine, niched buildings facing onto it. These are traditionally thought to have been the ruler's dormitory—a building with an audience chamber and a water channel that runs into a narrow internal

the water tumbling from one to another from the upper part of the city to the start of the terraces below. The bath beneath the torreón, the fourth from the top, is the finest in the quality of its stonework. Each bath has stone sides up to 1.5 meters (5 feet) high, with narrow door openings and some with small

119 A wall of superb ashlars on the north side of the torreón shrine has a gate with a curious lower opening flanked by unexplained holes.

120 Most authorities agree that Bingham's "king's group" was the Inca's lodging, with a private garden to the left and the "prison group" beyond.

passage. Beyond lie servants' quarters in more rustic masonry; and below the "king's group" is what may once have been a delightful walled kitchen garden—archaeologists found traces of maize and potatoes there.

This small enclosure reminds us of the Spaniards' descriptions of their first meeting with the Inca Atahualpa, on the day before they kidnapped him in the square of Cajamarca. He was at natural hot baths a short distance from the city, in a small palace of four chambers around a patio. There was a stone bath into which hot and cold water was piped. The Inca slept in a room with a corridor overlooking a walled garden. Its walls and roof beams were painted with red bitumen, but the chamber opposite was plastered white as snow and roofed by four false domes incorporated into a larger thatched dome. Two other chambers were for servants. All the eyewitnesses stressed the fine textiles that surrounded the Inca—carpets covering his stool and draperies held over him by a flock of women constantly in attendance.

121 Two chambers of the "king's group" open onto a small courtyard.

The holy character of Machu Picchu emerges most strongly on the ridge that rises northwest of the "king's group." This is the dominant feature of the inner city, and every building on it has obvious religious significance. The long staircase behind the "king's group" leads toward the Sacred Plaza at the heart of this complex. On one side of the plaza is the famous "temple of the three windows," looking down over the central squares. The three windows and their attendant niches are roughly trapezoidal, but with rounded lower corners and subtle, highly satisfying curves on their sides to widen the frames of the view. Bingham argued very plausibly that these great windows symbolized the three caves of Tambo-toqo, the mouths of the tunnels from which the legendary Ayar brothers emerged on their migration from Titicaca toward Cuzco. (In an early interpretation, Bingham wondered whether this part of Machu Picchu was from an older "megalithic" period. He noted that the Peruvian chronicler Santacruz Pachacuti Yamqui wrote that the first Inca, Manco Capac, ordered that in his birthplace his Indians "should build masonry with a form of opening, consisting of three windows, that signified the home of his fathers from whom he was descended. The first of these was called Tampo-ttoco, the second Maras-ttoco, and the third Sutic-ttoco." So, for a while, Bingham suggested that Machu Picchu might have been the first Manco's birthplace, and the actual Tambo-toqo—even though it was obviously on the wrong side of Cuzco and nowhere near Huanacauri hill.) This temple is a masma: three-sided, with the open side toward the plaza. A magnificent monolithic pier once supported

122 The long staircase from the Sacred Plaza down to the lower city.

the roof beams in the center of the open side; and the end walls have large sockets for the missing horizontal beams. On the side with the three windows, the building drops down far below its inner floor, which is level with the plaza. The outer face is thus 5.2 meters (17 feet) high, an imposing sight from below, with the three great windows apparently in an upper story and dominating all Machu Picchu.

The buildings around the Sacred Plaza are in monolithic style, with vast boulders so audaciously cut and fitted that they could only be the work of the most skilled Inca masons. The "principal temple," presumably to Viracocha, occupies the northern side of the Sacred Plaza. Huge blocks at the bases of its

123 The Sacred Plaza with the inti-huatana group above. The "temple of the three windows" to the right of the plaza and the "principal temple" in the center were open-sided masmas, and the U-shaped platform to the left may have been an observatory.

124 Because the openings of the "temple of the three windows" are slightly rounded, Bingham argued that they represented the caves of Tambo-toqo of the Inca origin legend.

125 The "temple of the three windows" from the east.

walls are foundations for neat coursed ashlars and symmetrical niches above. The side walls show vestiges of a sloping gable and notches for roof beams. Like the "temple of the three windows," the "principal temple" was evidently a masma, open on the side facing the square. The building measures 8 by 11 meters (26 by 36 feet). It is not clear whether a gigantic forest tree was found to span the open long wall, or whether this side once had a central pier, as did the adjacent temple. At the center of the back wall is an enormous stone altar 4.2 meters long, 1.4 meters high, and 0.9 meters wide (14 by 4½ by 3 feet), flanked by smaller stone benches or altars. This "principal temple" had a floor of sand, like the main square of Cuzco, which had been laboriously carried into the site. Across the plaza is a building of less brilliant masonry, traditionally thought to have been the house of the high priest.

A rock in front of the "temple of the three windows" is sculpted with steps and polished planes and carries the stepped symbol so familiar from the Tiahuanaco civilization of Lake Titicaca. At the center of the plaza are the remains of what Rowe felt was an ushnu, perhaps originally shaped like a woman's breast. To the west are semicircular foundations of a vanished enclosure. This observatory looks toward the rays of the setting sun and has a stunning view of the snowcapped Vilcabamba range. It also has interesting sight lines to a temple at Llactapata, a ruin glimpsed by Bingham when he did a tough walk from Vilcabamba to Machu Picchu, then investigated in the early

1980s by a team from the Cusichaca Project, and surveyed twenty years later by Hugh Thomson and Gary Ziegler who found that its "sun temple" was oriented to the solstices in the same way as Machu Picchu's.

The western wall of the "principal temple" was extended to the rear and enclosed one of the most perfect of Machu Picchu's many beautiful buildings. Bingham first identified it as the high priest's house; but he later decided that it was a royal mausoleum, with a bench for displaying the mummies of Inca rulers. Others call it an ornament chamber. It is quite small, only 7 by 4 meters (23 by 13 feet), but built of white granite cut and fitted with breathtaking brilliance. A great block forms the base of the wall to the left of this chamber's only door. Visitors are shown how this one stone has no fewer than thirty-two corners, in three dimensions, each fitting tightly with its neighbors; and the rock at the base of the opposite wall, to the right on entry, also has the same number of angles. The masons' virtuosity is manifested just as strikingly in the startlingly crisp and regular niches, in the turning of stones at the chamber corners, and in the precision and polish of every ashlar. Bingham boasted justifiably that this building in his discovery equaled, in proportions, beauty, and the artistic care with which it was built, any ancient building in the world.

The ornament chamber is at the edge of the most spiritual of all sectors of this holy city. A corridor leads around its northern end and then climbs some sixty steps, in four small flights, toward the summit of the inti-huatana. The Incas converted a natural outcrop of granite into a stepped pyramid, a form of ushnu. The temple that surrounds the crowning gnomon seems elevated by tiers of terraces or walls of natural rock. The mystery and expectancy of the approach is heightened by changes of direction, successive flights of steps, small walled courtyards, and clusters of buildings.

The inti-huatana itself is a simple pillar of stone rising from a roughly rectangular platform. It is the pinnacle of the ridge's natural bedrock. The gnomon rises 1.8 meters (6 feet) above its base, the highest such rock projection to survive among the Inca ruins of Peru. It is also the most powerfully elegant, a masterpiece of sculpture, rising in tapering planes from its curving base in a single strong upward thrust.

No one knows the precise ceremonial that took place at the inti-huatanas of Machu Picchu, Pisac, or other shrines. One assumption is that these gnomons were used to record movements of the sun, inti. Garcilaso de la Vega explained that "for all their simplicity, the Incas realized that the sun completed its course in a year, which they called *huata*. The noun means 'a year,' but used as a verb, similarly pronounced and accented, it means 'to tie.'" In the first dictionary of Quechua, Diego González Holguín wrote that inti-huatanan meant "place well lit [or benefited] by the sun." But modern writers follow Garcilaso in

126 The snowcapped Vilcabamba mountains beyond the Sacred Plaza, seen from within the "temple of the three windows," with the "principal temple" on the right.

translating it as "hitching post of the sun." It was first used in this way by the British travel writer Clements Markham in 1856 describing gnomons at Pisac, then by George Squier twenty years later. They considered the rock posts to be some form of sundial. This was first queried by the German archaeologist Max Uhle, in 1910 before the discovery of Machu Picchu, and later authorities agreed with him in failing to see how these gnomons could work as sundials. Reinhard argued that this famous one was connected to mountain worship because it appeared to replicate the shape of Huayna Picchu, and because at the summer solstice the sun sets over Pumasillo peak when viewed from it. It is at the crossing of a north–south line from Huayna

127 The approach to the inti-huatana. The trapezoidal openings on either side were partially filled by Inca masonry.

Picchu to Salcantay and east–west from Verónica to Mount San Miguel (near Pumasillo). Rowe agreed that it might have "symbolized the 'place of spirit' of the mountain on which it stands." Reinhard also wondered whether there could have been astronomical observations from here; or whether the Incas told the time by watching shadows move across it rather than monitoring its own shadow. However, none of these explanations fits inti-huatanas at Pisac or elsewhere.

Millones in 2001 reported a revival of the sundial interpretation, since the midday sun at Machu Picchu casts its maximum shadow in the southern winter and minimum in summer. The Incas had an accurate awareness of the

128 The inti-huatana.

seasons and equinoxes. Felipe Guaman Poma noted that they knew that the sun was further away than the moon and paid particular attention to eclipses. "They calculated the month, day, hour and precise moment for sowing their crops, observing the movements of the sun. They observed the way in which its rays illuminated the highest peaks in the mornings and how they penetrated the windows of their houses. Variations in its direction and intensity acted as a precise clock to regulate the sowing and harvesting of their foods." Sarmiento de Gamboa described four poles called sucanas on hills east of Cuzco as solar observatories "in order to know the precise time of sowing and harvesting... The whole became an instrument serving as an annual timepiece." Garcilaso wrote that, throughout the empire, "to ascertain the time of the equinoxes they had splendidly carved stone columns erected in the squares or courtyards before the temples of the sun... The columns stood in the middle of great rings filling the whole extent of the squares or open spaces. Across the middle of the ring a line was drawn from east to west by a cord... When the shadow fell exactly along the line from sunrise, and at midday the sun bathed all sides of the column and cast no shadow at all, they knew that that day was the equinox. They then decked the columns with all the flowers and aromatic herbs they could find, and placed the throne of the sun on it, saying that on that day the sun was seated on the column in all his full light."

Worship of the sun culminated at the solstices in June and December, in each of which there was a great Raymi festival. The young priest Cristóbal de Molina was privileged to observe Manco Inca's last Inti Raymi in 1535, shortly after the Spanish occupation of Cuzco. He wrote that "the Inca opened the sacrifices and they lasted for eight days. Thanks were given to the sun for the past harvest and prayers were made for the crops to come... They brought all the effigies of the shrines of Cuzco onto a plain at the edge of the city in the direction of the sun's rise at daybreak... As soon as the sunrise began they started to chant in splendid harmony and unison. While chanting each of them shook his foot...and as the sun continued to rise they chanted higher." The Inca presided from a rich throne, and it was he who opened the chanting. "As the sun was rising toward noon they continued to raise their voices, and from noon onward they lowered them, keeping careful track of the sun's course. Throughout this time, great offerings were being made. On a platform on which there was a tree, there were Indians doing nothing but throwing meats into a great fire and burning them up in it. At another place the Inca ordered [llama] ewes to be thrown for the poorer common Indians to grab, and this caused great sport. At eight o'clock over two hundred girls came out of Cuzco, each with a large new pot of...chicha that was plastered and covered. The girls came in groups of five, full of precision and order, and pausing at intervals. They also offered to the sun many bales of a herb that the Indians chew and call coca, whose leaf is like myrtle. There were many other ceremonies and sacrifices. Suffice it to say that when the sun was about to set in the evening the Indians showed great sadness at its departure, in their chants and expressions. They allowed their voices to die away on purpose. And as the sun was sinking completely and disappearing from sight they made a great act of reverence, raising their hands and worshipping it in the deepest humility." This great celebration was in the imperial capital Cuzco; but it gives an inkling of the rituals that were performed in the sun temples of Machu Picchu.

Modern visitors follow a route doubtless once used by Inca priests, leaving the inti-huatana to the north away from the Sacred Plaza. Ahead is a small hill called Uña Huayna Picchu ("small young peak"). Facing it, at the northernmost part of the town, along the path to Huayna Picchu, is a great thin slab of rock set

129 Northern Machu Picchu. Uña (small) Huayna Picchu is to the left; Huayna Picchu, center, rises above gabled masma buildings attending to the "sacred rock."

in a platform of Inca masonry—the "sacred rock." It replicates Mount Yanantin to the east [ill. 35], and from the opposite direction it mirrors Pumasillo far to the west. There is a sunken plaza in front of this shrine with fine examples of masmas on either side of it. These doubtless sheltered participants in the ceremonies from sun or rain [ills. 19 & 20]. One has had its roof restored, with beams slotted into the gables and the thatch tied down to bosses and eye-bonders, and a trace of original clay plaster on its walls.

From the "sacred rock," the lower city stretches along the northeastern side of the central squares. This is the largest concentration of dwellings, with a series of wards arranged along a low ridge. These wards contain the greatest concentration of housing. Closest to the "sacred rock" is the so-called "upper group," which overlooks the main square. It is enclosed by a wall with only two gates, the main one a double-jambed door toward the plaza. Within this perimeter is an irregular group of houses and courts, of relatively rustic workmanship. To the south is the "three doors group" or "group of identical houses," named because three identical buildings overlook the square. Each of these has one double-jambed door toward the square, with other gates leading onto courtyards within the compound. The doors over the square stand above three handsome tiers of terraces. It is possible to

130 Each cancha enclosure of the "residential group" may have housed an ayllu clan.

imagine participants emerging from them for some ceremony. As with other important compounds, these gates are protected within by vertical cylinders in the jambs to secure vanished doors. On the inner side of each of the three courtyards is a fine three-doored building, and on the flanking sides are back-to-back, open-fronted masmas. The entire group is well isolated by its enclosure wall. Richard Burger and Lucy Salazar describe this sector as high-status canchas, with a cluster for each family of the Cuzco elite.

Behind the "three doors group," to the north, is the largest building in Machu Picchu, too long and narrow to be a kallanka, possibly a dormitory for agricultural workers since a staircase nearby leads down to the terraces.

131 The lower, eastern side of Machu Picchu contained residential enclosures for the elite, some with high-gabled double-sided masmas (to the right).

With eight doors on one long wall, it is similar to the barracks-like tambo at the junction of the two roads entering Machu Picchu from the south. Near here, Bingham's men excavated a rubbish midden that showed signs of long occupation, with sherds from well over a hundred pots. The side of the hill facing northeast has the feel of a residential district, with terraces of 150 identical simple houses, courtyards, internal streets, rock-outcrop shrines, caves, tombs, and short terraces overlooking the steep mountainside. This was doubtless accommodation for *yanacona* (servants).

The finest of these clan compounds is across the square from the "temple of the three windows." A splendid tall gabled building dominates the center

132 The stone projections identified by Bingham as household mortars may have had a ceremonial rather than a practical function.

133 A carved rock shrine on the easternmost edge of Machu Picchu, near terraces above the Urubamba river.

of this ward. It is a double masma, with a high central wall supporting the roof apex, and piers in the center of each open side. The buildings around it have flat stone walls and were once hip-roofed, with the thatch rising from each of the four walls in a near pyramid. Bingham called this the "mortar group" because of a building that faces the double masma to the east. In its floor are two round stone projections whose tops are carved to form shallow, flat cups. Bingham took these to be "permanent and unbreakable mortars or grinding stones, where maize could be ground and frozen potatoes crushed under the smooth-faced mullers, or rocking stones, which have been used throughout the central Andes since time immemorial. Near the mortars we actually found one of the ancient mullers which had been rocked here centuries ago." Salazar agrees with Bingham; but Victor Angles felt that they were not sufficiently concave for grinding: "Up to now [Bingham's stones] have not been explained; but it is clear that they were not mortars." One theory is that these were mirrors to observe "circular astronomical phenomena"—although it is unclear why the star-gazers could not simply look up at the night sky.

The Incas, like all Andean Indians, were orderly, docile, honest, and law-abiding by European standards. Their communal spirit and unquestioning obedience to authority greatly facilitated the Spanish Conquest. However, despite their natural good behavior, their society demanded abso-

lute conformity to established laws and customs. Any transgression or deviation was punished implacably. The chroniclers describe a scale of harsh punishments for crimes ranging from treason and murder to adultery, abuse of royal possessions, sorcery, and common theft. Guaman Poma described one prison as "constructed below ground in a form of crypt, very dark, where they raised snakes, poisonous serpents, pumas, jaguars, bears, foxes, dogs, wildcats, vultures, eagles...—creatures that could be used to punish criminals and delinquents." Lesser crimes might be punished by "tying the hands and feet with a cord and twisting it to obtain confession." For very serious crimes there was execution by stoning, clubbing, or—as seems possible at Ollantaytambo—being hurled from high precipices. Cobo spoke of habitual criminals being "executed by hanging with their heads downward and left hanging in this way until they died."

Bingham identified one group of buildings in Machu Picchu as its prisons: the ward to the southeast of and below the residential sector of high-status canchas. This group is overlooked by an imposing three-story building, which could conceivably have housed the prison governor or legal authority. It is an admirable structure that makes good use of the steep slope to give access to each floor. Its gables, walls, windows, and niches are intact, and the stepped

134 A vault, or passageway, within Bingham's "prison group."

135 The offertory stone and central outcrop of the "prison group."

136 Bingham imagined prisoners confined in the tall niches of his "prison group"; others feel that they may have held mummies or similar images.

cornice that once held the upper floor is clearly visible. The view from the top story is superb. The basement and the rocky vaults and caverns alongside could have been the subterranean prisons that once held dangerous beasts. A large, flat rock in the small courtyard outside has been carved to resemble a reclining condor. The head, knobbed beak, and white collar of the largest of all flying birds are clearly visible. Above this rock are niches large enough to take prisoners—they even have holes in their stone walls through which the cords described by Guaman Poma could have passed. There is another row of nine

137 Coursed masonry blends into bedrock of the central spur of the "prison group."

full-length niches along the wall that faces westward toward the upper city. These might also have been used for some form of incarceration.

As so often in Machu Picchu, nothing is certain. I think that the "prison group" probably had a religious purpose. The condor stone looks like a sacrificial altar, with grooves to carry off fluids. The tunnels and caverns under the rock outcrops—which remind one of Kenko above Cuzco—may have been used for theatrical priestly processions rather than as dungeons. Even Bingham admitted that the niches with holes in their sides were just the right size and shape to hold mummy bundles: "Each of these three niches was large enough to receive such a bundle and was provided with a stone

138 The offertory stone shaped like a condor's beak.

bar-hold so that the mummy could be tied in, or taboo sticks could have been fastened in front of each niche to ward off any interference with the mummy. Each niche in turn had three little niches, one on the back wall and one on each of the side walls. The little niches were probably for the reception of offerings, articles presumed to be of value and interest to the departed." The

stone platform below could have been used to dry the mummies in the sun, to maintain their preservation.

One of the holiest of Machu Picchu's many shrines was discovered only in 1936. This is the so-called Cave of the Moon, on a densely forested mountain-side far below the pinnacle of Huayna Picchu. It is reached by a 40-minute walk

139 The upper cavern of the Cave of the Moon, on the flank of Huayna Picchu.

down a fine Inca road that plunges around the western flank of Huayna Picchu. This is a dramatic journey, vertiginous where the slippery trail clings to granite cliffs. The cave is in deep cloud forest. When it finally comes into view in a break in the tropical vegetation, it is as unexpected as the first sight of Petra's tombs at the end of their ravine. It is almost as theatrical as the famous Jordanian ruin.

There are two caverns in the Cave of the Moon, with the upper and lower chambers linked by an ornamental façade. The upper cavern has five full-height niches and several smaller ones. The interior is completely filled with the most brilliant masonry, remarkable even among Inca ruins for the skill of its cutting. The niches are particularly impressive. The five large ones have double jambs, with their recessed edges carved from single stones—which is far more difficult than having different blocks interlocking at the inner angle. A lateral chamber of this upper group has a long screening wall with three fine trapezoidal doorways, 1.6 meters (5¼ feet) tall, with a similar door at the south end. One doorway leads to a passage and stair down the rock face to the lower cave group. Here again, the cavern is associated with an ornamental façade that faces south, above the cave's entrance, with niched wings projecting on either side. Opposite, a rock outcrop has been sculpted into a huge throne, with a view of the tall forest and the entrance to the sacred cave. There are other carved

140 The cave of Choquequilla, above the Huarocondo river near Ollantaytambo.

and masonry-lined caves, notably at Choquequilla near Anta and Huarocondo 52 kilometers (32 miles) along the railway from Cuzco. These were evidently more than burial mausoleums. As with so many structures at Machu Picchu, they were shrines, manifestations of the Incas' worship of the earth deity Pachamama and physical marvels—mountains, waterfalls, rock outcrops, and caves.

141 The ruins of Vitcos palace are on a low spur overlooking the Vilcabamba river as it flows northeastward toward the Urubamba.

11. Vitcos and the Inca Trail

WHEN HIRAM BINGHAM WAS IN LIMA IN 1909 (after visiting Choquequirao), the Peruvian historian Carlos Romero advised him to seek Inca ruins in the Vilcabamba region. Romero told Bingham about recently discovered documents that mentioned places in Vilcabamba's forests and mountains. It was this that inspired Bingham and his Yale classmates to organize the famous expedition of 1911. And when Bingham was shown the ruins of Machu Picchu, he spent only a few hours at the site that later made him famous. His expedition hurried on to its objective: the discovery of Inca ruins in Vilcabamba. (The name Vilcabamba is applied to five places: the region or province northwest of Cuzco, between the Urubamba and Apurímac rivers; a mountain range that is the watershed in this region; a river that flows into the Urubamba downstream from Machu Picchu; and two towns, one founded by Manco Inca and the other Vilcabamba la Nueva, a post-Conquest Spanish mining settlement.)

When Manco Inca's rebellion of 1536–37 failed, he retreated from Ollantaytambo to the valley of the Vilcabamba river. Manco hoped that the barrier of the Vilcabamba mountains, the gorges of the Urubamba, the densely forested terrain, and some hasty obstructions on the road would prevent pursuit by the dreaded Europeans. His first refuge was a place called Vitcos, high up the Vilcabamba river. But Manco was mistaken to think that this was beyond the reach of the Spaniards. As early as July 1537 the dashing conquistador Rodrigo de Orgóñez pursued the fugitive Inca and came within a few minutes of capturing him at Vitcos. Manco escaped by night in the arms of his swiftest runners; but Orgóñez led off thousands of the Inca's family and followers, tens of thousands of llama and alpaca, and a haul of other booty. After such a close shave, Manco decided that Vitcos was too exposed and started to build another capital called Vilcabamba, at lower altitude and deeper in the security of the Amazon forests. He established a neo-Inca state in this small corner of his father's former empire.

In 1542 Manco gave sanctuary to seven Spaniards who had fled from defeat by the Pizarro faction in one of the conquerors' civil wars. The Inca lodged these fugitives at Vitcos and treated them as his friends; they in turn taught him swordsmanship and riding. But when, in 1545, these Spaniards learned that the political climate in Peru had turned against the Pizarros, they decided to return to Spanish Peru and hoped to gain kudos by killing the exiled Inca. So

they stabbed Manco Inca to death, at Vitcos, while playing a game of quoits—and also wounded and almost killed his young son Titu Cusi, who managed to hide. The murderers galloped off toward Cuzco; but they ran into a force of Manco's soldiers and were themselves destroyed.

Manco was succeeded by three sons, who ruled the remote kingdom successively for twenty-eight years after his death. The second of these was Titu Cusi, who grew into a shrewd ruler and endearing extrovert. Throughout the 1560s he kept the Spanish authorities at bay with protracted diplomatic negotiations, giving occasional concessions but never emerging from his Vilcabamba enclave. One concession was to allow missionaries into his tiny kingdom. Two of these were Augustinian friars: an inflexible zealot called Marcos García and then the gentler Diego Ortiz. These were allowed to build two small churches, in the upper part of Vilcabamba west of Vitcos. They begged to see the town of Vilcabamba, the retreat built by Manco Inca; and in 1570 Titu Cusi let them make the two-day walk to his religious and administrative capital. It was while they were there that Titu Cusi dictated an autobiographical memoir—this was rediscovered three centuries later, and Carlos Romero showed a copy to Bingham.

Back at their churches near Vitcos, the friars brazenly led their congregation of converted Indians up the hill to the shrine of Chuquipalta beside Vitcos, with each boy carrying a piece of burning firewood. In the words of the Augustinian hagiographer Antonio de la Calancha, writing in the 1630s, Chuquipalta was "a temple of the sun, and inside it was a white stone above a spring of water. The devil appeared here and it was the principal *mochadero* in these montañas. There was a devil, captain of a legion of devils, inside a white stone called Yurac Rumi within that sun temple." (*Mochar* was a kissing gesture to the sun that formed part of Inca rituals; *montaña* described the forested hills on the Amazonian foothills of the Andes; *yurac* in Quechua means "white" and *rumi* "stone.") The missionaries' acolytes set fire to the temple's thatch and burned and "exorcized" this sacred shrine. Titu Cusi's captains were understandably furious at this sacrilege and wanted to kill the Augustinians. But the Inca was surprisingly lenient: he expelled the austere Friar Marcos, but allowed the more amenable Friar Diego to continue his ministry at his church a half-day's walk away.

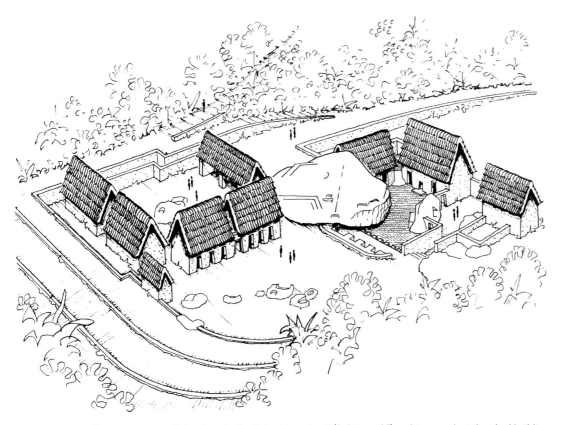

142 In Vincent Lee's reconstruction of the Chuquipalta shrine, Yurac Rumi ("white rock") and its attendant thatched buildings are seen from the southeast.

Titu Cusi's younger brother Tupac Amaru was living amid the priests and holy women in Vilcabamba town. When this brother suddenly succeeded, he and his generals were determined to revert to the traditional Inca way of life. They not only ordered the death of Friar Diego, but broke off relations with Spanish Peru and killed an envoy. This reactionary attitude provoked the dynamic new Spanish viceroy Francisco de Toledo: he launched an invasion of Vilcabamba by an overwhelmingly powerful Spanish force, which occupied both Vitcos and Vilcabamba town. Tupac Amaru fled to hide among forest tribes down the Urubamba; but he was pursued, captured, and led back to Cuzco for a hasty trial and execution on September 24, 1572.

After discovering the ruins of Machu Picchu in July 1911, Hiram Bingham pressed on down the Urubamba trail and into the Vilcabamba region. With characteristic energy, good luck, and help from local people, he rapidly discovered Vitcos. Ascending the Vilcabamba river, he was taken up a hill above a village called Puquiura. "Here before us was a great white rock. Our guides had not misled us. Beneath the trees were the ruins of an Inca temple, flanking and partly enclosing the gigantic granite boulder, one end of which overhung a small pool of running water... Densely wooded hills rose on every side. The remarkable aspect of this great boulder and the dark pool beneath its shadow had caused this to become a place of worship. Here, without doubt, was Calancha's 'principal *mochadero*' of these forested mountains. It is still venerated by the Indians of the vicinity."

Chuquipalta is still a place of supreme beauty, calm, and sanctity. Thick woods cover the steep flank of the hillside above; but below are grassy meadows leading down to a stream, farm, and more Inca ruins. The rock Yurac Rumi itself is a great lozenge of granite, with a surface of some 21 by 10 meters (69 by 33 feet) and a height of 8 meters (26 feet). Inca masons made this into a majestic sculpture. They left most of its sweeping curves and smooth top untouched but straightened a side wall and carved other surfaces to create rectangular planes, a staircase of bedrock, and an inset with a row of eight square pegs surmounted by other bosses reminiscent of the celestial Southern Cross. The dark pool below the rock has given way to swampy grass.

In mid-1571 Titu Cusi was at Vitcos, where the renegades had murdered Manco a quarter-century earlier. Calancha wrote that the Inca spent the day "mourning the death of his father with heathen rites and impudent superstitions. At the end of the day he started fencing (which he had learned to do in the Spanish manner) with his secretary Martín Pando. He sweated heavily and caught a chill. He ended it all by drinking too much wine and chicha [maize beer], became drunk, and woke with a pain in his side, a thick tongue—he was a very fat man—and an upset stomach. Everything was vomiting, shouting and drunkenness. The Inca passed the night bleeding from the mouth and nose." Pando, a mixed-race friend, and others gave Titu Cusi a brew of white-of-egg and sulfur to restrain his bleeding. But when he drank this, "the sickness rose to its full pitch, and he expired." His distraught subjects lynched Pando, who had administered the fatal medicine; and they took Friar Diego Ortiz down toward Vilcabamba town, and he was killed and buried (head-down in a pit) shortly before he reached it.

143 Geometric planes are carved on the southern side of Yurac Rumi, with a narrow offertory channel incised on its gently sloping surface.

144 In Inca times, the rock of Yurac Rumi overlooked a mysterious pool below its eastern edge.

hispanan. They are at an altitude of 3,080 meters (10,105 feet), a 45-minute climb from the village of Puquiura on the Vilcabamba river.) Vitcos is on a promontory—a favorite location for the Incas—although with less spectacular views than the ridge saddles of Choquequirao, Pisac, Ollantaytambo, or Machu Picchu. The palace was probably built by Manco's great-grandfather Pachacuti, since Vilcabamba was one of the first provinces occupied by that great conquering Inca.

Vitcos is a modest place, hardly a "palace" in European terms. Approaching from the hill, the narrow neck of its saddle is blocked by a long rectangular building with three doors on its outer face and two behind. This gives onto a plaza, beyond which the widening spur is blocked by another structure, a terrace of four houses, each with three trapezoidal doors onto the plaza and other gates to the three passages between them: a screen with fifteen doors in total. The residential area at the end of the promontory consists of a dozen small houses around two square courtyards. Most of the site was ruined and overgrown with weedy grasses and shrubs; but it, too, has been cleaned and drastically restored.

Having discovered Machu Picchu and Vitcos in those amazing weeks in 1911, Bingham was told about other ruins far to the northwest. He pressed

Bingham spent two days excavating at Chuquipalta in 1912; it was remapped by the American architect-explorer Vincent Lee in 1982 and 1984; but despite other surveys, attempts at looting, and many visits, the second excavation was not until 2008. This was done by the Chicago archaeologist Brian Bauer, who found evidence of the massive fire of 1570, as well as early floors, remains of roofing thatch, and Inca and colonial-era ceramics. Peru's archaeological authority, the National Institute of Culture, plans to restore the pond and even reconstruct the simple temple buildings. This could violate the aura of mystery of this isolated and largely untouched ruin.

Bingham knew from Calancha, whom he quoted, and other sources that Manco's palace of Vitcos was nearby. He easily located its ruins twenty minutes' walk away, on a spur of the same hill that contains Chuquipalta and its white rock. (The hill slope is now often called Rosaspata and the shrine Ñusta-

on for a week, through tough terrain and often drenched in rain, and made a third remarkable discovery: remains of Inca structures choked by dense tropical forest, at an "alluvial fan" called Espíritu Pampa that was far lower in altitude than his earlier finds. This was later proved to be part of Manco's new capital and Tupac Amaru's spiritual retreat, the town of Vilcabamba. (Bingham himself tried, in vain, to show that Manco's "lost city" was not here, but at his first spectacular discovery Machu Picchu.)

To the Incas, Vitcos was near the end of a string of shrines, royal retreats, and forts in the hills along the Vilcanota–Urubamba river and its tributaries. Northwest of Ollantaytambo, this chain of ruins is along what we now call the Inca Trail, then comes Machu Picchu itself, beyond it Llactapata (a place glimpsed by Bingham in 1912 and then cleared and mapped by the British David Drew in 1982 and Hugh Thomson and Gary Ziegler in 2002), with Vitcos

145 Yurac Rumi from the west. Buildings of the Chuquipalta shrine would have stood on either side of it, with the sacred pool below it to the left.

146 The sheer northern face of Yurac Rumi is carved with bosses resembling the Southern Cross stars and a row of square pegs.

a day's walk to the northwest. Another switchback trail runs southwestward behind Mount Yanama toward Choquequirao.

Visitors who have time and stamina should approach Machu Picchu by the high Inca road, the famous Inca Trail. This is a walk of great beauty, through a national park full of lush flora (particularly orchids, bromeliads, and lichens) and bird life, and with breathtaking views. This is the only way to see six fascinating Inca ruins—each different from one another—and long stretches of Inca roads. The culmination of three or four days of sometimes punishing climbing, very cold nights, and a 43-kilometer (27-mile) walk is to gaze down on Machu Picchu and enter the legendary lost city through its Intipunku gate.

The third Yale Peruvian Expedition of 1914–15 cut its way along this road, southward from Machu Picchu, and discovered three ruins for which Bingham

147 Vitcos before reconstruction, looking south from the residential cluster to the neck of the spur.

VITCOS

Vincent Lee made a plan and
reconstruction drawing of
the modest palace of Vitcos,
on an artificially leveled spur
overlooking the Vilcabamba river.

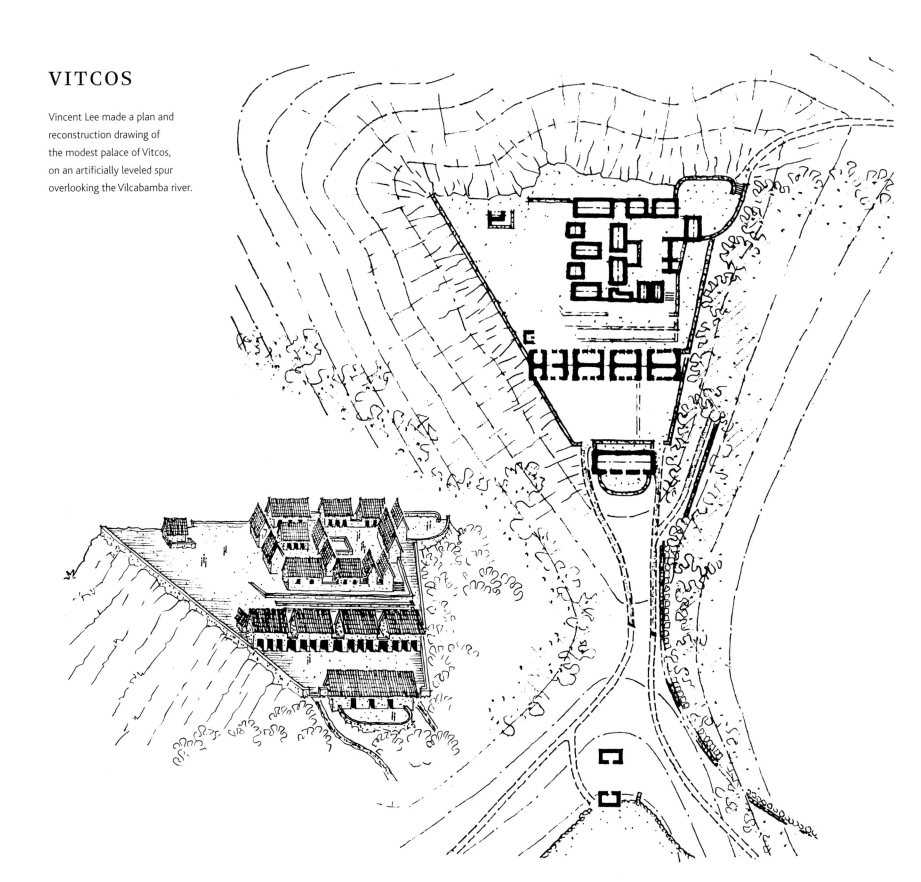

invented Inca names. These sites were cleared and investigated again by the Peruvian archaeologist Luis Valcárcel in 1934, and were carefully mapped in 1939–40 by the Fejos expedition financed by the Swedish millionaire Axel Wenner-Gren. The Fejos expedition discovered two more sites quite close to Machu Picchu, which it named Wiñay Wayna and Intipata. (This Inca road was badly overgrown and crumbling when I first attempted it in 1960. I fell off, and spent a night in a tree and half a day clambering down to the river.) The Inca Trail is now excellently restored and given annual repairs by tourist porters, all of whom come from a village called Patacancha.

Many walkers start by crossing the Urubamba on a bridge at Kilometer 88 on the railway. Their first visit is to an urban complex called Patallacta (or sometimes Llactapata) on a crescent-shaped bluff where the Cusichaca stream joins the Urubamba. This is one of the largest settlements in the region, with a curving residential area of twenty-three blocks of buildings containing 109 chambers, arranged along tidy streets. From this town a road runs up the Cusichaca valley to a venerable shrine called Pulpituyoq, a great sculpted boulder reminiscent of the Yurac Rumi white rock at Chuquipalta near Vitcos, enclosed by a curved wall and a series of temple chambers. These sites were thoroughly explored between 1978 and 1982 in a project led by the British archaeologist Ann Kendall. The urban complex Patallacta and the fort of Willkaraqay facing it were excavated and restored. Dr. Kendall got local people to clear and revive some 10 kilometers (6 miles) of skillfully engineered Inca irrigation channels, which transformed their farming. This led to the foundation of the Cusichaca Trust, which restores ancient terraces and irrigation all over Peru.

Further up the Cusichaca, at Huallabamba village where there is another oval rock-outcrop shrine, the trail turns northwestward up a side

149 A fine double-jambed doorway in the palace buildings at Vitcos.

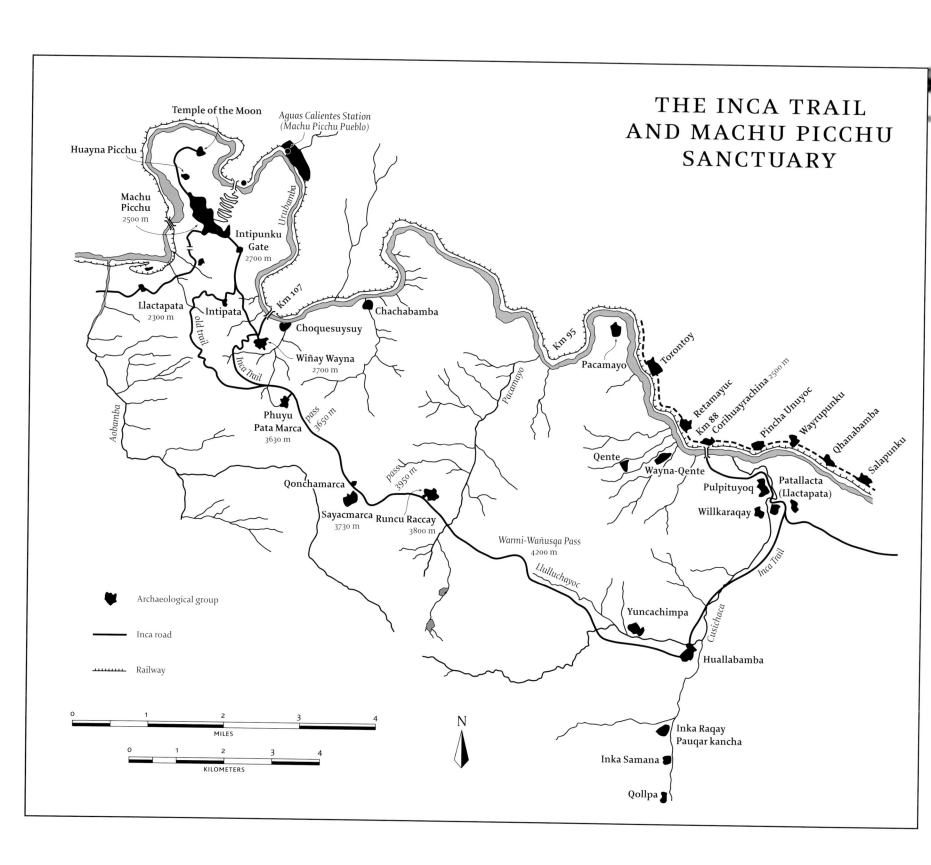

THE INCA TRAIL
AND MACHU PICCHU
SANCTUARY

Temple of the Moon

Aguas Calientes Station
(Machu Picchu Pueblo)

Huayna Picchu

Machu
Picchu
2500 m

Intipunku
Gate
2700 m

Km 107

Chachabamba

Llactapata
2300 m

Intipata

Choquesuysuy

old trail

Wiñay Wayna
2700 m

Inca Trail

Km 95

Pacamayo

Torontoy

Retamayuc

Km 88
Corihuayrachina 2500 m

Pincha Unuyoc

Wayrupunku

Qhanabamba

Salapunku

Phuyu
Pata Marca
3630 m

pass
3650 m

Qente

Wayna-Qente

pass
3950 m

Pulpituyoq

Patallacta
(Llactapata)

Qonchamarca

Willkaraqay

Sayacmarca
3730 m

Runcu Raccay
3800 m

Warmi-Wañusqa Pass
4200 m

Llulluchayoc

Aobamba

Urubamba

Pacamayo

Archaeological group

Inca road

Railway

Cusichaca

Inca Trail

Yuncachimpa

Huallabamba

0   1   2   3   4
MILES

0   1   2   3   4
KILOMETERS

N

Inka Raqay
Pauqar kancha

Inka Samana

Qollpa

151 Patallacta (sometimes called Llactapata) after excavation and restoration by Ann Kendall's Cusichaca Project in the early 1980s. This urban complex occupies a crescent platform, overlooking the Cusichaca stream where it joins the Urubamba river—seen in the distance, with the railway to Machu Picchu on its far bank.

152 Phuyu Pata Marca ("town in the clouds," a name given by Hiram Bingham) occupies a pyramid of seven terraces linked by a fine straight stairway. Six ritual "baths" or fountains mark the source of a sacred stream which flows past Wiñay Wayna to join the Urubamba at Choquesuysuy.

153 The western slope of Phuyu Pata Marca was photographed by Martín Chambi in 1941, after the Paul Fejos expedition cleared and mapped the site.

154 An open-fronted masma in the lower group in Wiñay Wayna, with slots for the cross beam and bar-holders to tie down the thatch. Photograph by Martín Chambi, 1941.

155 With its cascade of liturgical "baths," window in the lower group to admire or worship the waterfall, and hillside of curved terracing, Wiñay Wayna is the finest ruin on the Inca Trail. (Photograph by Chambi, shortly after first clearance in 1941.)

valley and then over a formidable 4,200-meter (13,800-foot) pass. This is the steepest and toughest climb on the Inca Trail. Breathless and weary travelers joke that it is aptly called Warmi-Wañusqa, which means "Dead Woman Pass." The road then drops steeply to its lowest point at 3,600 meters (11,800 feet) and a complex called Runcu Raccay. This circular structure on a large terrace appears to have been a check-point, for it is in a strategic location; but it might also have been a viewing platform to venerate the lovely Pacamayo valley below.

Peter Frost, a British author who knows the Inca Trail better than anyone, was sure that the route was planned to inspire pilgrims. "There was nothing happenstance about the stunning combinations of scenic and man-made beauty. The Incas wanted those who walked this way to reel in awe as they crested the passes and rounded the corners. They designed the trail like a dramatic narrative, with a series of troughs, slow buildups and climaxes, each greater than the last, until the stunning finale, when travelers look down from Intipunku upon Machu Picchu."

After another pass, the next goal for walkers is Sayacmarca ("inaccessible town"; which Bingham in 1915 called Cedrobamba, "cedar plain"). A steep stairway climbs from the path to this expertly engineered complex on a rocky ridge. There is religious significance in Sayacmarca, with a rock containing bas-relief carvings—a rarity for an Inca site—and three ceremonial water channels at the base of the outcrop. A dozen chambers, passages, and retaining walls fill the ridge, but there is still room for a large platform from which to admire—and worship—the view westward down the Aobamba valley and its rugged mountain scenery. Beyond here is a beautiful stretch of road skirting the fertile but marshy Chacilcocha plain, which passes through the first of several tunnels (16 meters or 52 feet) long, behind a rock overhang, before surmounting the third pass.

The next ruin is a ceremonial site on a spur with commanding views. Phuyu Pata Marca ("town in the clouds") was also located by Bingham, on the slope of Mount Corihuayrachina (or Qoriwayrachina: "place where gold is washed"). Perched above a pyramid of seven terraces that contour the spur like the layers of an architect's model, Phuyu Pata Marca's dozen buildings are tightly fitted onto its rocks. Below the terraces is a cascade of six superbly carved ritual baths, a foretaste of similar waterworks lower down the mountainside. Here the views are even more spectacular, from the Urubamba up to the snowy range around Mount Yanantin and south toward Salcantay. Crowning the hill above is a cemetery where Inca priests are thought to have been buried.

Beyond here the roads fork. The higher road leads to a complex called Cantupata (discovered only in 1985), and a series of Inca huts and shelters,

before descending to Machu Picchu. But most walkers continue down to two beautiful sites, Wiñay Wayna and Intipata. The Trail descends a gorge, on a wide stretch of paved road with a dizzying staircase of hundreds of steps (many carved from bedrock), and a 4-meter-long (13-foot) tunnel.

Wiñay Wayna ("forever young" because of its perpetual orchids) is the third-largest settlement in this region, after Patallacta and Machu Picchu. It was seen and named by Fejos, and excavated by the great indigenous Peruvian archaeologist Julio Tello in 1942. There are three inspiring religious features. The upper cluster of buildings, rebuilt in the 1990s, has fine masonry, a double-jambed bay, and a curved temple that admires the lovely snowcapped Mount Verónica. From here water once cascaded down a stunning staircase of nineteen baths. And from the last structure in the lower group, a trapezoidal window looks back up the mountain to frame a Wagnerian waterfall! Jean-Pierre Protzen commented that anyone who doubted that the Incas worshipped the natural world and appreciated beauty has only to visit Wiñay Wayna and admire this spectacle. This lovely ruin also has one of the finest curving slopes of terracing in all Peru; and it faces Intipata ("sun terrace"), with a hillside of similarly spectacular terracing.

The water in Wiñay Wayna's baths and waterfall rises at Phuyu Pata Marca, and then plunges down to join the Urubamba at an extraordinary site called Choquesuysuy. This stream was clearly sacred, and the buildings, terraces, and channels on either side of it in Choquesuysuy were built with the care lavished on temples in Machu Picchu. Some have niches, doors, and windows edged in fitted ashlars. Choquesuysuy has been carefully restored, and it is clearly visible across the river from Kilometer 107 on the railway.

There is a series of interesting ruins upstream from here: the large residential complex of Chachabamba with great open masma houses, at Kilometer 104; Pacamayo with terraces and some buildings, at Kilometer 95; Wayna-Qente, with four agricultural sectors and housing of a dozen chambers; then Qente with terracing beside the Urubamba a kilometer long and rising 250 meters (820 feet); upriver, the Trail starts at the bridge of Corihuayrachina at Kilometer 88, with the curving ruins of Patallacta above. The right bank of the Urubamba also has a string of small sites, notably a tambo called Wayrupunku with a guarded gate where the canyon narrows near the bridge. Further upriver at Kilometer 84, not far below Ollantaytambo, is Salapunku. This was the Incas' outer defense of the Machu Picchu sanctuary. A wall runs down the hillside to a gate through a two-story building, one that clearly controlled access by travelers or pilgrims. Downriver from here is the heart of the Sacred Valley of the Urubamba, dominated by the incomparable Machu Picchu. It is a region that lay miraculously undisturbed for four centuries.

156 A view southeast from the first and highest pass on the Inca Trail shows snow-clad peaks of the Huayanay range towering above the Cusichaca river.

157 Choquequirao from the truncated hill, after restoration. A cascade of baths and water channels link the upper and lower plazas. Photograph by Hugh Thomson.

12. Choquequirao

THE ENIGMATIC RUINS OF CHOQUEQUIRAO (CHOQUEQUIRAU) are being promoted by the Peruvian tourist authorities as "the second Machu Picchu." The two great ruins do have much in common. Both are in the forested Vilcabamba hills, with Choquequirao 90 kilometers (60 miles) as the condor flies southwest of the most famous ruin in the Americas—but the condor would have to soar high above the cordillera between the snowcapped Mounts Salcantay and Pumasillo. Both complexes are on saddles of spurs jutting out over river canyons. The hill at the end of Choquequirao's spur is lower than the horn of Huayna Picchu, but the view over the Apurímac is even more breathtaking than that over the Urubamba: a sheer drop of 1,800 meters (5,900 feet) to the raging river, which looks like a silvery ribbon as it slices through range after range of densely wooded hills toward the western horizon. Although Choquequirao is much smaller and its masonry less beautiful than Machu Picchu's, both places have the attributes of royal estates: stone buildings, watercourses and fountains, kallankas, sacred outcrops, and nestling in hillsides tamed by tiers of terraces. Also, in the words of the explorer-architect Vincent Lee, "both sites evoke much the same feeling of reverence for and celebration of wild Nature and the splendors of the high mountain world."

Choquequirao has thirteen clusters of ruins, separated due to the steep slopes and uneven terrain. There is an upper and lower sector, perhaps reflecting the hanan and hurin divisions of most Inca communities. To the north of the lower plaza are three large houses that have two levels, a central wall, doors on both stories, and protruding stones that once supported external wooden stairs. Below these, a magnificent six-door kallanka has alternating large and small niches separated by stone pegs in its inner wall. At the opposite end of this plaza, a screen of shrines with five double-jambed gateways leads to a "truncated hilltop." This remarkable feature involved prodigious earth-movement. It formed a great conical trunk surrounded by terracing, with a flat oval top measuring about 55 by 30 meters (180 by 100 feet). The result was a natural ushnu with amazing views in every direction, which could have served for solar, astronomical, and mountain worship.

The upper plaza may once have been beside a spring, and the site is full of splendid irrigation channels. One culvert runs down a wall to the lower plaza, and there is a cascade that Hiram Bingham called "the giant staircase."

An isolated building known as the "house of the falling water" or "pavilion" is set in the midst of beautiful terracing and seems to be for water rituals reminiscent of those in Wiñay Wayna on the Inca Trail. In size, and with its upper and lower plazas and quantity of terracing, Choquequirao resembles Wiñay Wayna more than the larger and more complex Machu Picchu.

Choquequirao's temperature is remarkably warm but well ventilated, with frequent mists and showers, thanks to interplay between cold winds blowing down from glaciated mountains and hot air rising from the canyon. The surrounding woods are full of orchids, bromeliads, ferns, and the semi-tropical vegetation which Peruvians charmingly call the *ceja de selva* ("eyebrow of the forest"). The many terraces here would have yielded excellent maize. So there are fine rectangular storehouses, similar to those on the hill opposite Ollantaytambo. These have good ventilation from lateral vents, and platforms for pouring in produce.

The stone in this part of Vilcabamba is metamorphic with a high content of quartzous clay. This cannot be cut into the tightly fitted masonry for which the Incas are famous. So walls in Choquequirao are built of fieldstone set in mortar: only doorways, bosses, and other features are of hard stones carried in from distant quarries. The pirca masonry in the falling-water pavilion is still embellished with a coat of plaster. There is a surprise in the flight of terraces west of the ceremonial plaza. Its stones are set in upright rows and in their midst are twenty-three large stylized llamas picked out in white stones. Such stones and stonework (but not the decorative llamas) are exactly the same as in ruins of the Chachapoya people of northern Peru. We know that this warlike tribe was pacified by Huayna Capac; and Cieza tells us that he moved a quantity of them to the Cuzco region as mitimaes. However, the French archaeologist Patrice Lecoq noticed that these figures replicate an Inca textile of a train of llamas, so that they may have been intended to be seen and venerated from afar.

Choquequirao is not mentioned in any early chronicle. The name first appeared in literature in a report of 1710 by one Juan Arias Díaz Topete, who was sent by the authorities in Guamanga (now Ayacucho) to investigate the abandoned Vilcabamba region. Topete mentioned Choquequirao as one of four places in that Inca province (of which one has never been located). Cosmé Bueno wrote in 1768 (in a description of the bishopric of Cuzco) that "a few years

158 A screen of buildings separates the lower plaza from the truncated observatory hill (right) and a breathtaking view down the valley of the Apurímac. (Hugh Thomson)

159 The two-story buildings and kallanka below them, heavily shrouded in vegetation before their cleaning and restoration. (Hugh Thomson)

ago some people, attracted by a tradition that there was an ancient town called Choqquequirau, crossed the Apurímac on rafts and penetrated the montaña [montane forest]. They found a deserted place built of quarried stone, covered in jungle and very hot. Sumptuous houses and palaces were recognized." This was the start of a protracted treasure hunt. For a century and a half, Choquequirao was "the lost city of the Incas." It was mentioned by the historian Pablo José Orcaín in 1790; and in the early days of the Peruvian Republic, a local landowner called Tejada searched it for treasure. The indefatigable French diplomat-traveler Eugène de Lavandais, Vicomte de Sartiges, in 1834 was determined to get there because he thought that it had been the capital of Tupac Amaru, Manco Inca's son. Sartiges succeeded, with two Peruvian companions and a team of trailcutters, by an incredibly difficult route: from Cuzco over a high pass on the flanks of Mounts Soray and Salcantay, then down to Huadquiña on the Urubamba (passing close to the then-unknown Machu Picchu), then cutting up through matted forest followed by high grasses and bamboo-like *zagua*, toward a pass northwest of Salcantay. The expedition suffered terribly from cutting grasses, thirst, and clouds of black-fly and mosquitoes. They then had a tough descent from the glaciers of Mount Yanama. The journey took five days, and they then spent a week clearing some of the vegetation that choked the fabled ruin. Sartiges wrote a brief description of Choquequirao. He admired the "Egyptian" appearance of the double-jambed entrances of the portico beneath the truncated hill; but his burrowing into it yielded no Inca objects. The next visitor was another French diplomat and artist, Léonce Angrand, who in 1847

was lured by a rumor that "immense treasures were buried among the ruins when the last survivors of 'the race of the sun' retired to this savage asylum." Angrand reached the ruin by the same punishing route as Sartiges, but he left a far more scholarly account of the site, with good plans and drawings. He noticed stone rings that are set into the inner wall of the kallanka, and surmised that these were used to tether wild animals such as pumas (they were probably for fixing the ends of back-looms).

The great Peruvian naturalist and cartographer Antonio Raimondi was on the upper Vilcabamba river in 1865 but did not reach Choquequirao, a very difficult 35 kilometers (22 miles) to the south. Raimondi, however, lent his prestige to the view that it was the last refuge of Manco and his sons; as did the other distinguished nineteenth-century geographer Mariano Paz Soldán. Various adventurers tried to reach the "lost city"—one failed, another said that he had walked nearby, and a third boasted that he spent five months there—without volunteering any details of his visit.

In 1908 J. J. Núñez, prefect of Abancay, raised thousands of dollars to finance a massive treasure-hunting expedition that planned to dynamite the ruin. This venture approached from the south, zigzagging down 2,000 meters (6,600 feet) from Cachora, a village off the main Cuzco–Ayacucho road, into the deep canyon of the Apurímac. An aged Chinese had the courage and strength to swim the turbulent river, so that Núñez's team could build a flimsy bridge (90 centimeters or 3 feet wide, of six telegraph cables). They spent three months doing this, cutting 19 kilometers (12 miles) of trails up the steep and densely wooded northern slope, and then clearing and searching the ruin. The eminent Peruvian historian Carlos Romero published notes of this survey; but there was no Inca treasure. In the following year Hiram Bingham was in Abancay on his way home overland from a conference in Chile. Prefect Núñez suggested that Bingham should visit the ruin—partly to lend respectability to his own hoped-for looting. Bingham later admitted that "we were not on the lookout for new Inca ruins and had never heard of Choqquequirau"; but he made the journey and was enthralled by what he saw. He described it all in an article in *The American Anthropologist*: the arduous journey, luxuriant cloud-forest vegetation, stunning views, and fascinating buildings. Bingham's description of the site was very competent and supported by photographs and plans. This was his first taste of jungle-shrouded Inca ruins. It inspired the Yale Peruvian Expedition of 1911 that made him eternally famous as the discoverer of Machu Picchu.

For most of the twentieth century, Choquequirao was forgotten, eclipsed by the famous ruins on the other side of the watershed. When I went there in 1960, the bridge over the Apurímac had gone: I had to swing across on an *oroya*, suspended under the armpits from a curved stick running along a strand of wire, with my legs dangling above the swirling waters. After a two-day climb up the little-used trail, I stayed in the tiny hut of a hospitable old couple, and they helped me cut through to the ruins. These were heavily overgrown, and there was plenty of rain. It was not until 1986 that the study and restoration of this beautiful site started in earnest. Although Sendero Luminoso (Shining Path) guerrillas were active in the Apurímac valley, the Peruvian tourism authority sent the Cuzco architect Roberto Samanez to survey Choquequirao. The archaeologists Julinjo Zapata and then Percy Paz, of Cuzco University, later cleared, excavated, and restored the great ruin. Because this complex was largely built of fieldstone in clay, the restorers had no qualms about rebuilding many Inca structures to the roof line with modern mortar. Vincent Lee had two seasons there, in 1995 and 1996, walking out by the punishing rollercoaster Inca Trail northward to Arma and the Vilcabamba river—this path's ascents add up to 8,000 meters (26,000 feet) and the descents to 8,500 (28,000 feet), which makes the Inca Trail seem like an afternoon stroll. Lee discovered new terraces and a cluster of buildings hidden in the forest below Choquequirao, and others investigated outlying ruins (notably Pincha Unuyoc and Cota Coca) a few kilometers to the north. Gary Ziegler mapped trails to the north and northeast (the Yanama route used by the French in the nineteenth century), but his team could find no Inca road directly southeastward toward Cuzco. There is now a modern suspension bridge over the Apurímac, the trails are in good shape for mules or horses, and the restored ruins look superb. So visitors can now enjoy "Peru's second Machu Picchu" which was for so long thought to have been the lost city of the Incas.

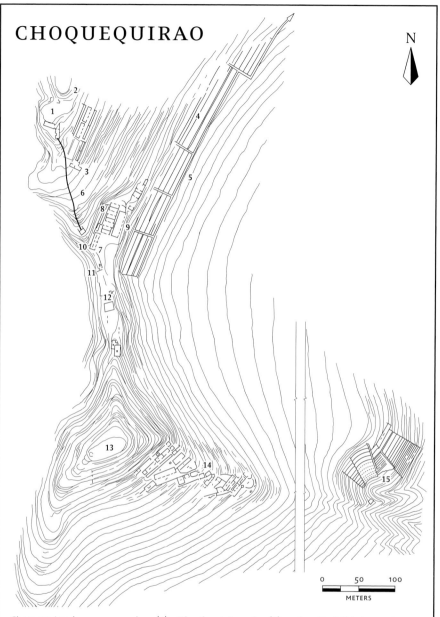

CHOQUEQUIRAO

N

Choquequirao has an upper plaza (1) with a fountain spring (2), and on the hill below a giant stairway (3). An aqueduct (6) flows down to the main fountain (11). The main, lower plaza (7) is approached from the Apurímac by a cedar-flanked road (5) below curved terraces (4). Beside it are a great kallanka hall (9), a lesser hall (10), and imposing two-story buildings (8). A screen of buildings and a gate (12) lead to a truncated observatory hill (13), on whose eastern ridge is a group of terraces and buildings (14). Some 350 meters (1,000 feet) below these is Capuliyoc, with terraces decorated with llamas (15). (After Copesco, Cuzco.)

161 The deep gorge of the Apurímac river was crossed by the Incas' most famous suspension bridge.

13. Saihuite

ONE OF THE MOST IMPORTANT FUNCTIONS of the Inca priesthood was prediction and divination. A few shrines in different parts of the empire were venerated as places where priests could converse with the spirit world. Spanish missionaries were naturally determined to crush such manifestations of a rival religion—but they were slightly in awe of indigenous sorcerers who might be in communication with the true devil. Cristóbal de Molina admitted the possibility that some of the predictions might be correct: "There were other shamans who had charge of the huacas [shrines], and among these were some who at certain shrines spoke with the devil and received his answers. They would tell the people whatever they wanted to learn...and on a few occasions they gave true answers." Another priest, Pablo José de Arriaga, agreed: "Huaca villac means 'he who speaks with the shrine': this [villac] is its chief priest, he who is responsible for guarding the huaca and speaking to it. He tells the people what he pretends it has told him—although sometimes the Devil really does speak through the stone."

One of the most holy oracle shrines was located above the canyon of the Apurímac. This mighty river, whose name means "great speaker" or "lord oracle," was probably named after this famous oracle shrine. According to Hernando de Santillán (a Spanish administrator who was particularly knowledgeable about the Incas) the coastal oracle of Pachacamac, the holiest of all pre-Inca shrines, told Topa Inca Yupanqui that it had four "sons": oracle shrines that would tell the Inca whatever he wanted to know. One of these overlooked the Apurímac near Andahuaylas. Francisco Pizarro's secretary Pedro Sancho reported that when the invading Spaniards passed this place on their march to Cuzco, they found a temple full of silver slabs "twenty feet [6 meters] long by a foot [30 centimeters] wide and an inch or two thick [2.5–5 centimeters]."

By far the most detailed description of the Apurímac shrine came from the conqueror's young cousin Pedro Pizarro. He learned about it from a soldier called Francisco Martín, who had been captured by Manco Inca's men and had actually seen his captor consult the oracle. "Manco Inca made the devil speak to him in front of this Francisco Martín, who says that he heard the voice of the devil answering what Manco Inca had asked him. The Inca said to Martín: 'Look how my god speaks to me!' For here at Apurímac there was a highly painted hall, inside which a thick pole was erected, thicker than a very fat man. This

pole had many pieces broken off it, and it was covered in the blood of sacrifices offered to it. It was completely encircled by a band of gold, the width of a hand, which was welded to it in a form of inlay. In front, it had two golden breasts the size of a woman's, fixed to the same band. They had this pole clothed in very delicate women's clothing, with many gold *copos* which are a form of pin that the women of this land used... Beside this thick pole there were other smaller ones in a line on either side, occupying the entire chamber from end to end. These poles were also bathed in blood and dressed in mantles like the large one, so that, with their copos, they resembled statues of women. The [Indians] said that the devil spoke to them from the large idol, and they called it Apurímac. The guardian of this was a lady called Asarpay, a sister of these Incas. She later jumped to her death from a very high pass on the descent toward the bridge over the river Apurímac. She covered her head and threw herself into the river where it runs near this cliff, from a height of over two hundred *estados* [315 meters or over 1,000 feet], calling on Apurímac, the idol whom she had served." The priestess's suicide was a protest against the Spanish desecration of her shrine.

The remains of this important oracle are probably those still visible at a hacienda called Saihuite. These are on rolling hills high above the Apurímac canyon, beside the main road between Cuzco and the coast, near the town of Curahuasi 45 kilometers (28 miles) from Abancay. Tough Andean horses graze here, on meadows often broken by lichen-covered outcrops [ill. 5]. Photographing these beautiful rocks, Edward Ranney was struck by the intimate relation between the monuments and their surroundings. The Argentinian artist César Paternosto painted Saihuite and exclaimed lyrically that such shrines are "an efflorescence" of the bedrock from which they are sculpted.

The most striking of the Saihuite shrines, known as the principal or upper stone, looks from a distance like a huge broken flint or a gigantic kettledrum. The stone stands 2.6 meters (8½ feet) high, and its oval surface varies from 3 to 4 meters (10 to 13 feet) in diameter. Its curving rim has notches that once held either a golden cladding or an elaborate textile. Cristóbal de Albornoz, one of the priests instructed to discover and destroy Inca idolatry, noted that many shrines had individual, distinctive clothing of the finest cloth—not least the sacred origin rock on the Island of the Sun in Lake Titicaca.

162 The complex carvings on the principal, or upper, stone of Saihuite may have been a topographical model.

As one approaches closer, the jagged top is seen to be covered in an intricate mass of carving: numerous figures, some in high relief, others almost free-standing. There are human beings armed with arrows, pumas, llamas, vicuñas, snakes, frogs, monkeys, lizards, and even a crab. The faces of all but one of these figures have been smashed, presumably by some Spanish zealot charged with the extirpation of indigenous "idolatry." The sole survivor is a puma who crouches severely at one side of the rock, almost as its guardian spirit. Between the figures is a labyrinth of tiny altars, stairways, gates, and platforms. A most important feature is the network of grooves and channels that doubtless once carried liquids past the various figures, in some complicated ceremony of divination. All the grooves run down from the stone's highest point. The stone itself has been tilted by erosion or treasure-seekers, so that the channels

163 Terraces, channels, and small creatures cover the upper Saihuite stone. Notches along its rim may have held a golden cladding.

do not now run freely; but it is easy to imagine the mysterious rites that once took place at this oracle. Other places, such as the rocky shrine of Kenko above Cuzco, have similar carving and divination channels; but nothing is as elaborate as the upper stone of Saihuite, and no other stone stands so dramatically isolated. It has been suggested that the rock's surface is a map or the model of a town. To the nineteenth-century Austrian traveler Charles Wiener, it was "a faithful reproduction of the region of the Andes and the works of the Peruvian architects and engineers: a form of topographical synthesis."

Over the brow of the hill, the land slopes down toward the distant Apurímac. There are more Saihuite stones here, notably a mighty carved boulder known locally as Rumihuasi ("stone house"). This rock, 6.1 meters (20 feet) wide, has been split, perhaps by lightning. The Incas had previously smoothed and shaped it into a gigantic sculpture. It is geometrical and abstract, with altar tables and small flights of steps, but its purpose was clearly prediction or divination. Eight shallow dishes are carved into its upper surface, and from one of these runs a groove intended for ritual effluents. The groove divides at the edge of the stone into two channels that end in rectangular basins.

Other rock outcrops in this area are similarly carved with channels and rectangular planes. Wiener reported a cyclopean wall almost sunk into swampy

ground. He also described and sketched a large Inca hall half a day's ride across the hills to the north. This building, known as Incahuasi ("Inca's house"), looks across the great cleft of the Apurímac toward Vilcabamba and the Inca ruin of Choquequirao. It is a tall structure with three levels of niches one above the other. It corresponds best to Pedro Pizarro's description of the temple containing the Apurímac Oracle. But the extraordinary rocks of Saihuite have a more powerful religious presence; and their location is closer to the foundations of the famous suspension bridge that once carried the royal Inca highway across the Apurímac.

In addition to shrines devoted to prediction and divination, the Incas worshipped at many isolated landscape shrines and carved rock outcrops, the symbolism and meaning of which are only partially understood. In the immediate vicinity of Cuzco there were over 300 of these huacas, located on ceques that radiated from the temple of the sun and created a pattern—possibly symbolic of the Inca calendar. Huacas were specific places or objects, distinguished by some special peculiarity, in which supernatural forces and spirits resided. To the Quechua Indian, even a small stone or stick from the vicinity of his home huaca could serve as a talisman, enabling him to carry the protective power of his huaca with him. Most huacas possessed the power of speech, or oracle. Some possessed demonic power, were feared, and destroyed if possible.

Caves and rocks, particularly those near rivers, streams, or springs where the sound of rushing water spoke as the oracle, were the most prevalent huacas. These were often carved with shapes that embodied the power of the sun, the mountains, or the earth's forces, or were related to them. Virtually all carving of the huacas was non-representational, made to mark the presence of man without depicting him, and was often in the form of ceremonial seats or niches. Some of the most precise work, such as that at Quillarumi, or the inti-huatana at Machu Picchu, appears to have been dedicated to the worship of the sun, to mark specific points of the solar year. Other carvings were more symbolic, such as the recurrent stepped design, the puma, and the incised channels used for offertory rites and divination ceremonies. Rarely, as far as we know, was representational carving employed, as on the principal, or upper, stone of Saihuite.

It was the Incas' acts of worship and ritual that endowed these shrines with meaning. Many of the small huacas outside Cuzco were cared for by the clan groups living near them, thus enabling much of the population to serve as their own priesthood. In addition, participation in public ceremonies relating to the Inca calendar and ancestor worship, annual initiation rites of noble youths at Huanacauri hill, and pilgrimages to religious sites like the Island of the Sun provided involvement in rituals and assured cultural continuity.

164 Offertory, or divination, channels on Rumihuasi, one of the stones of Saihuite.

165 The limestone outcrop of Kenko, a shrine above Cuzco, contains zigzag divination channels that pour into a labyrinth of passages and caverns.

166 The outcrop of Kenko is covered in carvings as well as natural faults and crevices. Its caverns and passages may have housed mummies and been associated with funerary rituals.

167 An outcrop at Kenko resembles a seated puma.

168 The offertory channel of the rock shrine at Urco ends in the head of a snake.

169 The puma on the summit of Puma Orco, 50 kilometers (30 miles) south of Cuzco.

170 A small round structure stands above the large rock shrine at Urco, located upstream from Calca in the Vilcanota-Urubamba valley.

171 An altar stone at the mouth of the cave shrine of Choquequilla, near Pachar, upriver from Ollantaytambo. The top of the stone was destroyed by vandals. The stepped design is repeated at the base and sides of the altar.

172 A semicircular cut at Quillarumi, on the Anta plain northwest of Cuzco.

173 A ceremonial seat below the cave openings at Puma Orco.

174 A stepped design at Quispihuara shrine, north of Sacsahuaman.

175 The "tired stone" at Sacsahuaman is actually an outcrop of bedrock.

176 The eastern face of the third carved stone at Saihuite.

177 An unusual stepped form, with a small square opening, on the western face of Saihuite's third stone may have been used for solar observations.

178 A gnomon at Intihuatana, downstream from Machu Picchu.

179 A ceremonial stairway is carved on the face of the Chingana stone at Chinchero.

180 A late-Inca shrine located to the north of Yurac Rumi, near Vitcos and the Vilcabamba valley.

181 The third rock shrine in a valley northeast of Chinchero toward the Yucay valley is carved with over a dozen niches and low platforms, undoubtedly dedicated to ritual use.

182 The shrine or ushnu of Tarahuasi has one of the finest stretches of polygonal retaining walling in Peru as well as a platform of full-height trapezoidal niches.

14. Tarahuasi

THE ROAD FROM CUZCO WEST TOWARD THE COAST drops dramatically into the mighty canyon of the Apurímac. As we have seen in discussing Saihuite, Apu-rímac means "lord-oracle"; and on the Cuzco side of the canyon was a royal lodging called Rimac-tampu ("oracle's inn"), a name that Spaniards have contracted to Limatambo. Two kilometers (1¼ miles) south of the modern town of Limatambo—76 kilometers (47 miles) from Cuzco—is a magnificent but isolated ruin, just off the main road on a farm called Tarahuasi.

The ruin does not look like the remains of a tambo inn or lodging. There is a long terrace wall of strongly rusticated polygonal masonry. In its center a monumental stairway leads up to the terrace, and above the stair is an earth-filled platform projecting from the hillside. The Incas clad three sides of this rectangular platform with masonry of the very highest quality. A solemn line of tall, trapezoidal, sentry-box niches adorns its three faces: twelve along the front looking down over the valley, and eight in each side wall. The two walls are imposing, almost theatrical. It is a place for ritual, with mummies or liveried attendants in the tall niches. On the lower terrace, the masons diverted themselves by having the cellular polygonal blocks radiate around a perfect octagon and a hexagon.

At the time of the Conquest, this hill was called Vilcaconga, and the chronicler Miguel de Estete mentioned that on this hillside the Peruvians had an idol also called Vilcaconga. Such an idol would have corresponded to the famous Apurímac oracle, across the river canyon at Saihuite. The ruins of Tarahuasi look more like a shrine to this idol than part of an inn, and no further building-remains were found here when the site was excavated and restored by Luis Valcárcel and J. M. Franco Inojosa in the 1930s. One theory is that this was an ushnu platform.

The slope of Vilcaconga played an important role during Pizarro's march toward Cuzco at the start of the Conquest. Hernando de Soto had pushed ahead of Pizarro, Almagro, and the slower part of the small invading army. He decided to hurry forward with his force of forty mounted men in order to be the first to reach Cuzco. His horsemen successfully forded the Apurímac and climbed the eastern wall of its canyon, on the last lap. They rested for two days at Rimac-tampu. On November 8, 1533, they set off up the hill of Vilcaconga. As Juan Ruiz de Arce recalled: "We were marching along with no thought of a line of battle.

We had been inflicting very long [daily] marches on the horses. Because of this we were leading them up the pass by their halters, marching in this way in groups of four." The Spaniards paused in the midday heat to feed the horses some maize. At this moment three or four thousand Inca warriors appeared along the crest of the hill. They charged down, completely covering the hillside. Soto shouted to his men to form line of battle, but it was too late. The Indians hurled a barrage of slingstones and missiles, which caused some Spaniards to scatter. Others ran to their horses, mounted, and tried to spur them up to the crest of the hill. "The horses were so exhausted that they could not catch breath sufficiently to attack such a multitude of enemy with any dash. [The Indians] never stopped harassing and worrying them with the javelins, stones and arrows they were firing. They exhausted them to such a degree that the riders could hardly raise their horses to a trot, and some not even to a walk. As the Indians perceived the horses' exhaustion, they began to attack with greater fury." For once the Indians had caught the Spaniards in hand-to-hand combat, at a time and place where the dreaded horses could not function. They killed five Spaniards—two on their horses, and three before they could mount—and wounded seventeen. The dead Spaniards all had their heads split open by stone battle-axes. It was the conquerors' worst defeat in the initial invasion.

As night fell, the remainder of Soto's force huddled on a hillock and tried to tend their wounded. Diego de Trujillo wrote: "We were in great hardship that night, for it snowed and the wounded men complained greatly of the cold. The Indians, who kept us encircled with many fires all round us, shouted at us: 'We do not want to kill you by night, but rather by day, so that we can have sport with you!'" The Spaniards spent the night on guard, armed and fearful. Then, in the middle of the night, they heard the distant sound of a Spanish trumpet. No noise could have been more welcome. Francisco Pizarro had, with amazing foresight, sent a further force of cavalry ahead to reinforce Soto. These men had hurried forward and at Rimac-tampu they were told about the battle of Vilcaconga. Their trumpeter Alconchel sounded his bugle like a foghorn in the night, and the two forces managed to link up in the darkness. So, when the mists cleared next day, Soto's battered force was miraculously doubled. It charged into action with characteristic courage, and the Inca army was soon dispersed.

183 This stretch of polygonal masonry has several examples of stones arranged like petals around a central hub.

A chastened Hernando de Soto rested his men near the top of the ascent and awaited the arrival of his leader. Pizarro came the following day and the combined force marched forward toward Cuzco. It was at this moment that the young Manco Inca first made contact with the invading Spaniards. He was a prince of the royal faction that had been defeated by Atahualpa's generals. He was therefore a fugitive, "fleeing from Atahualpa's men to prevent their killing him. He came all alone and abandoned, looking like a common Indian." He seemed younger than his twenty years and was wearing a yellow cotton tunic. The Spaniards were delighted to have in their midst so important a pretender to the Inca throne, particularly as he regarded them as his saviors in the Peruvian civil war. The Spaniards had with them Atahualpa's most senior general, the formidable old warrior Chalcuchima. They had him in chains and under guard, for they suspected that he wanted to avenge the murder of his Inca, Atahualpa. Manco Inca now told them that

Chalcuchima had passed a message to his fellow general Quisquis in Cuzco. Chalcuchima was thus responsible for the ambush by Quisquis' men on the slope of Vilcaconga.

Pizarro delivered a chilling announcement to his prisoner Chalcuchima: "You have seen how, with the help of God, we have always defeated you Indians. It will be the same in the future... You can rest assured that you yourself will never see Cuzco again. For...I shall have you burned alive!" Chalcuchima was brought out into the square of a town called Jaquijahuana, at the top of the ascent of Vilcaconga. The Dominican friar Vicente de Valverde tried to make him accept a deathbed conversion to Christianity, but the warrior would have none of it. He declared that he had no wish to become a Christian, and found Christian law incomprehensible. So he was set alight. As he burned to death he called on the god Viracocha, and on his friend Quisquis, to avenge him.

15. Vilcashuamán

THE INCAS CONSIDERED VILCASHUAMÁN OR VILCAS as a central point of their empire. It lay halfway between Cuzco and the Pacific coast, and "they say that it is just as far from Quito to Vilcas as it is from Vilcas to the farthest limit of the Incas' conquests on the Maule river in Chile." It was the main crossroads, the place where the road from Cuzco to the coast crossed the highway running along the length of the Andes. Vilcas means "sacred" and Huamán is "falcon."

Vilcashuamán was once in the lands of the Chanca tribe, the people who tried to capture Cuzco in about 1440 and, after their defeat, were overwhelmed in the first rush of Inca expansion. The chroniclers agree that Pachacuti and his son Topa Inca Yupanqui conquered this region and founded Vilcashuamán. A Spanish corregidor called Pedro de Carvajal described the place in 1586, stating that the rulers "founded in this location of Vilcas Huamán a city and frontier post with thirty thousand Indians as garrison. [They] began to construct forts and buildings in it. Parts of these and their foundations are visible at present, for they were all of cut stone." Pedro de Cieza de León also wrote that local people made these buildings, but under the direction of "masters from Cuzco to measure out the plans and show the way in which they must lay the stones and bricks in the building."

The most important structure in Vilcashuamán was the temple of the sun. It rose on one side of a vast square, with the temple to the sun itself and an adjacent temple to the moon all built of characteristically excellent masonry. Cieza wrote: "The temple of the sun, which was made of stones laid upon one another with great skill, had two main doorways. To enter them, there were two stone stairways which, by my count, had thirty steps each. Inside this temple there were rooms for the priests and for those who watched over the vestals, the mamaconas, who observed their vows faithfully." Inside the temple was a golden effigy of the sun. "The Indians tell that the image of the sun was of enormous value, and that there was great treasure both in the temple and buried." Such grandeur was an element of Inca policy. The corregidor Carvajal said that "The Incas worshipped [the sun and moon] and ordered all the Indians they were conquering to worship these gods and to destroy the stone idols that they already had."

Pachacuti, who conquered Vilcashuamán for the Incas, returned there at the end of his reign and started to build its many temples and structures.

Some chroniclers say that he died there. This could explain why his son Topa Inca Yupanqui chose this as the site for a personal palace. When the next ruler Huayna Capac was there, "he went up to pray on an elegant and excellent terrace that had been built for that purpose. They sacrificed, in their blind ignorance, the things that they usually sacrificed, killing many animals and birds."

Fifty years after the Conquest, Pedro de Carvajal wrote: "This temple or house that contained the sun effigy is still standing. It serves as a church, where Mass is…said for people at the royal market that is founded here." Three centuries later the ruins of Vilcashuamán were pathetically overgrown, fallen and buried under the houses of a Peruvian village. It was just possible to imagine the disposition of the original temple. The parish church of Saint John the Baptist used to occupy most of the temple building along the south side of the large square. The French diplomat Léonce Angrand sketched the church in 1849 and showed clearly how its adobes rose above a wall of Inca masonry that contained five trapezoidal doors or niches. The Inca wall is still there, built of dark granite in beautiful courses of rectangular ashlars, but the church has been rebuilt on a north–south axis with its end wall against the Inca façade. A Spanish colonial arch, fluted pilasters, and a cornice have been added, superfluously, to the austere Inca door.

The original temple occupied the crown of the hill on which Vilcashuamán is built. This great building was raised in three tiers, which have now been lovingly restored. The upper level is a smooth coursed wall. The middle level has a satisfying pattern of niches, some the height of a man, alternating with smaller ones at shoulder level. The lowest terrace has a curious arrangement of alternating salient and entrant stretches—a plan peculiar to Vilcashuamán. Such regular buttressing may have given added strength to the terrace walls. The lines of terraces project northward at one side of the church to form another platform, and it is here that we can see them best. A fine stretch of the middle and lower levels rears above the detritus of centuries. As Cieza observed in the 1540s, "What can be seen are only the foundations of the buildings and the walls and enclosures of the shrines…and of the temple with its stairways. For it has fallen into ruin and is overgrown with grass, and the storehouses have fallen down. In a word, it was once what it no longer is; and by what it is, we can judge what it was."

184 A terrace wall with tall niches is one of the few remains of the sumptuous sun temple at Vilcashuamán.

The most spectacular surviving structure in Vilcashuamán once faced the sun temple, in the middle of the great square, but is now separated from it by streets of the modern village. This ruin is a stepped ushnu. It rises in four terraces of superb masonry, a building unique among Inca ruins, more like a small version of the mighty stepped pyramids of Mexico. It was a monument worthy of South America's most powerful ruler. Carvajal said of the square that it was "very large, capable of holding twenty thousand men. The Inca ordered it built by hand, and he drained a very large lake that used to be there for this purpose." And Cieza de León wrote that "to one side of this plaza, toward the rising sun, there was a shrine of the [Inca] lords, made of stone and surrounded by a low wall from which a smallish terrace emerged, some six feet [1.8 meters] wide, with other terraces successively mounted upon it, until on the summit there was the throne to which the lord went to make his oration. This throne was made of a single rock, so large that it measures eleven feet [3.4 meters] long by seven [2.1 meters] wide, and on which two seats had been cut for this purpose. They say that this stone used to be covered in ornaments of gold and precious stones, to adorn this place that they venerated and esteemed so greatly. [There was similar decoration] on another stone, not small, which is still in the middle of this square. This is a form of font, where they killed and sacrificed young animals and (so they say) children, whose blood they used to offer to their gods. Some of the treasure that was buried in these terraces has been found by Spaniards."

Carvajal left a vivid description of this ceremonial. He wrote that the ushnu was "a platform surrounded by masonry, five *estados* [roughly 8 meters or 26 feet] high. It has a stone staircase, admirably made and cut in a theatrical manner. This is where the Inca used to go in person to be seen, and on top of it were two large stone seats,

185 The famous ushnu administrative platform is the best surviving Inca stepped pyramid.

covered in gold at that time, where the Inca and his wife used to sit, as if on tribunes, and from which they worshipped the sun… He would sit there under a great canopy of plumage of a thousand colors, and the posts on which this awning rested were of gold. Twelve very aged captains of his own lineage used to carry the canopy." They then sacrificed chosen llama kids, richly adorned,

to the creator deity Viracocha, the sun Inti, the earth Pachamama, and the lightning Illapa.

The majestic ushnu still stands, and the stone block with the Inca's two seats is still at the top of the theatrical staircase. But the building fell into a sorry state of disrepair: treasure-seekers dug into its terraces; and vegetation prized apart the Inca stones. (I myself once spent two days cutting away the worst of these bushes with a machete.) One detail was revealed by the damage to the ushnu. Its casing of dark granite masonry was arranged in tidy courses wherever it was visible. However, where the terraces tumbled, this revealed that hidden walling is of polygonal masonry—a sure sign that the Incas themselves valued coursed masonry above polygonal. The outer wall was ransacked for building blocks. It was largely intact in Angrand's and Wiener's drawings, but is now just a short stretch beside the gate at the foot of the stairs. Beside is the village children's football field.

The walled enclosure of the ushnu has the remains of a large Inca hall, known locally as the house of Topa Inca, on the side away from the square. In Wiener's plan he marks "unrecognizable ruins" and a "temple" 100 meters (330 feet) farther west. We know from Cieza and other authors that the Incas had a large royal palace at Vilcashuamán. A close relative of the Inca ruled over this prosperous and strategic province. The local tribes had to supply levies of up to 40,000 people for his service, and "solely to guard the gates there were forty gatekeepers." There were also, according to Carvajal, 500 acllas working for the temple and a further 500 mamaconas for the Inca. Cieza also described a vast depot of 700 storage huts at Vilcashuamán.

186 The double-seated throne atop the ushnu.

Ever since its conquest and foundation by Pachacuti and Topa Inca, Vilcashuamán was an important garrison city. It was mentioned as a valuable prize in the civil war between Huascar and Atahualpa on the eve of the Spanish Conquest. When Pizarro advanced toward Cuzco in late 1533, Atahualpa's troops planned to mount a resistance in Vilcashuamán. They were frustrated by the speed of a force of Spanish cavalry under Hernando de Soto: these dashed past the Indian sentries and galloped into Vilcashuamán early on October 29. Atahualpa's men were away hunting. Diego de Trujillo described the action: "They had left their tents, their women and a few Indian men in Vilcas and we captured these, taking possession of everything that was there, at the hour of dawn which was when we entered Vilcas. We thought that there were no more troops than those who had been there. But at the hour of vespers...they came from the steepest direction and attacked us, and we them. Because of the roughness of the terrain, they gained on us rather than we on them. Some Spaniards distinguished themselves...by winning a height from the Indians and defending it strongly. On that day the Indians killed a white horse belonging to Alonso Tabuyo. We were forced to retreat to the square of Vilcas and all spent that night under arms. The Indians attacked next day with great spirit. They were carrying banners made from the mane and tail of the white horse they had killed. We were forced to release the booty of theirs that we were holding—the women and Indians who were in charge of all their flocks. Then they withdrew." Although neither side won this battle, the Indian army had failed to stop a small force of Spanish horsemen. The Incas withdrew toward Cuzco. Another Spaniard wrote: "Counting those who went, those who

187 Divination grooves on an altar at the eastern edge of Vilcashuamán.

to meet the Spanish viceroy and then made a progress along the royal highway toward Cuzco. He paused at Vilcashuamán and there were emotional scenes as the Indians paid homage and tried to relive their glorious past. Eleven years later a stern new viceroy, Francisco de Toledo, took this road and also paused at Vilcashuamán. Guaman Poma wrote that the viceroy outraged local chiefs by usurping the privileges of an Inca ruler: "He reached Vilcashuamán and mounted the steps to the throne and usnu of the Inca, and was received thus, like the Inca himself, by all the chief lords. And he ordered the oldest and most important chief to mount the usnu."

After the Spanish Conquest this region declined, like so much of Peru. Carvajal's report of 1586 admitted that "the Indians of this province [of Vilcas] were in far greater numbers than they are now. The natives say that the reason for their diminution was the excessive work they are forced to perform in the mercury and silver mines and the sugar mills. In addition, it is caused by the personal service they go to do in the city of Guamanga [Ayacucho] and on the cattle ranches and other work in which they labor. Since these are outside their lands, and there are changes of climate in the places where they go to work, they are exposed to many diseases, from which the greater part of them have died."

remained there, and the natives of the district, a vast quantity of Indians had assembled. We all agreed that there could have been twenty-five thousand Indian warriors." With the retreat of this army, the invading Spaniards were able to spend two days picking their way, unmolested, down the spectacular descent of almost 2,000 meters (over 6,500 feet) to the hot gorge of the Pampas river far below.

Vilcashuamán had two brief moments of glory after the Conquest. Both were poignant reminders of the vanished grandeur of the Incas. In 1558 Manco Inca's son Sayri Tupac decided to leave his father's refuge of Vilcabamba and to live in Spanish-occupied Peru. He went down to Lima

Vilcashuamán is now a small village, remote on its hilltop, perched on the ruins of the great Inca city, and surrounded by rolling country with few trees and little population. When I first visited Vilcashuamán in the 1960s, the site was overgrown with weeds, its stones pillaged, and village houses straggling over Inca ruins. It is surprising that the first excavation of so famous a ruin was not until the early 1980s, by archaeologists from the university in Ayacucho. Then for a decade it became too dangerous because this was the heartland of the Shining Path insurgency. Study and restoration resumed in the twenty-first century, and Vilcashuamán is once again an outstanding monument.

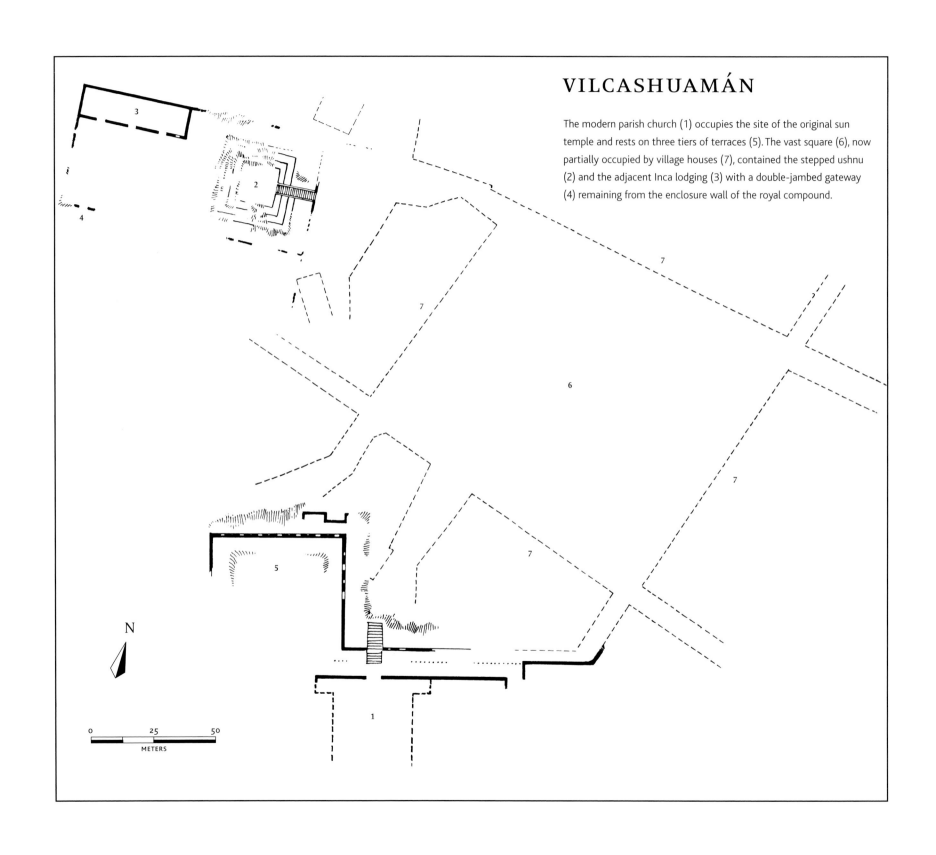

VILCASHUAMÁN

The modern parish church (1) occupies the site of the original sun temple and rests on three tiers of terraces (5). The vast square (6), now partially occupied by village houses (7), contained the stepped ushnu (2) and the adjacent Inca lodging (3) with a double-jambed gateway (4) remaining from the enclosure wall of the royal compound.

N

0   25   50
METERS

189 The view west from Vilcashuamán's ushnu, toward the Pampas river. One gateway remains from the walled enclosure around the palace courtyard.

190 The surviving central wall of the temple of Viracocha looks from a distance like a great aqueduct. It supported the largest known Inca roof.

16. Temple of Viracocha, Raqchi

THE INCAS' LEGENDARY CREATOR GOD, VIRACOCHA, was said to have originated in Lake Titicaca. After creating the world, Viracocha moved northward, down the Vilcanota valley toward Cuzco. The legend went on to say that the god moved through the land with his followers, creating all known living things. At Manta, in what is now southern Ecuador, Viracocha told his companions that he was leaving but would eventually return to them. "Having said this he went to sea with his two servants, moving across the water as if it were land, without sinking." At the very outset of the Conquest, some native Peruvians identified Europeans with Viracocha because of this legend. They may have hesitated to attack Pizarro's Spaniards in case these might be the returning Viracocha—although they were soon disabused and learned that the conquistadors were mere brutal mortals. Throughout colonial times, however, ordinary Indians often addressed Spaniards as "Viracocha." (There is a complex relationship between the Incas' two creator deities, the Sun Inti and Viracocha: both originated in Lake Titicaca and animated people throughout the land. Chroniclers differ about which of these appeared to Pachacuti and helped him defeat the Chanca.)

Spanish priests and missionaries were delighted by this legend, because the deity corresponded admirably to the single creator god of Christianity. The Viracocha of Inca legend, when transcribed by Spanish chroniclers, came to sound more and more like an apostle from the New Testament. Juan de Betanzos, a Spaniard who married an Inca princess, asked his Indian informants about Viracocha's appearance. They said that he had been "a man of tall stature who wore a white robe that fell to his feet and was belted. He wore his hair short, with a form of crown [tonsure] on his head like a priest's, and wore no hat. In his hands he carried an object that now appears to them like the breviaries that priests carry... They told me that he was called Kon Tiki Viracocha Pacha-yachachic, which means 'God, Creator of the World.'"

Betanzos went in the 1540s to see a famous statue of Viracocha at a place then called Cacha (now Raqchi). Cieza visited this place a few years later, and effectively debunked his compatriots' idea that the statue showed Viracocha looking like Saint Bartholomew or another apostle—not that this stopped later chroniclers from repeating the identification. Cieza wrote: "I went to see this idol, for some Spaniards affirm that it might have been an apostle. I have heard many say that it held [rosary] beads in its hands but, unless I am blind, this is nonsense. For although I examined it carefully, I could see no such thing. It simply had its hands above its hips, with the arms folded, and on its belt signs that signified that the robe it wore was fastened with buttons." Betanzos and Cieza agree that the statue was cut from a single block of stone, roughly 4 meters (13 feet) high and 80 centimeters (2½ feet) wide. Not surprisingly, the church had this sacred image destroyed, soon after they had seen it.

The creator god Viracocha performed a celebrated miracle at Raqchi, as he moved northward from Lake Titicaca down the upper Vilcanota valley. He was insulted by the local Canas people. To demonstrate his divinity, he summoned down fire from heaven. The hill behind Raqchi was consumed by fire, which the god then proceeded to quench with his staff. The local people were suitably impressed and cowed. The scorched hillside, with volcanic pumice or tuff that Cieza described as being as light as cork, is still visible. It is the base of the volcano Kinsachata; and the name Canas signifies "light" or "fire" in both Quechua and Aymara.

Suitably awed, the Canas people erected the famous statue to Viracocha, with a temple around it that was enlarged by successive Incas. Betanzos was amazed. He wrote that the temple was "so large that there is no larger building in all the land" and gave a description that exactly corresponds to the present ruins. The main building was a vast rectangular hall with two pitched roofs supported by a monumental central wall. Its scale is impressive. The plan measures 92 by 25 meters (302 by 82 feet) and the great dividing wall is 12 meters (39 feet) tall and 1.65 meters (5½ feet) thick. The roofed area was enormous, for a people without the arch. It covered 2,323 square meters (25,000 square feet) and is thus the largest surviving hall built by the Incas. The roof has vanished, but much of the central wall still stands, towering over the river valley like some gigantic Roman aqueduct. It is easily visible from the road or railway linking Titicaca and Cuzco, between the towns San Pablo and San Pedro.

Enough remains of the temple to deduce its original construction techniques. The central wall provides the clues. It consists of eleven rectangular "piers" supporting the solid upper part of the wall. The piers are built of fine Inca masonry—polygonal but arranged in rough courses—to a height of some 2.8 meters (9 feet). Above this, the piers and the wall they support are of adobe.

191 A row of round stone and adobe piers on each side of the central wall took some of the weight of the gigantic roof. The towering central wall had regular openings, perhaps for zigzagging processions. Log lintels were set into the adobe above these openings, and there were apertures above these to relieve the weight of the adobe bricks and the roof beam above.

192 Raqchi's only surviving circular column stands near one of two gateways at the southern end of the temple. The pier and central wall are capped with modern roof tiles to protect the adobes from rain damage.

The ten openings between the piers are each 2.7 meters wide and were once spanned by wooden lintels. The third pier from the southern end shows signs of these lintels in its adobes: there were five or possibly seven wooden beams, relatively thin poles 10 to 15 centimeters (4 to 6 inches) in diameter. Adobe is a heavy material; and the high, thick central wall would have weighed heavily on these delicate wooden lintels. Gasparini and Margolies showed that the Incas solved this problem of thrust by having a large squarish opening above each lintel. The sides of these "windows" slope inward and follow the trapezoidal incline of the doorways below. Above the windows are other small openings, which in turn relieve pressure on the lintels of the windows themselves. Earlier observers assumed that these upper openings indicated that the temple had two or three stories. Careful observation by Gasparini showed that there was a system of beams supporting the enormous pitched roof; but he found no evidence of upper floors. The openings were simply to lessen the wall's weight-load, and to spread light in the temple's gloomy interior.

On either side of the eleven piers of the central wall were sturdy round columns. These are unique in Inca architecture. Round wooden poles were used to support roofs of kallanka halls at Huánuco and other towns; rectangular monoliths or masonry piers supported the open walls of masmas at Machu Picchu; and there were quadrilateral adobe columns in coastal Inca sites such as Tambo Colorado, and Incahuasi in the Cañete valley. But none of them compares with Raqchi's cylindrical columns. These begin, as does the central wall, with stone foundations. The highest surviving column rises to 6 meters (almost 20 feet), with its masonry base rising to a height of 3.3 meters (11 feet) topped by adobe. In the top of this column can be seen notches that once held beams: there are corresponding notches for the other ends of the

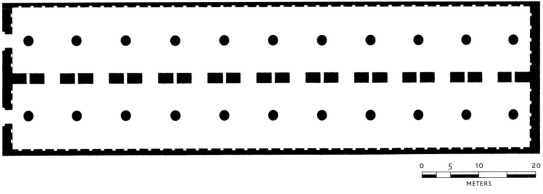

193 The plan of the great Viracocha temple at Raqchi, showing the central piers flanked by eleven pairs of circular columns.

Raqchi's magnificent temple was too holy to escape the wrath of Christian zealots. Garcilaso lamented that "although the temple was so curious in its construction, it was destroyed by the Spaniards, like so many other notable works found in Peru. They should have preserved these at their expense, so that in future centuries people might see the glorious things they had won by strength of arms and good fortune. But they have deliberately razed them to the ground, as if from jealousy, so that today only the foundations of the building remain."

The Viracocha shrine at Raqchi consisted of more than the towering four-aisled basilica. The sacred precinct included the lava flows of Viracocha's fiery miracle. A curtain wall 3.5 kilometers (2 miles) long runs along the crests of the surrounding hills and encloses an area of 80 hectares (198 acres). Groundwater flows from the base of the volcano, and the Incas characteristically harnessed this, with channels, two sets of "baths," and a shallow triangular lake (now sadly swampy). Looking out from a window that Garcilaso mentioned in the northeastern end of the temple, the volcano would have been mirrored in this lake; and in the opposite direction, it reflected the temple itself. Susan Niles noted that the Inca Huayna Capac loved using ornamental ponds in this way. Spanish archaeologists who excavated this area in the 1980s found a building beside the lake with a thick layer of ash, fragments of spondylus shells from the Pacific Ocean, and many identical dishes—all possibly from offerings burned by pilgrims. For Raqchi was named as an important pilgrimage destination, as was Vilcanota, 40 kilometers (25 miles) to the southeast on the road toward the holy origin shrine on the Island of the Sun in Lake Titicaca. The main highway, the Capac-Ñan, ran right through Raqchi, between the temple and the lake; and there is the ruin of a kallanka-like tambo to house pilgrims, one kilometer to the northwest.

beams near the top of the masonry in the central wall. Gasparini and Margolies argued convincingly that these beams were too weak to support an upper story: they must have been part of a frame of roof girders. The end walls of the temple were doubtless gabled to give further support to the roof.

Garcilaso de la Vega wrote a detailed but baffling description of the Viracocha temple. He said that it had four gates, with only one gate on the eastern wall open. From the ruins, the temple seems to have had two entrances in its southern short wall, but the northeastern end is too ruined to tell. Garcilaso also described a labyrinth of partitions within the temple: "These walls were spaced out at intervals of seven feet [2.1 meters] and each was three feet [90 centimeters] thick. There were twelve passages between these walls... On entering the temple by the main gate, people turned right down the first passage until they came to the wall at the right hand side of the temple; they then turned left down the second passage and went on till they came to the opposite wall. There they turned right again down the third passage, and by following the series of passages in the plan, went through the whole of the covered part of the temple, passage by passage, until they came to the twelfth and last... Instead of a high altar there was a square chapel with walls twelve feet [3.7 meters] long, covered in shining black flagstones fitted into one another and rising in a ceiling of four pitches. This was the most notable part of the whole structure. Within this chapel, there was a tabernacle in the thickness of the temple wall, and this contained the effigy of the Viracocha apparition." It is possible to imagine Garcilaso's zigzag approach to the Viracocha statue, by moving right and left around the columns and through the openings in the central wall. This would provide the twelve passages of Garcilaso's description. The British archaeologist Bill Sillar imagined pilgrims weaving through the temple in this serpentine way and added that its zigzag movement reminded him of a dance of the present-day Canas and Canchis during their pilgrimages.

Beside the temple is a series of five cancha-like courts, with twelve pairs of back-to-back houses arranged along a straight avenue beside a plaza. The alignment of walls and angles at Raqchi is highly accurate, so that the view down this avenue is satisfyingly symmetrical. These twinned houses echo the main temple in having stone in the lower part of their walls and adobe for upper walls and gables. They have rows of fine niches on their inner walls, as do pairs of ungabled houses on the south side of each court.

South of the enclosures are some eighty circular structures, each roughly 8 meters (26 feet) in diameter. These were assumed to be storage qollqas, even though they are significantly different from similar Inca structures elsewhere,

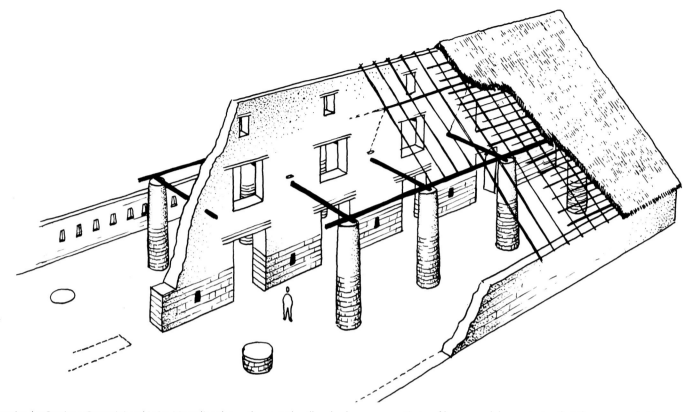

194 A reconstruction by Graziano Gasparini and Luise Margolies shows the central wall and columns supporting roof beams, and demonstrates that there was probably no upper story.

by being wider, sunk below ground, and possibly unroofed. Bill Sillar and the American Emily Dean discovered that these circular "tanks" were built by the pre-Inca Huari–Tiahuanaco culture and resemble pits in Pikillacta, a Huari site between here and Cuzco. Traces of red paint were found on the masonry bases of the temple's central piers, and this paint was in stepped designs— a Tiahuanacan motif, also noted by Bauer and Stanish on the sacred islands in Lake Titicaca.

Such archaeological evidence and remarks in the chronicles indicate that this had long been an important shrine. Cieza said that Pachacuti's father, Inca Viracocha, celebrated a treaty with the Canas chiefs, with great sacrifices, here at Cacha (as he called Raqchi). Once the Incas controlled this part of Peru, they enhanced the site and in a sense usurped its sacredness as an origin shrine or *pacarina*. This was a standard Inca tactic to cement their rule. It worked well with the Canas and related Canchis: these became such staunch supporters of the Inca that they were exempted from tribute. Betanzos said that Huayna Capac Inca built more structures in order to add to Raqchi's holiness, including the great temple; but when Sillar and Dean carbon-dated

straw from the temple's adobes, they found that it was slightly earlier than the sixteenth century when Huayna Capac reigned.

After the Conquest, Christian priests were happy for local people to embrace Saint Bartholomew as their patron. As we have seen, this itinerant apostle was identified as the figure in the temple's Viracocha statue. A nearby village became San Bartolomé de Tinta, and this was the base of the late eighteenth-century Inca descendant José Gabriel Condorcanqui. It was he who rebelled against oppressive Spanish rule, adopting the title Tupac Amaru II—after Manco's son, the last Inca, executed in 1572. He inspired his forces with a ceremony in the shrine of Raqchi, calling on his Inca ancestors and their holy spirits to favor his enterprise. For a time this Tupac Amaru controlled much of southern Peru, and in 1781 he besieged Cuzco itself; but he was betrayed, overcome, and brutally executed there in the same year. His legacy is to be hailed as a precursor of Peruvian independence from Spain, with a place in the national pantheon, his image on coins, and rebel movements such as the Uruguayan Tupamaros of the 1970s named after him.

195 The high plain of Huánuco from the hill where lines of qollqa storehouses still stand. Even from a distance, the ushnu platform dominates the vast central square.

17. Huánuco

WHEN FRANCISCO PIZARRO CAPTURED THE INCA ATAHUALPA at the outset of the Spanish Conquest, the Peruvian monarch told his captors that there was a province called Huánuco, ten days' march from where they were holding him at Cajamarca, and that it was rich in gold mines. Early in 1533, while the Inca's ransom was still being accumulated, Pizarro sent his brother Hernando to sack the coastal temple of Pachacamac and to explore the rich empire they planned to seize. During this reconnaissance, Hernando Pizarro climbed into the Andes to meet Atahualpa's most powerful general, Chalcuchima, and persuaded him that his Inca wanted him to return to Cajamarca with the Spaniards. This Pizarro brother thus had the privilege of traveling along the main Inca highway in the company of the empire's greatest military commander. When they reached Huánuco, the largest provincial city in this part of central Peru, they were entertained for two days with a series of festivities.

Surrounded by hills, Huánuco is on a stretch of flat puna—cold, treeless, upland savanna carpeted in pale-green ichu grass and watered by mountain streams, icy tarns, and mossy bogs. The ruins are at an elevation of over 3,700 meters (12,150 feet), near the headwaters of the Marañón, a river that becomes the Amazon, above the town of La Unión. The Incas built a stepped road that climbs for an amazing 963 meters (3,159 feet) from the river to Huánuco's puna [ill. 10]. Miguel de Estete, who was with Hernando Pizarro on this reconnaissance, noted that the road near Huánuco was paved with flagstones, and had "channels to carry water: they told us that this was done because of the snows that fall on this region at certain seasons of the year."

During Manco Inca's first rebellion, an Inca army attempted to invest and capture the Spaniards' new coastal city Lima. Their magnificently plumed phalanxes advanced bravely toward the half-built Spanish town. But at sea level, on the open coastal plain, they were no match for Spanish cavalry and they fell in their thousands, cut down by European horsemen with steel swords and lances. One Inca general, Illa Tupac, survived this disaster and established himself as warlord of the region around Huánuco. He successfully attacked a column led by Alonso de Alvarado as it advanced to relieve Cuzco in 1537. In the following year he organized a revolt by tribes of the Conchucos region north of Huánuco. Thousands of Indians swept down on the northern coastal town of Trujillo, killing any Spaniards they could catch. At the time of Manco Inca's

second rebellion, in 1539, Illa Tupac still controlled this strategic part of the central Andes and his men surprised some Spaniards on a snow-covered plain north of Lake Junín. When Gonzalo Pizarro, the youngest of the Pizarro brothers, marched past here in mid-1539, "he had to fight the Indians of the province of Huánuco. These came out in battle against him, and placed him in [much] danger," but he continued northward to Quito.

A later chronicler wrote that "in 1539, because of the war that the rebel Illa Tupac was waging in this province, the Marquis Francisco Pizarro sent the illustrious captain [Alonso] Gómez de Alvarado, who founded it [as a Spanish municipality on August 11]. It was later depopulated." Its altitude saved Huánuco. The Spaniards in 1539 started to build European houses in the enormous central square: foundations of a handful of these and a tiny Franciscan chapel can still be seen. But the place was too remote, high, rainy, and cold for Spaniards. Within a few months, the conquerors moved to a warmer, lower location 80 kilometers (50 miles) to the east, and this is the town now called Huánuco. The old Inca city, known today as Huánuco Pampa, remained undisturbed on its high puna, hardly pillaged by later builders, unoccupied and, being on firm ground, little buried by sediment. With remains of over 3,500 structures covering 2 square kilometers (500 acres), it is the largest undamaged Inca ruin. Its stone buildings are merely tumbled by the ravages of time and earthquakes.

Illa Tupac is one of the unsung heroes of Peruvian resistance. Cieza de León said that he caused "much mischief" but was finally captured "with great difficulty" in 1542; another chronicler said that he was still active in 1544. Pizarro sent Francisco de Chaves to pacify this region and his punitive expedition was a bloodbath. He swept through the province of Huánuco and the Conchucos, sacking towns, destroying fields, and hanging men, women, and children indiscriminately. Cieza wrote: "The war was so cruel that the Indians feared they would all be killed, and prayed for peace." A few years later, after Chaves had died, a royal decree ordered that his estate make amends—for it was admitted that he had slaughtered 600 children under three years of age and had burned or impaled many adults.

Spanish chroniclers were impressed by the magnificence of Huánuco. Cieza said that the area had been conquered by Pachacuti's son Topa Inca Yupanqui.

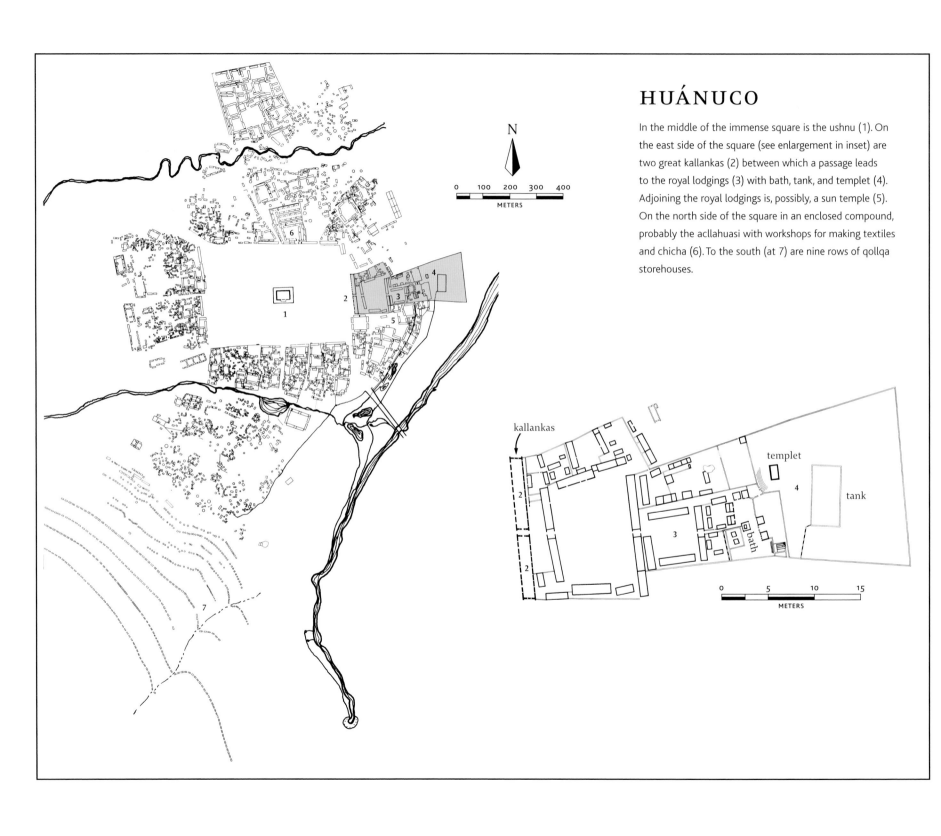

HUÁNUCO

In the middle of the immense square is the ushnu (1). On the east side of the square (see enlargement in inset) are two great kallankas (2) between which a passage leads to the royal lodgings (3) with bath, tank, and templet (4). Adjoining the royal lodgings is, possibly, a sun temple (5). On the north side of the square in an enclosed compound, probably the acllahuasi with workshops for making textiles and chicha (6). To the south (at 7) are nine rows of qollqa storehouses.

N

0   100   200   300   400
METERS

kallankas

templet

tank

bath

0   5   10   15
METERS

At Huánuco he ordered the building of "the palace of such excellence that we can still see." This "admirably built royal palace was made of very large stones skillfully joined... Beside it there was a temple to the sun with many vestals and priests. [Huánuco] was so important in the times of the Incas that there were always over thirty thousand Indians to serve it." In his gazetteer of Spanish Peru, Vázquez de Espinosa was struck by the mighty ushnu that stands in the middle of the square. He described this as a "fortress all of hewn stone and two estados [well over 3 meters or 10 feet] high, like a well-planned stronghold that could hold four thousand men." Two great kallankas along one side of the square were "halls so large that each could hold a horse race, and with many doors: these must have been where important Indians or chiefs sent by the kings would have lodged. They now serve as stables for cattle." Behind the halls a line of stone gates, some with "royal arms" of carved pumas on their lintels, led into a series of courtyards of what were clearly the lodgings of the Inca himself. Vázquez also noted a walled enclosure nearby that he (correctly) guessed to have been the convent of holy women.

Despite their remoteness, the ruins of Huánuco were visited and described by some early travelers: the Austrian Charles Wiener, the German Ernst Middendorf, the Swiss J. J. von Tschudi, the Peruvian–Italian Antonio Raimondi, and the Englishman Charles Reginald Enock. All of them tried to deduce the original functions of the labyrinths of fallen stones. Emilio Harth-Terré, an architect from Lima, made careful surveys and analyses of the buildings between 1934 and 1960. Back in the 1560s, the Spanish colonial authorities wanted to learn more about Inca systems of government and (particularly) taxation, so they instituted detailed enquiries known as *visitaciones*. Huánuco is the only place for which two of these precious reports survive. This led the American historian John Murra to inspire archaeologists to excavate the site, to see whether the written evidence could help them interpret the ruins. One of these, Craig Morris, worked at Huánuco from the mid-1960s until the early twenty-first century, when his weak heart prevented him from returning to such high altitude. The result is an admirable picture of the best-preserved important provincial Inca city.

All the buildings of Huánuco radiate outward from the immense rectangular plaza, which was built on a scale to delight a modern totalitarian dictator. It is some 550 meters (1,800 feet, or a third of a mile) in length, and 370 meters (1,200 feet) wide, making this great space twenty-four times the size of a standard Spanish city square. It is not a perfect rectangle, possibly because important roads leave from its four corners. Harth-Terré wondered whether the Incas made the plaza so large to accommodate, shear, and slaughter herds of llamas and alpacas: colonial records speak of the famous herds of Huánuco and its herdsmen who were active throughout the Inca empire.

The square is dominated by the powerful mass of the stone-clad ushnu. This is one of those buildings that epitomizes Inca architecture: massive, built of painstaking masonry, unadorned, and of a size and with design details that are not easily explained. The platform is long and squat. The central structure is some 30 by 50 meters (100 by 165 feet) in plan, but it rises to a maximum of 4 meters (13 feet) above its terrace. Its core is a terreplein of solid earth, above which the retaining walls rise to form a low parapet. These walls are of the finest masonry, with courses of ashlars that diminish as they rise [ill. 23].

The ushnu is approached from the south by a broad monumental staircase, but this leads to two surprisingly narrow doorways through the parapet wall. Bold sculptures of crouching felines (or possibly monkeys) flank them. An elegant cornice projects outward around the entire building. Within the parapet are niches, two of which face the entrances. These may have been seats for attendants watching the doorways, or they could have served as steps for standing officials who faced outward to address a crowd in the plaza below. The Spanish *visitación* inquiry of 1562 spoke about the uses of the city square and the powers of the Inca's provincial governor (*tocricoc*). It declared that "this official assembled in the square all the chiefs and leaders of that land and many other Indians and, in the presence of all, told them to observe how he administered justice." This confirmed the definition of ushnu in one of the earliest Quechua dictionaries as "a judge's tribunal made of an erected stone."

The Huánuco ushnu rests on a base of two low terraces. When the archaeologists cleaned and restored these, they noticed that they counteracted any optical illusion caused by the plaza sloping down to the east: without these terraces, the stone platform might appear to tilt in the opposite direction. The archaeologists also investigated two small buildings at the southeastern corner of the outer terrace and concluded that these were not, as was popularly imagined, built by the Spaniards during their brief occupation. However, a construction at the eastern end of the ushnu probably was of post-Conquest date: John Rowe suggested that it might have been the remains of a *picota*—the ornamental pillar (sometimes used as a gibbet) that was the symbol of every Spanish municipality—since the walls of the ushnu would have heightened the drop for any victim hanged from it.

The most important buildings of Huánuco are at the eastern end of the plaza. Two magnificent kallankas frame the entrance to a compound that was almost certainly the royal lodgings. Craig Morris was in charge of the restoration of the kallankas—those halls that Vázquez de Espinosa described as large enough to contain horse races. The interior of one is 84 meters (276 feet) long and the other 75 meters (246 feet), while both are 9.7 meters (32 feet) wide. Morris's team did an admirable job of rebuilding walls that had suffered from

197 The easternmost gateway of the royal compound.

198 Gates decorated with pumas lead to courtyards of the Inca's residence.

centuries of use as stabling for cattle. They cleared the original floor and discovered circles of stones that had once enclosed the bases of wooden pillars supporting the enormous thatched roofs. The various functions of these halls have already been discussed (page 31), but it is interesting to note that the kallankas of Huánuco formed the outer wall of the so-called Incahuasi or Inca's palace. The alley between the halls looks directly through a succession of gateways in the palace compounds; and from the depths of the palace the sun sets over the ushnu along this line of vision.

The royal palace of Huánuco corresponds admirably to Murúa's or Garcilaso's descriptions of an Inca's residence (page 40). Courtyard follows courtyard in the manner of the Turkish sultan's palace and harem of Topkapi in Istanbul, or the lodgings of the Chinese emperors in the Forbidden City

199 A plaza and sunken bath beyond the royal enclosure.

of Beijing. As Murúa explained, senior grades of officials were allowed to penetrate only as far as certain gates. The inner area was for the monarch alone, and it is within the innermost courtyards that we see the passage leading to an adjoining compound that may once have housed the chosen women. Cieza wrote that the "vestal virgins" were located alongside Huánuco's royal palace. The line of gates is built of fine masonry and adorned with crouching pumas in high relief. The walls and buildings of the courtyards are of more rustic stonework, not because they were of later date, but probably because they were once plastered and painted.

It is an interesting reminder of Inca cleanliness (that so impressed dirty European conquerors) to find a stone bath in the inner courtyard, as well as the remains of a huge shallow cistern measuring 103 by 40 meters (338 by 130 feet). The archaeologists cleared away bushes that were destroying the gates, and restored the Inca bath and its system of pipes and channels. They also restored a delightful building north of the axis of gates and the innermost courtyard. This "templet" or "tabernacle" has three double-jambed niches facing east. Harth-Terré noticed that the niches were aligned to catch the rays of the rising sun on the March and September equinoxes.

The complex of buildings immediately south of the Incahuasi may well have been the temple of the sun, with the quarters of some chosen women discreetly hidden between the inner part of the temple and the inner quarters of the royal palace. The gates of the courts of the "temple" complex are aligned on an axis exactly parallel to that of the Incahuasi. The second court has a well

in its center that would correspond to the one in Cuzco's Coricancha. This could have been the font that received the daily sacrificial libations offered to the sun by the mamaconas. The first court has enough buildings to correspond to the temples of the lesser celestial deities: Venus and the Pleiades, thunder, rainbows, and the moon.

At the far end of the second court are two "sentry boxes" which flank the gate leading onto what may have been the quarters of the temple's holy women. One aged chief declared to the Spanish inquiry of 1562 that "they used to place in Huánuco girls who were going to be beautiful, [to serve] as mamaconas. The Inca would give some of these, whom he did not keep for himself, to be wives of Indians whom he chose [to honor]." This same chief also remarked that "they used to bring to the store at Huánuco, pots and pitchers and other pottery vessels." When the archaeologists excavated the sealed enclosure, they found tons of pottery and an abundance of food remains. Their conclusion was that they had found a vast kitchen complex for the preparation of chicha and food for public banquets. Fasting was an important element of Inca religion, as it is in the Christian Lent and the Muslim Eid; and it was normal to end a fast with an enormous *taqui* dance and banquet. Cieza described the Hatun Raymi ("great feast") that marked the end of the harvest of potatoes, corn, quinoa, and oca: "It was observed in many provinces and was the principal feast of the entire year... It lasted fifteen or twenty days, during which there were great taquis or drinking feasts and other celebrations." There was sacrifice of many llamas, guinea pigs, pigeons, and other animals. "The mamaconas came forth richly attired and with a great quantity of the chicha that they considered sacred... After having eaten and drunk repeatedly and all being drunk, including the Inca and the high priest, joyful and warmed by the liquor, the men assembled a little after midday and began singing in a loud voice songs and ballads that had been composed by their forebears." The Inca rulers organized them "to make the people joyful, giving them solemn banquets and drinking feasts, great taquis and other celebrations such as they use, completely different from ours. In these the Incas show their splendor, and all the feasting is at their expense." Garcilaso wrote that on the night before one regular festival, "the women of the sun busied themselves with the preparation of enormous quantities of a maize dough called *zancu*, of which they made little round loaves the size of an apple... The flour for this bread...was ground and kneaded by the chosen virgins, the wives of the Sun, who also prepared the rest of the food for the feast. The banquet seemed a gift from the Sun to his children...and for that reason the virgins, as wives of the Sun, prepared it."

On the northern side of the great square is a securely walled compound containing fifty rectangular buildings arranged in neat rows. These were low buildings with rustic pirca walls and narrow doors. Excavation revealed

200 The unfinished templet on the eastern edge of Huánuco.

over 300 spindle whorls and numerous bone awls and other tools used to manipulate threads in looms. There were also a number of copper pins used by Andean women to fasten their cloaks. It thus became evident that these were workshops for textiles—for cloth was the fundamental item of tribute, royal patronage, and trade in Inca Peru. This compound, rather than the enclosure alongside the royal palace, may therefore have been the acllahuasi housing the acllas or mamaconas engaged in making the Inca's cloth. In commenting on this textile factory compound, Murra and Morris quoted a sixteenth-century litigation recently discovered in a Bolivian archive. In it, a chief of Huancané on the north shore of Lake Titicaca recalled bitterly that the Inca had transplanted a thousand weavers and other mitimaes laborers into his district. His ancestors had resented these immigrants, but dared not complain against a royal order. The Huánuco compound, with its single entrance, could just as well have held such transplanted laborers as the beautiful chosen women of the acllahuasi.

201 The view south from the royal residence to the entrance gate.

An informant to the 1562 inquiry said that "in the time of the Inca they used to offer to the sun feathers from the [Amazon forests] and colored seashells, and llamas and marrow fat, guinea pigs, chicha and coca... And they gave all this of their own free will...for no one forced them." It is therefore no surprise to find that the important regional center of Huánuco had a magnificent battery of qollqas. They are arranged in nine rows on the gentle slope of Chumipata hill, half a kilometer (a third of a mile) south of the city. The foundations of 497 qollqas can be counted, some circular and some rectangular. Craig Morris

excavated 120 of these buildings and reroofed one of them with an imitation of its original conical thatch. The excavations revealed very few items of military equipment. But Morris calculated that the qollqas could have held a million bushels of potatoes, maize, and other tribute foods.

North of the acllahuasi compound is a district that Harth-Terré called the herdsmen's ward because it contains a number of circular corrals. North of it, beyond the Ayararacra stream, is the best-preserved of the residential wards. It is a fine example of Inca planning, with a series of canchas and a grid of streets

202 An enclosure north of the central square held mamaconas' workshops.

grouped around a central square. Far off, at the southwestern corner of the square, on the road leading to the storehouses, is a notable group of houses arranged along four square courtyards. Harth-Terré called this complex the "house of the chasquis" (postal runners), although it was not on the main highway which crossed the square from northwest to southeast.

From his work at Huánuco, Morris was able to confirm six main characteristics of provincial highland Inca centers. They were often on new sites, settlements that developed quickly in archaeological terms. Their official Inca ceramics differed markedly from the local wares of the surrounding districts. They were invariably on main roads, depending for defense on the mobility of Inca armies rather than fixed fortifications. This led to a preoccupation with storage and buildings for temporary lodging or non-residential activities. They had royal palaces and temples, but no cemeteries. And many were rapidly depopulated after the fall of the Inca empire.

203 The temple platform of Ingapirca from the north.

18. Ingapirca

THOUGH THE NORTHERN PART OF THE INCA EMPIRE was particularly rich and important, few Inca ruins survive in what is now Ecuador. The most notable is an isolated temple complex known as Ingapirca. It is in rolling, bare, and often misty hills of the Andes, at an altitude of 3,160 meters (10,370 feet). Although remote from any town, Ingapirca is only a short distance east of the main north–south highway, near modern Cañar. It is some 35 kilometers (22 miles) due north of Cuenca, which was once the sumptuous Inca city Tumibamba.

The most striking feature of Ingapirca is a platform faced with fine coursed masonry. The ashlars are gently rusticated with the joints countersunk in the finest Inca manner. This was clearly the work of master masons trained in Cuzco. The platform has straight sides and semicircular ends, a plan seen in no other Inca building. Graziano Gasparini noticed that the ends have diameters of 12.35 meters (40½ feet), while the entire platform is precisely three times this length. The plan thus consists of three circles in a line, with the triangular spaces between the circles filled in to give straight sides.

There could be some religious significance in the fact that the circular module is repeated three times. The platform is aligned roughly from east to west, and the three circles could correspond to the three positions of the sun: *anti* (or *punchao*) for dawn and the east, *inti* for the full overhead sun, and *cunti* for the western sunset. The Antisuyo and the Cuntisuyo (Condesuyo to the Spaniards) were the eastern and western quarters of the Inca empire. In this context it is worth recalling Cristóbal de Molina's account of the chanting at the Inti Raymi in Cuzco, which rose during the morning and fell in the afternoon, echoing in intensity the sun's path across the heavens. The three circles remind us of Garcilaso's description of the solar columns that were erected throughout the empire. In front of temples of the sun there were stone columns in a line from east to west. When the columns' shadows fell along this line at sunrise, but at midday the sun bathed all sides of the column without casting a shadow, they knew that it was an equinox. Very possibly the terreplein of Ingapirca was such a solar observatory or temple, with its curving ends clad in coursed ashlars reminiscent of curving walls of temples in Machu Picchu, Pisac, or Cuzco itself.

A rectangular gabled building stands athwart the Ingapirca platform. It is of typical Inca design, with the crest of the roof supported by a solid wall that divides the building into two identical halves. This central wall occupies the diameter of the middle circle of the platform's plan. The building has good, coursed ashlars on the lower part of its four walls, with adobes in the triangular portions of the gables—almost as if it were originally planned as a hip-roofed building and the gables were added later. It is known locally as the "guardian's house" but was clearly far more important: it is difficult to imagine it being used for any purpose other than a religious one.

The platform is reasonably tall—its height varies from 3.15 to 4.1 meters (between 10 and 13½ feet)—and it is approached by an elegant system of stairs in the middle of the south side. Five steps lead to a double-jambed trapezoidal gate in the outer casing of the platform. Inside this gate, the visitor faces the foundation of the central building, in which there is a trapezoidal niche. Identical staircases rise to right and left, to reach the eastern and western ends of the platform, which are otherwise separated by the dividing wall of the central building.

The remainder of the Ingapirca complex is unremarkable, consisting of rectangular courts and buildings, some with niches, but all typically Inca. The site was visited by a number of earlier travelers. Two Spanish inspectors, the naval officers Jorge Juan and Antonio de Ulloa, made a cursory sketch in 1736. But the best early plan was done three years later by Charles-Marie de La Condamine, their colleague on a team sent by the scientific academies of France and Spain to calculate the earth's circumference by surveys on the equator near Quito. (Their brilliant measurement of our planet was one basis for the entire metric system of weights and measures.) The polymath Alexander von Humboldt visited the site in 1803 and pondered the uniformity, quantity, and geographical spread of Inca architecture. (He also studied fine buildings of coursed Inca masonry at a nearby hacienda called Cuchicaranqui, now Hacienda San Agustín de Callo.) Ingapirca then lapsed into abandon, used as farm buildings, overgrown, and occasionally gouged by treasure-hunters, until 1966 when it was acquired by the archaeological museum of the Central Bank of Ecuador. Excavation started under the American Gordon Hadden; but the main restoration was in the 1970s by a Spanish team led by José Alcina Franch.

Ingapirca is in the territory of an ancient tribe called Cañari, who resisted Inca expansion and—when finally defeated—were slaughtered at a place called

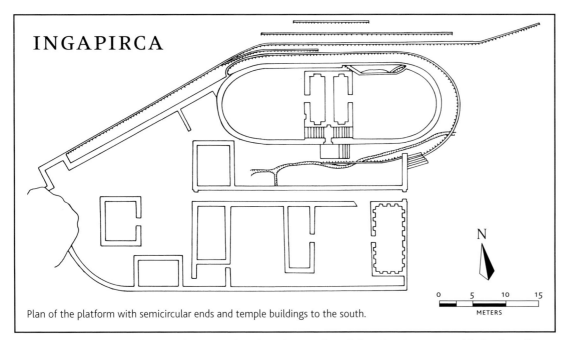

INGAPIRCA

Plan of the platform with semicircular ends and temple buildings to the south.

Yaguar Cocha ("lake of blood"). The Spanish archaeologists found that the site had long been a religious center of the Cañari people, and they excavated a deep tomb full of Cañari and Inca skeletons and artifacts. There is no direct reference to the ruin in the chronicles, unless it was part of Hatun Cañar (Upper Cañar) where, according to Gaspar de Gallegos, "they say that in the time of Huayna Capac there were great towns of the Indians and that this was the main capital of the Cañari. This seems to be so, for there are still today [1582] great and very sumptuous buildings, among which is a very strong tower." The region was conquered by Pachacuti's son Topa Inca Yupanqui. That great Inca started to organize roads and towns on the Inca model, but it was his son Huayna Capac who developed the province. Huayna Capac loved this northern part of the empire and contemplated building a second capital at either Tumibamba (modern Cuenca) or at Quito.

The soldier-chronicler Pedro de Cieza de León traveled through this town in 1547 and was amazed by his first view of Inca architecture. "The temple of the sun was of stones put together with the subtlest skill, some of them large, black and rough, and others that seemed of jasper... The fronts of many of the buildings are beautiful and highly decorative, some of them set with precious stones and emeralds; and the inside walls of the temple of the sun and the palaces of the Inca lords were covered with sheets of the finest gold... The roofing of these buildings was of thatch so well laid that, barring a fire, it would last for ages... Whatever I say, I cannot give an idea of the wealth the Incas possessed in these royal palaces, in which they took great pride, and where many

silversmiths were kept busy... The woolen clothing in the storehouses was so numerous and so fine that, had it been kept and not lost, it would be worth a fortune... These famous lodgings of Tumibamba, which were situated in the province of Cañari, were among the finest and richest to be found in all Peru, and the buildings the largest and best... Today all is cast down and in ruins, but it can still be seen how great they were." The buildings that were ruins in Cieza's day are now swallowed up by the prosperous city of Cuenca. The German archaeologist Max Uhle excavated what he could in 1922; and further foundations revealed in the 1980s are now on show in the heart of the city.

Tumibamba and the province of the Cañari were the scene of the first catastrophe in the destruction of the Inca empire. A sixteenth-century report from this town told how the Inca Huayna Capac, "a noble lord, well regarded and loved by all, and spirited in war," finished his conquests of what is now southern Colombia, and came to reside for ten years at Tumibamba because of its perfect climate. It was during those years that the Inca was informed about the arrival of a foreign ship off the coast of Ecuador. The ship was Pizarro's, from his second voyage, the reconnaissance of 1527–28, during which he had his first glimpse of the mighty empire he was later to conquer.

Shortly after the sighting of the first Europeans came their most deadly legacy. "At this time a terrible disease and epidemic occurred, in which an innumerable quantity of people died of a pox in which they all developed an incurable leprosy. This lord Huayna Capac died of it and they embalmed him and took him to Cuzco for burial. His death was greatly lamented among the natives." "They say that a great pestilence of smallpox struck, so contagious that over two hundred thousand people died of it in all the districts, for it was general." Smallpox (and possibly measles) were European diseases against which American indigenous peoples had no hereditary immunity. It is now thought certain that this deadly epidemic swept across Colombia from the Caribbean, passing from tribe to tribe before the arrival of the Spaniards themselves. It killed not only the Inca, but also his heir and most of his government. The result was a disputed succession between two of his surviving sons, Huascar in Cuzco and Atahualpa in Quito. Their fatal civil war left the Inca empire weakened, divided, and vulnerable to the invasion that destroyed it.

205 Back-to-back chambers in the middle of the temple platform, looking south.

Glossary

of Quechua words and names, with alternative modern spellings.

aclla (ajlla, aqlla): young woman chosen to serve the Inca

acllahuasi (ajllahuasi, aqllawasi, akllahuaci): house of the Inca's chosen women

amaru: snake

anti (ante): the east, dawn

apachita (apacheta): pass, cairn of sacrifices on a pass

Aucaypata (Huacaypata, Waqaypata): square in central Cuzco

ayllu (ayllo): clan, lineage (*see also* panaca)

camayo: expert, specialist

cancha (kancha): enclosed compound, courtyard

capac: chief, great

Carmenca (Karminqa): district of Cuzco

Cassana (Casana, Qasana): a royal palace in Cuzco

ceque (zeq'e, zeque): radiating line of shrines

chaca (chaka): bridge

chasqui (chaski): courier, postal runner

chicha: fermented beer, usually of maize

chullpa (chulpa): funerary tower

Coati (Koati): an island in Lake Titicaca

Colcampata (Qollqampata): district and palace in Cuzco

collca: *see* qollqa

Cora Cora (Qoraqora): a palace in Cuzco

Coricancha (Qoricancha, Qorikancha): the sun temple in Cuzco

Corihuayrachina (Qoriwayrachina): a site on the Inca Trail

cumbi: fine cloth

curaca (kuraca): headman, chief

Cusipata (Kusipata): a square in Cuzco

hanan and hurin: moieties, upper and lower districts respectively

hatun: large, great

Hatun Rumiyoc (Jatun-rumiyoc): a palace in Cuzco ("great stone")

huaca (waka, waqa): shrine

huaina (wayna): young, new

huaman (waman): falcon

Huanacauri (Huanacaure, Wanakauri): sacred hill near Cuzco

Huari (Wari): pre-Inca culture associated with Tiahuanaco

huarmi: *see* warmi

huasi (wasi): house, building

huatana (watana): hitching post, gnomon

huauque: totem

Huchuy Cosco (Uchuy Cosco, Huchuy Cuzco, Juchuy Qozqo, Huchuy Qosqo): a ruin near Chinchero

ichu: tough highland grass, used for thatch

illapa: thunder

Inca (Inka): an Andean tribe or people, and their empire and ruler

    Some Inca emperors, in sequence:

    —Manco Capac (Manko Qhapaq, Manku Qhapaq): legendary first Inca

    —Mama Ocllo (Mama Ucllu): sister-wife of Manco Capac

    —Viracocha (Wiracocha, Wiraqocha): eighth Inca (also a creator god)

    —Pachacuti (Pachakuti Inca Yupanqui, Pachakuteq, Pachacutec, Pachakutej, Pacakoti): ninth Inca

    —Topa Inca Yupanqui (Tupac Inca, Thupa Inka): tenth Inca

    —Huayna Capac (Huaina Capac, Wayna Qhapaq): eleventh Inca

    —Huascar (Washkar): twelfth Inca

    —Atahualpa (Atawallpa): Huascar's brother, executed by Pizarro

    —Manco Inca: Huascar's brother, who rebelled against Spanish rule

Incallacta (Inkallaqta): a ruin near Cochabamba, Bolivia

inti: sun

inti-huatana: hitching post of the sun

kallanka (callanca): long rectangular building, barracks

Kenko (Qenquo, Q'enqo): a shrine above Cuzco

kero: a decorated beaker, usually wooden and often post-Conquest

llacta (llaqta): town, settlement

llautu: woolen head band, royal diadem

mamacona (mamacuna, mamakuna): holy woman

Mañay Raqay (Manyaraki): a district of Ollantaytambo

marca (marka): tower, fortified settlement

masma: open-sided building

mita (mit'a): labor service

mitma (pl. mitimaes) (mitmaq, mitayoc, mijmaq): tribute payers, often resettled as colonists

moya: garden, orchard, pleasure garden

Muyuc Marca (Muyu Marca, Muyumarka): a tower in Sacsahuaman

pacarina (paqarina): place of origin

Pacaritambo (Pacarectambo, Paqareq Tanpu, Paqarejtanpu, Paqari-tampu): origin site near Cuzco

pacha: land, time

Pachacamac (Pachakama): a pre-Inca shrine south of Lima

Pachamama: Mother Earth

pampa (bamba): plain

panaca (panaqa): royal clan, lineage

paqcha (paccha, pajcha): ritual bath, fountain, device for pouring libations

pata: terrace, platform, plateau

phutu: niche

Pilco Caima (Pilco Kaima, Pilco Kayma): a building on the Island of the Sun, Titicaca

pirca: walling of fieldstone in clay

pirua (pirwa): storehouse (*see also* qollqa)

Puca Pucará (Pukapukara): a ruin near Cuzco

pucará (pukará): fort

puna: high-altitude savanna

punchao: sun idol, dawn

puncu (punku): gate

puquio (pucyu, pucjiu): spring, well

pururauca: a venerated rock, petrified deity

qollqa (collca): storehouse

quilla (killa): moon

quipu (khipu, qhipu): knotted-string record

Quishuar-cancha (Kiswar Kancha): holy garden of Coricancha

racay (raqay): hall, shed

Raqchi (previously called Cacha) (Racche, Racchi, Rajch'i): Viracocha temple
    southeast of Cuzco

rimac (corrupted to "lima"): oracle

Rimac-Tampu (Rimaq Tanpu, Limatambo): ruin of an oracle or tambo above the Apurímac

rumi: rock, stone

runa, runakuna: ordinary man, people

Runcu Raccay (Runku Raqay, Runturaqay): a site on the Inca Trail

Sacsahuaman (Sacsayhuaman, Sacsaihuaman, Saqsaywaman, Sajsawaman):
    temple-fortress above Cuzco

Saihuite (Saywite, Sayhuite): an oracle near the Apurímac

Sallac Marca (Sayac Marka, Sayaqmarka): a tower of Sacsahuaman

sinchi: warrior, hero

Suntur-huasi (Sondorhuaci): round tower, on Cuzco plaza and elsewhere

suyu (suyo, svio): a quarter or region of the Inca empire

tambo (tampu, tanpu): post-house, inn

Tambo Machay (Tanpumach'ay, Tampumachai): ruin and spring near Cuzco

Tambo-toqo (Tamputoco, Tanput'oqo, Tambotoco): place with caves of Inca origin legend

tapia: compacted clay walling

Tawantinsuyu (Tahuantinsuyu): the Inca empire, of the four quarters

Tiahuanaco (Tiwanaku, Tiahuanacu): pre-Inca civilization, associated with Huari;
    ruin in Bolivia south of Lake Titicaca

tiana: throne, stool

urco: hill

ushnu (usnu, usno): ritual/administrative platform or pillar

Vilcabamba (Willkapampa): region/river/town/mountain range northwest of Cuzco

Vilcanota (known to the Incas as Willcamayu, "sacred river"): river that waters the Yucay
    valley (also called Sacred Valley), then becomes the Urubamba, and is a headwater
    of the Ucayali–Amazon

Viracocha (Wiracocha, Huiracocha, Wiraqocha): founder deity; also an Inca ruler

warmi (huarmi): woman

Xaquixahuana (Jaquihahuana, K'aq-ya Qhawana): town, battlefield, north of Cuzco

yanacona: retainer, servant

Abbreviations

used in the notes and bibliography

AA *American Anthropologist.*

BAE *Biblioteca de autores españoles desde la formación del lenguaje hasta nuestros días,* ed. Manuel Rivadeneira, 71 vols., Madrid, 1846–80.

BAE (CONT.) *Continuación,* ed. M. Meléndez Pelayo, Madrid, 1905–.

BRAH *Boletín de la Real Academia de la Historia,* Madrid.

CDIHE *Colección de documentos inéditos para la historia de España,* ed. M. Fernández de Navarrete and others, 112 vols., Madrid, 1842–95.

CIAH *Cuadernos de Investigación, Antropología, Huánuco.*

CLDRHP *Colección de libros y documentos referentes a la historia del Perú,* ed. Carlos A. Romero and Horacio H. Urteaga: first series, 12 vols., Lima, 1916–19; second series, 10 vols., Lima, 1920–34.

CLERC *Colección de libros españoles raros ó curiosos,* 25 vols., Madrid, 1871–96.

GP *Gobernantes del Perú, cartas y papeles, siglo XVI...,* ed. Roberto Levillier, 14 vols., Madrid, 1921–26.

HAKL. SOC. The Hakluyt Society: first series, 100 vols., Cambridge, 1847–98; second series, Cambridge, 1899–.

HSAI *Handbook of South American Indians,* ed. Julian H. Steward, Smithsonian Institution, Bureau of American Ethnology Bulletin 143, Washington, DC, 1946–63.

RGI *Relaciones geográficas de Indias,* ed. M. Jiménez de la Espada, 4 vols., Madrid, 1881; in BAE (CONT.), vols. 183–185 (1965).

RH *Revista histórica,* Instituto Histórico del Perú, Lima, 1906.

RIAC *Revista del Instituto Arqueológico del Cuzco.*

RMN *Revista del Museo Nacional,* Lima, 1932–.

RSAC *Revista de la Sección de Arqueología,* University of Cuzco.

RU *Revista Universitaria,* Cuzco, 1912–.

Notes

THE CATCHLINES FOR CITES TO QUOTATIONS consist of the last few words quoted. If the cite to a text quotation is a Spanish source, an additional cite to a published English translation may be given. A volume number, where applicable, is given first, followed by a colon and a page number.

Photographer's Preface

6 *Cusco Histórico*, Lima: Casa Editorial SA, 1934
See also essays by Edward Ranney:
"Images of a Sacred Geography," in *The New World's Old World*, Albuquerque (NM): University of New Mexico Press, 2003
"Martín Chambi, de Coasa y Cusco," in *La Recuperación de la memoria, el primer siglo de la fotografía*, Peru, 1842–1942, Lima: Patronato de Telefónica & Museo de Arte, 2001
"New Light on the Cusco School: Juan Manuel Figueroa Aznar and Martín Chambi," in *History of Photography*, vol. 24, no. 2, London and Philadelphia: Taylor and Francis, 2000

1. Inca Architecture

11 "appreciate them": Bernabé Cobo, *Historia del Nuevo Mundo*, bk. 14, ch. 12, BAE (CONT.) 92:260.

11 "ninety years": Miguel de Estete, *Noticia del Perú...* (ca. 1540), CLDRHP, 2 ser., 8 (1924):47.

12 "everything efficiently": Cobo, *Historia del Nuevo Mundo*, bk. 12, ch. 12, BAE (CONT.) 92:77–78.

12 "miraculous involved": Ibid., bk. 13, ch. 11, 92:166.

15 "in Cuzco" "obedient to him": G. Diez de San Miguel, *Visita...a la Provincia de Chucuito...*, 92–93.

17 "buildings": Alexander von Humboldt, *Vue des cordillères et monumens des peuples de l'Amérique* (Paris, 1810), 114–115.

17 "solutions": Graziano Gasparini and Luise Margolies, *Arquitectura Inka*, 330.

18 "and appearance": Juan de Betanzos, *Suma y narración de los Incas*, BAE (CONT.) 209:47.

19 "of the gutter": Pedro Sancho, *Relación para S. M. ...*, CLDRHP, 1 ser., 5:192.

19 "been involved!": Cobo, bk. 14, ch. 12, BAE (CONT.) 92:261.

22 "with the top": Cobo, bk. 14, ch. 12, BAE (CONT.) 92:262.

22 "Inca in Cuzco": Diez de San Miguel, *Visita...Chucuito*, 92.

22 "their empire": Cobo, bk. 13, ch. 19, BAE (CONT.) 92:197.

24 "shaping stones": Jean-Pierre Protzen, *Inca Architecture and Construction at Ollantaytambo*, 188.

24 "imagine": Protzen, "Inca architecture," in L. L. Minelli (ed.), *The Inca World*, 212.

24 "one another" "number of rooms": Cobo, bk. 14, ch. 3, 92:241–242.

26 "readily worked" "overlapping tiles": E. George Squier, *Peru*, 394–395; Garcilaso on thatch: *Comentarios reales de los Incas*, pt. 1, bk. 6, ch. 4, Livermore trans., 1:321.

26 "sheet of flame": *Relación del sitio del Cuzco...*, CLERC, 13:19.

26 "almost suffocated": Cristóbal de Molina (el Almagrista), *Relación de muchas cosas...*, CLDRHP, 1 ser., 1:175.

26 "same fashion": Garcilaso de la Vega, pt. 1, bk. 6, ch. 4, Livermore trans., 1:321.

31 "open air": Garcilaso, pt. 1, bk. 6, ch. 4, Livermore trans., 1:320–321, and bk. 7, ch. 9, 1:424.

31 "for that purpose": *Noticia del Perú*, 32.

31 "on their horses": F. de Jerez, *Verdadera relación...*, BAE (CONT.) 26:332.

31 "very skillfully": Pedro de Cieza de León, *Crónica del Perú*, pt. 1, ch. 81, Onis–von Hagen edn., 101–102.

31 "drinking celebrations" "level and clear": Pedro Pizarro, BAE (CONT.) 168:214.

32 "anywhere on earth": Molina (el Almagrista), BAE (CONT.) 209:69.

32 "or assemblies": Ibid., 68.

32 "climbs to it": Jerez, BAE (CONT.) 26:330.

32 "into their midst": Cristóbal de Mena, *La conquista del Perú*, in A. Pogo, "The Anonymous 'La Conquista del Perú,'" *Proceedings of the American Academy of Arts and Sciences* (Boston), 64 (July 1930):242.

32 "began to kill": P. Pizarro, *Relación del descubrimiento y conquista...*, BAE (CONT.) 168:178.

32 "aforesaid purpose" "and lay feasts": Cieza, pt. 1, ch. 89, Onis–von Hagen edn., 127.

33 "in its honor": Miguel Cabello de Balboa, *Miscelánea Antártica*, pt. 3: *Historia del Perú*, ch. 21, 1951 edn., 365.

33 "invoked their god": Felipe Guaman Poma de Ayala, *Nueva corónica y buen gobierno*, ed. Métraux, 262.

33 "sacrifice of chicha": Cristóbal de Molina (of Cuzco), *Relación de las fábulas y ritos de los Incas*, ed. Morales, 46.

33 "sun on the plaza": Ibid.; also Cobo, bk. 13, ch. 14, 4:39.

34 "for the Inca": Guaman Poma, pt. 1, ed. Bustios Gálvez, 1:218–219.

34 "to the Spaniards": Diego de Trujillo, *Relación del discubrimiento...*, 54. The rape was hinted at in Fernández de Oviedo and in Mena, but the more official report of Francisco de Jerez mentioned only "a large, strong house surrounded by tapia [hardened mud] walls, with gates, in which were many women spinning and weaving clothing for Atahualpa's army" (BAE (CONT.) 26:326).

38 "take his pleasure": Cieza, pt. 2, chs. 38, 40, Onis–von Hagen edn., 210, 215. It was Betanzos who clearly stated that Viracocha's fortress of Caquia Xaquixahuana was on a crag seven leagues from Cuzco and above the town of Calca in the Yucay

valley (Suma, ch. 6). On the strength of this, Rowe supposed that it was the ruin now called Huchuy Cosco, which is in precisely this location ("Inca Culture at the Time of the Spanish Conquest," HSAI 2:204; "What Kind of Settlement...," 68).

38   "magnificent buildings" "their jurisdictions": Pedro Sarmiento de Gamboa, chs. 40, 41, Markham trans., 121, 124.

38   "he went hunting": Cobo, bk. 13, ch. 14, Pardo edn., 4:34, 36.

38   "his household": Sarmiento, ch. 54, Markham trans., 153.

40   "marvelous skill": Martín de Murúa, Historia general del Perú, bk. 3, ch. 3, ed. Bayle, 2:165–166.

40   "and fruits": Garcilaso, pt. 1, bk. 6, ch. 2, Livermore trans., 1:315.

40   "space for mortar": Ibid., bk. 6, ch. 1, 1:313.

40   "his government" "lodging of the Inca": Guaman Poma, pt. 1, ed. Bustios Gálvez, 1:245, 481.

40   "most remarkable": Sancho, Relación, CLDRHP, 1 ser., 5:192–193.

40   "and other metals": Estete, Noticias del Perú, 45.

40   "like azoteas": P. Pizarro, Relación del descubrimiento del reyno del Perú (1571), trans. Philip Ainsworth Means, New York: The Cortes Society, 1921, 355.

41   "vast halls" "with astonishment": Garcilaso, pt. 1, bk. 7, ch. 10, Livermore trans., 1:426.

41   "up to the roof": Pedro Pizarro, Relación, BAE (CONT.) 168:192.

41   "in the Cassana": Garcilaso, Comentarios reales de los Incas, pt. 1, bk. 7, ch. 10, Livermore trans., 426.

41   "had been razed": Garcilaso, pt. 1, bk. 6, ch. 2, Livermore trans., 1:427.

41   "house or lodging": Ibid., pt. 2, bk.1, ch. 32, 2:701.

41   "preserved it": Ibid., 427.

42   "belongings and ornaments": Cobo, bk. 12, ch. 4, 3:155.

42   "and the Incas": Cristóbal de Castro and Diego Ortega Morejón, Relación y declaración... (1558), CLDRHP, 2 ser., 10:135–136.

42   "and drank there": P. Pizarro, Relación del descubrimiento...del Perú (1571), trans. Philip Ainsworth Means, New York: The Cortes Society, 1921, 251.

43   "roofs are missing": Cobo, bk. 12, ch. 30, 3:287–288.

43   "or twelve years": Ibid.

43   "so many items": Sancho, Relación, CLDRHP, 1 ser., 5:195; Estete [Narrative of a Journey to Pachacamac], BAE (CONT.) 26:47.

43   "and of coca" "leather chests": P. Pizarro, CDIHE 5:271–272.

43   "prior cooking": Guaman Poma, pt. 1, ed. Bustios Gálvez, 1:251.

43   "each different province": Cobo, bk. 12, ch. 30, 3:287–288.

43   "not be provided": Cieza on Vilcashuamán storehouses: Crónica, pt. 2, chs. 44, 84, 89; Onis–von Hagen edn., 68, 114, 127.

45   "of foodstuffs": Cobo, bk. 12, ch. 30, 3:287–288.

45   "various products": John V. Murra and E. Craig Morris, "Dynastic Oral Tradition...," World Archaeology, 7:273; Morris, "Master Design of the Inca," Natural History (December 1976), 63.

45   "of the tyrant": litigation in the Bolivian National Archive, Sucre, quoted in Murra and Morris, "Dynastic Oral Tradition...," 277.

46   "their sacrifices": Blas Valera, Relaciones de las costumbres antiguas de los naturales del Pirú, BAE (CONT.) 20:157.

2. Island of the Sun

49   "and so it was": Sarmiento de Gamboa, Historia indica, ch. 7, Markham trans., 32–33. See also Molina (of Cuzco), Relación, 13–15; Betanzos, Suma, ch. 1, BAE (CONT.) 109:9, Hamilton-Buchanan trans., 7.

49   "for that age": Cobo, Historia del Nuevo Mundo, bk. 59, ch. 18, Pardo edn., 4:77. See also Garcilaso, Comentarios reales, pt. 1, bk. 3, ch. 25, Livermore trans., 1:189–190.

49   "confused": Betanzos, Suma, ch. 11, Hamilton-Buchanan trans., 40.

49   "teaching the people": Cobo, Historia del Nuevo Mundo, bk. 59, ch. 18, Pardo edn., 4:77. See also Garcilaso, Comentarios reales, pt. 1, bk. 3, ch. 25, Livermore trans., 1:190.

49   "his great majesty": Cobo, bk. 13, ch. 18, 4:78.

49   "have seen them": Ibid., 79.

50   "to the south": Charles Stanish and Brian Bauer, "Pilgrimage and the geography of power in the Inka empire," in Richard L. Burger et al., Variations in the Expression of Inka Power, 56.

52   The two plans of Pilco Caima (or Kayma): Squier, 342; Gasparini and Margolies, Arquitectura Inka, 270. See also Charles Wiener, Pérou et Bolivie, 411; Adolph Francis Bandelier, The Islands of Titicaca and Koati, 176.

52   "shades of red": Squier, Peru, 345.

52   "sea in front" "beautiful in nature": Ibid., 346.

53   "illume the world": Squier, 366.

53   "in the island": Cobo, bk. 13, ch. 18, 4:82–83. Similar descriptions occur in the works of two of Cobo's contemporaries, Alonso Ramos Gavilán and Antonio de la Calancha (see the bibliography).

53   "rain was needed": Ibid., 84.

3. Tambo-toqo and Huanacauri Hill

55   "Rich Opening" "you make offerings": Sarmiento de Gamboa, Historia indica, ch. 12, BAE (CONT.) 135:216, or Markham trans., 55–52. See also Cieza de León, Crónica, chs. 6–7, Onis–von Hagen edn., 32–33; Molina (of Cuzco), Relación, 64; Garcilaso, Comentarios reales, pt. 1, ch. 16, Livermore trans., 1:43; Betanzos, Suma, ch. 4, BAE (CONT.) 209:13, Hamilton-Buchanan trans., 15–16; Guaman Poma, Nueva corónica, ed. Bustios Gálvez, 1:166, 188; Informaciones que mandó evanter el Virrey Toledo, CLERC, 16:196.

55   "nobility and knighthood": Sarmiento, ch. 12, Markham trans., 52.

55   "sons": Cobo, Nuevo Mundo, bk. 13, ch. 25, Pardo edn., 4:122; Molina (of Cuzco), 65–81; Molina (el Almagrista), Relación, BAE (CONT.) 209:73–74; Garcilaso, pt. 1, bk. 6, ch. 24.

57   "wealth of treasure": Cieza, pt. 2, ch. 28, Onis–von Hagen edn., 150. See also Joan de Santacruz Pachacuti Yamqui, Relación de antigüedades, BAE (CONT.) 209:286.

57   "gold and silver": Guaman Poma, pt. 2, Dilke trans., 110. See also Bartolomé de Las Casas, De las antiguas gentes del Perú, ch. 16; John H. Rowe, "An Introduction to the Archaeology of Cuzco," Peabody Museum Papers, 27:41–43.

4. Sacsahuaman

59   "was in it" "necessary food" "the world exists": Cieza de León, Crónica, pt. 2, ch. 51, Onis–von Hagen edn., 153–154.

59 "others laid them": Sarmiento de Gamboa, *Historia indica*, ch. 53, Markham trans., 152.

59 "roll downhill": Garcilaso, *Comentarios reales*, pt. 1, bk. 7, ch. 29, Livermore trans., 1:470.

59 "sight as this!": Sancho, *Relación*, 5:193.

60 "rather than men!": Garcilaso, pt. 1, bk. 7, ch. 27, BAE (CONT.) 133:285.

60 Source of the stone for Sacsahuaman: Carlos Kalafatovich Valle, "Geología del grupo arqueológico de la fortaleza de Saccsayhuaman y sus vecinidades," Saqsaywaman 1:64–65; Gasparini and Margolies, *Arquitectura Inka*, 299–300.

60 "in their places": Garcilaso, pt. 1, bk. 7, ch. 28, BAE (CONT.) 133:286, Livermore trans., 1:467–468.

60 "level or uniform": José de Acosta, *Historia natural y moral de las Indias*, bk. 6, ch. 14, BAE (CONT.) 73:194, quoted in Garcilaso, pt. 1, bk. 7, ch. 27, Livermore trans., 1:465.

60 "into place": Vincent R. Lee, *The building of Sacsayhuaman* (Wilson, WY, 1987), 2.

60 "obliquely" "more beautiful" "as in Spain": Sancho, *Relación*, CLDRHP, 1 ser., 5:193–194. The restorers in 1968 were led by Luis A. Pardo and the architect Oscar Ladrón de Guevara Avilés. They were amazed to find the entire southern wall of Sacsahuaman buried under a century of deposits, with many of its stones tumbled into the Pucrumayo stream. They rebuilt a gate and called it Rumipuncu ("stone gate"). See their "Trabajos de limpieza y consolidación, estudio e investigación," Saqsaywaman, 1 (1970):30.

60 "as above it": Garcilaso, pt. 1, bk. 7, ch. 29, Livermore trans., 1:469.

61 "of it remain": Luis E. Valcárcel y Vizcarra, "Cuzco Archaeology," HSAI 2:178–179. See also his reports, "Sajsawaman redescubierto," RMN, vols. 3–6 (1934–37), and Squier, *Peru*, 473.

61 "in one day": Sancho, *Relación*, 193.

62 "lost inside": Garcilaso, pt. 1, bk. 7, ch. 29, Livermore trans., 1:469. See also Juan Ruiz de Arce, *Relación de servicios...*, BRAH 102:368.

62 "have mentioned": Garcilaso, 1:471. An anonymous chronicle called *Noticias cronológicas del Cusco*, written in about 1740, said that the destruction of Sacsahuaman started in 1537. The ecclesiastical council of Cuzco, in a decision dated October 6, 1559, ordered stones from the temple-fortress to be brought down to build the cathedral; but on May 13, 1561, the town council (*cabildo*), under Lieutenant-Governor Licentiate Antonio de Gama, prohibited the removal of stones for house-building, on pain of a fine of one hundred pesos de oro (Víctor Angles Vargas, *Historia del Cusco*, 1:122).

62 "faced blocks": Carolyn Dean, "The Inka married the earth," *The Art Bulletin*, September 2007.

62 "what is was": Garcilaso, *Comentarios reales*, pt. 1, bk. 7, ch. 29, Livermore trans., 471.

62 "of this land!": Cieza, pt. 2, ch. 51, Onis–von Hagen edn., 155.

62 "see the ruins": Sarmiento, ch. 53, Markham trans., 152.

64 "top of a hill": Sancho, *Relación*, 5:193. In their descriptions, both P. Pizarro and Cieza say that Sacsahuaman had only two towers (Pizarro, BAE (CONT.) 168:196–197; Cieza, pt. 2, ch. 51, Onis–von Hagen edn., 154–155).

64 "lords of Cuzco": Sancho, Ibid., Means translation (1917), 157. On the geology of the Rodadero: Isaiah Bowman, *The Andes of Southern Peru* (New York, 1916); Kalafatovich Valle, "Geología del grupo arqueológico...," *Saqsaywaman*, 1:66–68.

64 "know what to do": Titu Cusi Yupanqui, *Relación de la conquista del Perú...*, CLDRHP, 1 ser., 2:67.

64 "few of them": *Relación de los sucesos del Perú* (1548), GP 2 (1921):393.

64 "speed": Titu Cusi Yupanqui, *Relación*, 68.

65 "was indeed brave": Francisco de Pancorvo's testimony in support of Francisco Pizarro's claim against the Crown, Cuzco, October 7, 1572, GP 2:153.

66 "close combat": *Relación del sitio del Cuzco*, 30.

66 "with determination": Ibid.

66 "wine jar": *Relación de los sucesos del Perú*, 394. The exploits of Hernán Sánchez (who may himself have written the anonymous *Relación de los sucesos*) were repeated by Antonio de Herrera y Tordesillas (*Historia general*, Década V, bk. 8, ch. 5). Mancio Sierra de Leguízamo claimed to have been the first Spaniard to penetrate Sacsahuaman's terraces, in front of Juan Pizarro, in an enquiry held in Cuzco in 1572 (reply to question 31, GP 2:145), and repeated it in his will of September 18, 1589 (text in *Revista Peruana*, 2, 1879). Pedro Pizarro also mentioned that he fought alongside his cousin Juan.

66 "became exhausted": *Relación del sitio del Cuzco*, 31–2.

66 "stones and arrows": P. Pizarro, BAE (CONT.) 168:204–205.

66 "top of the tower": Ibid.

66 "on his head": Ibid. The brave orejón is sometimes called Cahuide, but this was not a Quechua name and does not appear in any contemporary source.

66 "on his arm": Ibid.

66 "not been touched": *Relación del sitio del Cuzco*, 32.

66 "fifteen hundred of them": Ibid., 33. Alonso Enríquez de Guzman said that three thousand were slaughtered during the capture of Sacsahuaman: *Libro de vida y costumbres...* (1543), trans. C. R. Markham, HAKL. SOC., 1 ser., 29 (1862):98.

66 "heap of dead men": Titu Cusi Yupanqui, *Relación*, 70.

66 "died in it": Cédula of Charles V, Madrid, July 19, 1540, *Colección de documentos inéditos para la historia de Hispano-América*, 3 (1928):75.

5. Coricancha

69 "well served": Mena, *La conquista del Perú*, Raúl Porras Barrenechea (ed.), 92.

69 "greatly at them": Ibid., 93.

69 "had on them": Ibid.

69 "if they did": Ibid.

69 "evidently been secured": Francisco de Jerez, *Conquista del Perú*, BAE (CONT.) 26:343.

69 "its shape": P. Sancho, *Relación*, 5:191

69 "we went in": Trujillo, *Relación*, Barrenechea edn., 63–64.

69 "monastery": Ruiz de Arce, *Relación de servicios* (ca. 1545), in R. Porras Barrenechea (ed.), *Los cronistas del Perú (1528–1650) y otros ensayos* (Lima, 1986); trans. Brian Bauer, *Ancient Cuzco*, 146.

69 "in the empire": Cobo, *Historia del Nuevo Mundo*, bk. 13, ch. 12, Pardo edn., 4:9.

69 "in Rome": Ibid.

69 "universe": Brian S. Bauer, *Ancient Cuzco: Heartland of the Inca* (Austin, Texas, 2004), 157.

70 "improve on them": Cieza de León, *Crónica*, pt. 1, ch. 92, Onis–von Hagen edn., 146.

70 "excellent quality": Ibid.

70   "said was the sun": P. Pizarro, BAE (CONT.) 168:192; also Betanzos, *Suma*, ch. 11, BAE (CONT.) 209:33, Hamilton-Buchanan trans., 47.

70   "four-year-old boy": Jerez, BAE (CONT.) 26:345-346; Betanzos said that it was the size of a one-year-old boy, dressed in miniature royal robes and regalia, surmounted by a gold disk and with golden sandals.

70   "magnificent specimens": Cieza, pt. 1, ch. 94, Onis-von Hagen edn., 255.

70   "those distant lands": Albrecht Dürer's journal for August 27, 1520, in *Albrecht Dürers Tagebuch der Reise in die Niederlande*, ed. Friedrich Leitschuh (Leipzig, 1884), 58.

71   "the present day": Molina (el Almagrista), BAE (CONT.) 209:75. G. Fernández de Oviedo (*Historia*, bk. 47, ch. 9, BAE (CONT.) 121:6) said that Rodrigo Orgóñez captured a sun image from the fugitive Inca, Manco, in 1537 and gave it to the puppet Inca, Paullu, but this must have been an insignificant object as no other chroniclers mentioned it.

71   "many precious stones": Cieza, pt. 1, ch. 92, Onis-von Hagen edn., 146. See also Cobo, bk. 13, ch. 12, BAE (CONT.) 92:168-169; Acosta, *Historia natural*, bk. 5, ch. 12, BAE (CONT.) 73:153; Guaman Poma, *Nueva corónica*, ed. Métraux, 258, 264; Santacruz Pachacuti, *Relación*, CLDRHP, 2 ser., 9:159-161; *Relación de las costumbres antiguas*, BAE (CONT.) 209:158.

71   "body of the idol": Francisco de Toledo despatch to King, March 20, 1572, in Roberto Levillier (ed.), *Gobernantes del Perú. Cartas y Papeles, siglo XVI* (14 vols., Madrid, 1921-26), vol. 4, 345; Sarmiento de Gamboa, *Historia indica* (1572), ch. 29.

71   "medallions": Ibid.

71   "food was consumed": P. Pizarro, BAE (CONT.) 168:192-193.

71   "made love to them": Cobo, bk. 13, ch. 12, BAE (CONT.) 92:169.

71   "who were many": P. Pizarro, BAE (CONT.) 168:193, or Means trans., 255.

71   "songs": Bernabé Cobo, *Historia del Nuevo Mundo*, bk. 13, ch. 37.

71   "on those occasions": P. Pizarro, BAE (CONT.) 168:193. See also Molina (el Almagrista), BAE (CONT.) 209:75; Cobo, bk. 13, ch. 12, BAE (CONT.) 92:169; Vázquez de Espinosa, bk. 4, ch. 76, 563. Cieza (pt. 1, ch. 92, Onis-von Hagen edn., 147) added that there were golden llamas and herdsmen as well as golden maize. Garcilaso (pt. 1, bk. 3, ch. 24, Livermore trans., 1:188) let his fertile imagination run riot, with the garden full of golden plants, trees, animals, reptiles, birds, and butterflies.

71   "octavos": Luis Fernández de Alfaro, *Relación del oro del Perú que recibimos de Hernando Pizarro...para Su Majestad...* (Seville, 1534), in José Toribio Medina (ed.), *La Imprenta en Lima (1584-1824)* (Santiago de Chile, 1904), vol. 1, 163-72, quoted in Brian S. Bauer, *Ancient Cuzco: Heartland of the Inca* (Austin, Texas, 2004), 146. Fernández de Alfaro was the official who recorded the items brought to Seville by Hernando Pizarro in February 1534. His inventory said that the maize cob weighed 10 marks, 6 ounces, 4 eighths. A marco de oro was 8 ounces (226.8 grams), so this weighed 5 pounds or 2.275 kilos. An onza was just over an ounce or 28.8 grams, so 6 onzas and 4 octavos would have been similar in weight.

72   "form of a pyramid": Garcilaso, pt.1, bk. 3, ch. 21, Livermore trans., 1:181.

72   "chief of the pururaucas": Cobo, bk. 13, ch. 16, Pardo edn., 4:58.

72   "kept in that place": Garcilaso, pt. 2, bk. 8, ch. 11, BAE (CONT.) 135:146.

72   "ancient edifice": Squier, *Peru*, 499.

72   "underground passages": Kubler, *Cuzco: Reconstruction of the Town and Restoration of Its Monuments* (Paris, 1952), 8. M. Uhle, "El Templo del Sol de los Incas en Cuzco," XXIII International Congress of Americanists, *Proceedings* (1930), 291-295; J. H. Rowe, "An Introduction to the Archaeology of Cuzco," *Peabody Museum Papers*, 27.

74   "of the square": Garcilaso, pt. 1, bk. 3, ch. 21, Livermore trans., 1:181. For comment on the restoration of Coricancha, see Gasparini and Margolies, *Arquitectura Inka*, 230-238; Oscar Ladrón de Guevara Avilés, "La restauración del Ccoricancha y Templo de Santo Domingo" (1966).

74   "tabernacles": Garcilaso, pt. 1, bk. 3, ch. 22, Livermore trans., 1:184.

74   "of the universe": Betanzos, *Suma*, ch. 11, BAE (CONT.) 209:31.

6. Pisac

79   "town of the Cuyos": Sarmiento de Gamboa, *Historia indica*, ch. 34, Markham trans., 107.

79   "all his glory": Squier, *Peru*, 529. See also Garcilaso, *Comentarios reales*, pt. 1, bk. 2, ch. 22, Livermore trans., 1:116; Cieza de León, *Crónica*, pt. 2, ch. 26, Onis-von Hagen edn., 172; Acosta, *Historia natural*, bk. 6, ch. 3, BAE (CONT.) 73:184. The Austrian traveler Charles Wiener also visited Pisac at about the same time as Squier, but left a more boastful account, claiming that he was the first white man to have discovered it. He made a drawing of the "fortress" in which it looks like a grandiose castle with the agricultural terraces as battlements (*Pérou et Bolivie*, 374).

79   "staircases": Protzen, *Inca Architecture and Construction at Ollantaytambo*, 281.

80   "his perilous way": Squier, 529.

80   "doors": Ibid., 530. A good modern description of Pisac is by Víctor Angles Vargas, *Pi'saq, metrópoli Inka* and his *Historia del Cusco*, 1:152-188. On the adobe buildings of Pisac, see Elizabeth L. Moorehead's "Highland Inca Architecture in Adobe," *Ñawpa Pacha*, 16:70-83.

7. Chinchero

87   "outlined": Betanzos, *Suma*, pt. 1, ch. 38, trans. Roland Hamilton and Dana Buchanan, 159.

87   "amphitheatres": Gasparini and Margolies, *Arquitectura Inka*, translated by Patricia J. Lyon (Bloomington, IN, 1980), 94.

87   "high-prestige": Susan Niles, *The Shape of Inca History*.

89   "immigrants": Stella Nair, "Witnessing the in-visibility of Inca architecture in colonial Peru," *Buildings and Landscapes: Journal of the Vernacular Architecture Forum* (vol. 14, 2007, 50-65), 51.

8. Moray

93   "they are filled": Garcilaso, *Comentarios reales*, pt. 1, bk. 5. ch. 1, Livermore trans., 1:241; Cobo, *Historia del Nuevo Mundo*, bk. 14, ch. 8, Pardo edn., 4:220; Sarmiento de Gamboa, *Historia indica*, ch. 30, Markham trans., 98; Guaman Poma, *Nueva corónica*, pt. 3, Dilke trans., 191.

93   "hot and humid": Hernando de Santillán, *Relación del origin...y gobierno de los Incas*, BAE (CONT.) 209:144.

9. Ollantaytambo

97 "ford was defended": *Relación del sitio del Cuzco*, CLERC 13:47.

97 "yet seen": Squier, *Peru*, 492.

97 "on all fours": P. Pizarro, *Relación*, BAE (CONT.) 168:209.

97 "well-armed warriors": *Relación del sitio del Cuzco*, 47, 48.

97 "hillsides and plains": *Relación de los sucesos del Perú*, GP 2:397.

97 "hear the shouting": *Relación del sitio del Cuzco*, 48.

97 "have been killed": P. Pizarro, 209.

97 "by either side": *Relación del sitio del Cuzco*, 49. See also *Relación de los sucesos*, 396–397.

97 "control of his army": Antonio de Herrera y Tordesillas, *Historia general…*, dec. V, bk. 8, ch. 6, Ballesteros and Gómez (ed.), 11:216.

98 "could not skirmish": *Relación del sitio del Cuzco*, 49.

98 "the horses' tails": Ibid., 50.

98 "with great spirit": P. Pizarro, 209.

98 "nothing else": *Relación del sitio del Cuzco*, 51.

99 "shrines and altars": Cieza de León, *Crónica del Perú*, pt. 4 (*La guerra de Las Salinas*), ch. 21, Markham trans., 87.

101 "wall ends": Squier, *Peru*, 494.

101 "scutiform": Emilio Harth-Terré, "Técnica y arte de la cantería incaíca," 158.

105 "project": Protzen, *Inca Architecture…Ollantaytambo*, 81.

105 "will never be": Ibid., 82.

106 "it was abandoned": Ibid., 94.

106 "which was not his": Sarmiento de Gamboa, *Historia indica*, chs. 32, 35, Markham trans., 103, 107–108. Pedro Gutiérrez de Santa Clara said that Tampu Apu was one of the four ayllus (noble clans) of Cuzco, and Santacruz Pachacuti described Apu Tampu as a pre-Inca chief who received the royal scepter (*Relación de antigüedades*, BAE (CONT.) 209:283). In the Inca origin myth, the cave of Tambo-toqo might have referred to this tribe. The spring above Cuzco called Tambo Machay may have meant "cave of the Tampus," according to L. E. Valcárcel y Vizcarra (*Machu Picchu…*, 25–26).

106 "people who were there": Sarmiento de Gamboa, ch. 40, BAE (CONT.) 135:245; or Markham trans., 121–122.

111 "single storey": Squier, *Peru*, 515.

111 "structure like it": Protzen, *Ollantaytambo*, 107.

111 "smiling valley": Squier, *Peru*, 515.

112 "most effectively": Protzen, *Ollantaytambo*, 129.

112 "not known": Ibid., 135.

114 "attempt to explain": Squier, *Peru*, 508.

114 "leaf fibers": Gutiérrez de Santa Clara, *Historia de las guerras civiles del Perú…*, bk. 3, ch. 63, BAE (CONT.) 165–167.

10. Machu Picchu

117 "incredible height": Bingham, *Inca Land*, 314.

117 "towards the east": Wiener, *Pérou et Bolivie*, 345.

117 "subterranean constructions": Augusto R. Berns, prospectus for the Compañía Anónima (Limitada), "Huacas del Inga" (Lima, 1887). Machu Picchu mountain also appeared on other maps, including those of Antonio Raimondi (1887) and Clements Markham (1910).

117 "muleteer": Bingham, *Inca Land*, 715.

120 "all-fours" "Indians": Bingham, "The discovery of Machu Picchu," *Harper's Magazine*, vol. 127, 1913, 711.

120 "exquisitely fitted together" "found in Peru": Bingham, *Inca Land*, 320 and 714.

120 "beautifully constructed houses": Bingham, *Lost City of the Incas*, 149.

121 "stones of a temple": Ibid., 174.

121 "other properties": María Rostworowski, "El repartimiento de Doña Beatriz Coya en el valle de Yucay," *Historia y Cultura*, 4, 1970, 153–267. The document found by John Rowe was explained in his "Machu Picchu a la luz de documentos del siglo XVI," *Histórica*, vol. 14, no. 1, 1990, 139–154.

121 "dense jungles": Cobo, bk. 12, ch. 12, Pardo edn., 3:185. Sarmiento de Gamboa said that Pachacuti defeated his brother Urco and killed him downstream from Ollantaytambo (*Historia indica*, ch. 33). He also said that Pachacuti's uncle was called Vicchu (Picchu?) because he defeated a tribe of that name (Ibid., ch. 23).

121 "rituals": Federico Kauffmann Doig, *Machu Picchu, tesoro inca* (Lima, 2005), 62.

129 "the lower ward": Cobo, *Historia del Nuevo Mundo*, bk. 12, ch. 24, Pardo edn., 3:257.

129 "entertainment they devised": Ibid., 258.

130 "in many folds": Kubler, "Machu Picchu," 53.

133 "entombed": Betanzos, pt. 1, ch. 32, Hamilton-Buchanan trans., 138.

134 "architecture": Carolyn Dean, "The Inka married the earth," *The Art Bulletin*, September 2007.

136 "450 years": Alfredo Valencia Zegarra, "Recent archaeological investigations at Machu Picchu," in Richard L. Burger and Lucy C. Salazar (eds.), *Machu Picchu: Unveiling the Mystery of the Incas* (Yale, 2004), 76.

136 "three tons": Bingham, *Lost City*, 170.

136 "defies description": Ibid.

139 "third Sutic-ttoco": Santacruz Pachacuti Yamqui, *Relación de antigüedades*, BAE (CONT.) 209:286; Bingham, *Lost City*, 209.

142 "means 'to tie'": Garcilaso, *Comentarios reales*, pt. 1, bk. 2, ch. 22, Livermore trans., 1:116.

142 "by the sun": Diego González Holguín, *Vocabulario de la lengua general de todo el Peru llamado lengua Qqichua del Inca* (1608), ed. Raul Porras Barrenechea (Lima: Universidad Nacional Mayor de San Marcos, 1952), entry for *inti-huactanan*.

144 "it stands": Rowe, "Inca culture at the Time of the Spanish Conquest," 328, note 39.

145 "of their foods": Guaman Poma, *Nueva corónica*, pt. 1, Bustios Gálvez edn., 1:165, or Dilke trans., 60.

145 "annual timepiece": Sarmiento, ch. 30, BAE (CONT.) 135:235–236, or Markham trans., 98–99. Garcilaso said that there were eight sucana columns on either side of Cuzco (pt. 1, bk. 2, ch. 22); Cieza de León said that there were many of these ruined observatory towers around Cuzco (*Crónica*, pt. 2, ch. 26); Acosta mentioned twelve pillars, one for each month (*Historia natural*, bk. 6, ch. 3, BAE (CONT.) 73:184).

146 "all his full light": Garcilaso, pt. 1, bk. 2, ch. 30, Livermore trans., 1:117.

146 "chanted higher" "deepest humility": Molina (el Almagrista), *Relación de muchas cosas…*, CLDRHP, 1 ser., 1:160, trans. J. Hemming, *The Conquest of the Incas*, 172–173.

149   "here centuries ago": Bingham, *Lost City*, 160.

149   "were not mortars": Angles Vargas, *Machupijchu*, 428.

149   "delinquents": Guaman Poma, pt. 1, Bustios Gálvez edn., 1:221.
The laws and punishments are summarized by Rowe, "Inca Culture at the Time of the Spanish Conquest," 271–272, and by S. F. Moore, *Power and Property in Inca Peru*, 165–174.

149   "obtain confession": Guaman Poma, Ibid., 222.

149   "until they died": Cobo, bk. 1, ch. 26, Pardo edn., 3:272.

152   "to the departed": Bingham, *Lost City*, 159.

11. Vitcos and the Inca Trail

155–56   "sun temple" "nose" "expired": Antonio de la Calancha, *Corónica moralizada del orden de San Agustín en el Perú* (Barcelona, 1630), bk. 4, ch. 5, 806, 812–13.

156   "vicinity": Bingham, *Lost City*, New York, 1948, ch. 5.

158   "alluvial fan": Bingham, "Along the uncharted Pampaconas," *Harper's Magazine*, August 1914, 461.

170   "Machu Picchu": Peter Frost, *Machu Picchu: Historical Sanctuary, Cusco, Peru* (Lima, 1995), 41; *Exploring Cusco* (5th edn., Lima: Nuevas Imágenes, 1999), 157.

12. Choquequirao

173   "mountain world": Vincent Lee, *Inca Choqek'iraw* (Wilson, WY, 1997), 10.

174   "recognized": Cosmé Bueno, *Descripción del obispado del Cuzco* (Lima, 1768).

174   "asylum": Léonce Angrand's notes, in Ernest Desjardins, *Le Pérou avant la conquête espagnole* (Paris, 1858), 137–145; also in Carlos Milla Batres (ed.), *Imagen del Perú en el siglo XIX* (Lima, 1972). The Vicomte de Sartiges wrote as M. E(ugène) de Lavandais, "Voyage dans les républiques de l'Amérique du Sud," *Revue des Deux Mondes*, Paris, (June 10, 1851): 1019–1041

175   "heard of Choqquequirau": Bingham, "The ruins of Choquequirau," AA 12 (1910):505–525.

13. Saihuite

177   "gave true answers": Molina (of Cuzco), *Relación de los fábulos y ritos de los Incas*, ed. Morales, 30–31.

177   "through the stone": Pablo José de Arriaga, *Extirpación de la idolatria del Pirú*, ch. 3, BAE (CONT.) 209:205.

177   "an inch or two thick": Sancho, *Relación*, CLDRHP, 1 ser., 5:157; Santillán, *Relación*, BAE (CONT.) 209:111. Cieza de León also mentioned this oracle of Apurímac and said that a quantity of gold was found near it (*Crónica*, pt. 2, ch. 28, ed. Aranibar, 98, or Onis–von Hagen edn., 152).

177   "whom she had served": P. Pizarro, *Relación*, BAE (CONT.) 168:190–191.

177   "efflorescence": César Paternosto, *The Stone and the Thread*, 60.

179   "synthesis": Wiener, *Pérou et Bolivie*, 289. See also Squier, *Peru*, 555.

14. Tarahuasi

191   "groups of four": Ruiz de Arce, *Relación de servicios*, BRAH 102:367.

191   "with greater fury": Sancho, *Relación*, CLDRHP, 1 ser., 5:159.

191   "sport with you!": Trujillo, *Relación*, 62.

192   "a common Indian": Molina (el Almagrista), *Relación*, 156.

192   "you burned alive!": Sancho, *Relación*, 164.

15. Vilcashuamán

193   "river in Chile": Vázquez de Espinosa, *Compendio*, bk. 4, ch. 70, para. 1476, BAE (CONT.) 231:365; or Clark trans., 546. Cieza de León also noted this central location (*Crónica*, pt. 1, ch. 89, Onis–von Hagen edn., 126). See also Pedro de Ribera and Antonio de Chaves, *Relación de la ciudad de Guamanga y sus terminus* (1586), RGI, in BAE (CONT.) 183:181.

193   "all of cut stone": Pedro de Carvajal, *Descripción fecha de la provincia de Vilcas Guaman…* (1586), RGI, in BAE (CONT.) 183:218. Cieza wrote that Vilcas had a population of 40,000 (pt. 1, ch. 89, Onis–von Hagen edn., 126), and there is confirmation of this figure in earlier royal decrees: "Ordenanza para el tratamiento de indios," Valladolid, November 1536, in Richard Konetzke (ed.), *Colección de documentos para la historia de la formación social de Hispano-América*, 1 (Madrid, 1953):180–181; and a royal instruction to Bishop Tomás de Berlanga, 1535, in Angel de Altolaguirre (ed.), *Colección de Documentos Inéditos Relativos al Descubrimiento, Conquista y Organización de las Antiguas Posesiones Españoles de Ultramar*, 10 (Madrid, 1897):466–467.

193   "in the building": Cieza, pt. 2, ch. 48, Aranibar edn., 159.

193   "vows faithfully": Ibid., pt. 1, ch. 89, Onis–von Hagen edn., 127. Vázquez de Espinosa, who preached in churches near here in the early seventeenth century, also mentioned the two staircases of thirty steps each. The district of Vilcashuamán had also been described in 1586 in a report by Luis Monzó, Pedro González, and Juan de Arbe, *Descripción de la tierra del repartimiento de San Francisco de Atunrucana y Laramati…*, RGI, in BAE (CONT.) 183.

193   "temple and buried": Cieza, 127.

193   "they already had": Carvajal, 218.

193   "birds": Cieza, pt. 2, ch. 64, Aranibar (ed.), 215.

193   "is founded here": Pedro de Carvajal, *Descripción fecha de la provincia de Vilcas Guaman…* (1586).

193   "judge what it was": Cieza, 127. Angrand left his valuable sketchbooks to the Bibliothèque Nationale, but some of his notes are in Ernest Desjardins, *Le Pérou avant la conquête espagnole* (Paris, 1858). His drawing of Vilcas is reproduced in Gasparini and Margolies, *Arquitectura Inka*, 121, and in Angrand, *Imagen del Perú en el siglo XIX* (Lima, 1972), 261–262. Wiener also made a good plan of the terraces (*Pérou et Bolivie*, 265).

194   "for this purpose": Carvajal, 218. There is another stepped ushnu at Curamba, between Andahuaylas and Abancay, which was also sketched by Angrand in 1847 (*Imagen del Perú*, 263).

194   "by Spaniards": Cieza, pt. 1, ch. 89.

195   "canopy": Carvajal, 218–219.

196   "forty gatekeepers": Cieza, pt. 1, ch. 89, Onis–von Hagen edn., 127.

196 "Then they withdrew": Trujillo, *Relación*, 60–61.

197 "Indian warriors": Ruiz de Arce, *Relación de servicios*, 366.

197 "mount the usnu": Guaman Poma, *Nueva corónica*, quoted in R. Levillier, *Don Francisco de Toledo, supremo organizador del Perú: su vida, su obra (1515–82)*, 1 (Madrid, 1935):440, loosely translated by Dilke in *Letter to a King*, 125. Viceroy Toledo held an inquiry into native taxation and the legitimacy of Inca rule, at Vilcas Tambo in 1571. The respondents confirmed that their region had been conquered by Topa Inca Yupanqui.

197 "them have died": Carvajal, 205.

16. Temple of Viracocha, Raqchi

201 "without sinking": Sarmiento de Gamboa, ch. 7, Markham trans., 36; Sarmiento de Gamboa, *Historia indica*, ch. 7, Markham trans., 35. Sarmiento wrote that Viracocha means "sea foam," and other chroniclers repeated his definition. Cieza had said that this was wrong, and that the Spaniards were called Viracocha because of the three envoys who reached Cuzco to loot Coricancha for Atahualpa's ransom: the inhabitants of Cuzco had been praying to Viracocha for deliverance from Atahualpa's army, so that the curious strangers were taken to be messengers from the god. Two words of the Inca god's titles recently achieved fame as the name of Thor Heyerdahl's raft Kon Tiki.

201 "of the World'": Betanzos, *Suma*, ch. 2, BAE (CONT.) 209:11, Hamilton-Buchanan trans., 10.

201 "with buttons": Cieza de León, *Crónica*, pt. 2, ch. 5, Araníbar edn., 9.

201 "all the land": Betanzos, pt. 1, ch. 45, Hamilton-Buchanan trans., 175.

203 Solution to the thrust problem: Gasparini and Margolies, *Arquitectura Inka*, 254–255.

204 "apparition": Garcilaso, bk. 5, ch. 22, BAE (CONT.) 133:179–180; or Livermore trans., 1:290–291. See also Gasparini and Margolies, 249–263; Squier, *Peru*, 403–414; Bingham, *Inca Land*, 129; Moorehead, "Highland Inca Architecture in Adobe," 86–89.

204 "building remain": Garcilaso, bk. 5, ch. 22, BAE (CONT.) 133:180–181.

17. Huánuco

207 "seasons of the year": Estete, quoted in Jerez, *Verdadero relación*, BAE (CONT.) 26:342; or in Oviedo, *Historia general*, bk. 49, ch. 12, BAE (CONT.) 121:76. The remark about Huánuco's gold is in ibid., ch. 9, 61.

207 "danger": Agustín de Zárate, *Historia del descubrimiento y conquista del Perú*, bk. 4, ch. 1, BAE (CONT.) 26:493.

207 "later depopulated": D. de Córdova Salinas, *Crónica franciscana de las provincias del Perú* (1651), bk. 1, ch. 15, Gómez Canedo edn., Washington, DC, 1957.

207 "much mischief" "great difficulty": Cieza de León, *Crónica*, pt. 4 (*La guerra de Chupas*), ch. 82, Markham trans., 293.

207 "prayed for peace": Ibid., ch. 17, 50.

209 "can still see": Ibid., pt. 2, ch. 57, Araníbar edn., 188.

209 "Indians to serve it": Ibid., pt. 1, ch. 80, Onis–von Hagen edn., 109. The figure of 30,000 for Huánuco's population was repeated by J. López de Velasco, *Geografía...*, BAE (CONT.) 248:240, by A. Vázquez de Espinosa, *Compendio*, bk. 4, ch. 51, para. 1361,

BAE (CONT.) 231:329; and by Garcilaso, pt. 1, bk. 5, ch. 4, Livermore trans., 1:484. This was perhaps the population of the surrounding district, because the surviving ruins do not look as though they could have housed so large a population.

209 "four thousand men": Vázquez de Espinosa, *Compendio*, bk. 4, ch. 51, para. 1361, BAE (CONT.) 231:929, or Clark trans., 486.

209 "stables for cattle": Ibid. The notion of herds in the plaza: E. Harth-Terré, "El pueblo de Huánuco Viejo," 4–5.

209 "administered justice": Íñigo Ortiz de Zúñiga, *Visita...a Huánuco*, in *Revista del Archivo Nacional* (1956), 43, 301. See also D. Shea, "El conjunto arquitectónico central en la plaza de Huánuco Viejo," CIAH 1:109–111; J. V. Murra and G. J. Hadden, "Informe presentado al Patronato Nacional de Arqueología...," CIAH 1:131–133.

209 "an erected stone": Diego González Holguín, *Vocabulario de la lengua general...llamada lengua qqechua* (1608) (Lima, 1952), 358.

212 "vestal virgins": Cieza de León, pt. 1, ch. 80, Onis–von Hagen edn., 109.

212 "whom he chose": Declaration by Chief Diego Xauxa, in Ortiz de Zúñiga, Murra edn., 1:37.

212 "pottery vessels": Ibid.

212 "other celebrations": Cieza de León, pt. 2, ch. 30, Onis–von Hagen edn., 183.

212 "by their forebears": Cieza de León, pt. 2, ch. 30, ed. Araníbar, 103–104; or Onis–von Hagen edn., 181–183.

212 "at their expense": Ibid., ch. 29, ed. Araníbar, 101; or Onis–von Hagen edn., 191.

212 "prepared it": Garcilaso, *Comentarios reales*, pt. 1, bk. 6, ch. 20, BAE (CONT.) 133:219–220; or Livermore trans., 1:357–358.

214 "no one forced them": Declaration by Chief Diego Xauxa, in Ortiz de Zúñiga, Murra edn., 1:4.

214 Morris on provincial cities: *Establecimientos estatales en el Tawantinsuyu* (Spanish trans. of his "State Settlements in Tawantinsuyu"), 127–141.

18. Ingapirca

218 "very strong tower": Gaspar de Gallegos, *Relación de...Sant Francisco Pueleusi del Azogue* (1582), RGI in BAE (CONT.) 184:175.

218 "great they were": Cieza de León, *Crónica*, pt. 1, ch. 44, Onis–von Hagen edn., 69–70, 73.

218 "spirited in war": Hernando Pablos, *Relación...de Cuenca*, RGI in BAE (CONT.) 184:267.

218 "among the natives": Ibid. Cieza de León tells about the news of Pizarro's arrival (pt. 1, ch. 64, Onis–von Hagen edn., 72–73).

218 "it was general": Cieza de León, pt. 2, ch. 69, 231. The epidemic was also reported by M. de Murúa, *Historia*, ed. Ballesteros Gaibrois, 1:103–104; Cabello de Balboa, *Miscelánea austral*, pt. 3, CLDRHP 2 ser., 2:128; Sarmiento de Gamboa, *Historia indica*, ch. 62, Markham trans., 167–168; Cobo, *Historia del Nuevo Mundo*, bk. 13, ch. 17, BAE (CONT.) 92:93; and others.

Bibliography

THE YEAR A WORK WAS completed is given in parentheses after its title if it was not published at the time. Abbreviations are listed on page 221.

Early Works

Acosta, José de, *Historia natural y moral de las Indias*, Seville, 1590; BAE (CONT.) 73 (1954). Trans. C. R. Markham, HAKL. SOC., 1 ser., 60–61 (1880).

Anon., *Relación de las cosas del Perú desde 1543 hasta la muerte de Gonzalo Pizarro* (ca. 1550; attributed to Juan Polo de Ondegardo, Rodrigo Lozano, or Agustín de Zárate); BAE (CONT.) 168 (1965):243–332.

Anon., *Relación del sitio del Cuzco y principio de las guerras civiles del Perú hasta la muerte de Diego de Almagro* (1539, often attributed to Vicente de Valverde, but more probably by Diego de Silva); CLDRHP, 2 ser., 10 (1934).

Arriaga, Pablo José de, *Extirpación de la idolatría en el Perú* (Lima, 1621); BAE (CONT.) 209 (1968): 191–277. Trans. L. Clark Keating, *The Extirpation of Idolatry in Peru*, Lexington (KY): University Press of Kentucky, 1968.

Betanzos, Juan de, *Suma y narración de los Incas* (1551); CLDRHP, 2 ser., 8 (1924); BAE (CONT.) 209 (1968):1–55. Trans. Roland Hamilton and Dana Buchanan, *Narrative of the Incas*, Austin (TX): University of Texas Press, 1996.

Cabello de Balboa, Miguel, *Miscelánea Antártica*, pt. 3: *Historia del Perú* (1586); CLDRHP, 2 ser., 2 (1920).

Calancha, Antonio de la, *Corónica moralizada del orden de San Agustín en el Perú*, Barcelona, 1638; Lima: Universidad Nacional Mayor de San Marcos, 1978.

Cieza de León, Pedro de, *Parte primera de la crónica del Perú*, Seville, 1553. Many Spanish editions. Trans. C. R. Markham, *The Travels of Pedro de Cieza de León*, HAKL. SOC., 1 ser., 33 (1864).

—*Segunda parte de la crónica del Perú, que trata del señorío de los Incas Yupanquis* (1554); ed. Carlos Araníbar, Lima, 1967. Many other editions. Trans. C. R. Markham, HAKL. SOC., 1 ser., 68 (1883).

—*The Incas of Pedro de Cieza de León* (combination of parts 1 and 2), trans. Harriet de Onis, ed. Victor W. von Hagen, Norman (OK): University of Oklahoma Press, 1959; also trans. Alexandra Parma Cook and Noble David Cook, *The Discovery and Conquest of Peru*, Durham (NC) and London: Duke University Press, 1998.

—*Tercera parte: Descubrimiento y conquista* (ca. 1554); ed. Rafael Loredo, in *Mercurio Peruano*, 27 (1946), 32 (1951), 34 (1953), 36–39 (1955–58).

—*La crónica del Perú*, pt. 4: *La guerra de Las Salinas, La guerra de Chupas, La guerra de Quito*. Many Spanish editions. Trans. C. R. Markham, *The War of Las Salinas*, HAKL. SOC., 2 ser., 54 (1923); *The War of Chupas*, HAKL. SOC., 2 ser., 42 (1918); *The War of Quito*, HAKL. SOC., 2 ser., 31 (1915).

Cobo, Bernabé, *Historia del Nuevo Mundo* (1653); ed. Luis A. Pardo, 4 vols., Cuzco, 1956; BAE (CONT.) 91–92 (1956). Trans. Roland Hamilton, *History of the Inca Empire* and *Inca Religion and Customs*, Austin and London: University of Texas Press, 1979, reprinted 1990.

Cuzco, *Actos de los libros de cabildos del Cuzco, años 1545 a 1548*, in *Revista del Archivo Histórico del Cuzco*, vol. 9, no. 9 (1958):5–13, 37–305.

—*Acta de la fundación del Cuzco* (March 23, 1534), in R. Porras Barrenechea, "Dos documentos esenciales sobre Francisco Pizarro y la conquista del Perú...el acta perdida de la fundación del Cuzco," RH 17 (1948):88–95; CDIHE 26:221–232.

Diez de San Miguel, Garci, *Visita hecha a la provincia de Chucuito en el año 1567*; ed. Waldemar Espinoza Soriano, Lima, 1964.

Estete, Miguel de, *Narrative of a Journey to Pachacamac*, in Francisco de Jerez (or Xerez), *Verdadera relación de la conquista del Perú* (Seville, 1534), BAE (CONT.) 26 (1947):338–343. Trans. C. R. Markham, *Reports on the Discovery of Peru*, HAKL. SOC., 1 ser., 47 (1872):74–94.

Garcilaso de la Vega ("El Inca"), *Primera parte de los comentarios reales de los Incas* (Lisbon, 1609); *Segunda parte de los comentarios reales de los Incas: Historia general del Perú* (Córdoba, 1617); BAE (CONT.) 134–135 (1960). Part 1, trans. C. R. Markham, HAKL. SOC. 41 (1869), 45 (1871). Both parts, trans. Harold V. Livermore, *Royal Commentaries of the Incas and General History of Peru*, 2 vols., London and Austin: University of Texas Press, 1966.

Guaman Poma de Ayala, Felipe, *Nueva corónica y buen gobierno* (?1580–1620); ed. L. F. Bustios Gálvez, 3 vols., Lima, 1956–66. Partly trans. Christopher Dilke, *Letter to a King*, London: Allen and Unwin, 1978; also trans. Jorge I. Urioste, ed. John V. Murra and Rolena Adorno, 3 vols., Mexico City: Siglo Veintiuno, 1980.

Gutiérrez de Santa Clara, Pedro, *Historia de las guerras civiles del Perú y de otros sucesos de las Indias* (ca. 1600); BAE (CONT.) 165–167 (1963–64).

Herrera y Tordesillas, Antonio de, *Historia general de los hechos de los Castellanos en las islas i tierrafirme del Mar Océano* (4 vols., Madrid, 1601–15); ed. Antonio Ballesteros and Miguel Gómez del Campillo, 17 vols., Madrid, 1934–56.

Jerez (or Xerez), Francisco de, *Verdadera relación de la conquista del Perú* (Seville, 1534); BAE (CONT.) 26 (1947):320–346. Trans. C. R. Markham, *Reports on the Discovery of Peru*, HAKL. SOC., 1 ser., 47 (1872):1–109.

Lizárraga, Reginaldo de, *Descripción breve de toda la tierra del Perú, Tucumán, Río de la Plata, y Chile* (ca. 1605); BAE (CONT.) 216 (1968):1–213.

López de Velasco, Juan, *Geografía y descripción universal de las Indias* (1571–74); ed. Justo Zaragoza, Madrid, 1894; BAE (CONT.) 248 (1971).

Mena, Cristóbal de, *La conquista del Perú, llamada la Nueva Castilla* (Seville, 1534); ed. R. Porras Barrenechea, in *Las relaciones primitivas de la conquista del Perú* (Lima, 1967), 79–101. Trans. Joseph H. Sinclair, *The Conquest of Peru, as recorded by a member of the Pizarro expedition* (New York, 1929).

Molina, Cristóbal de (el Almagrista), *Relación de muchas cosas acaesidas en el Perú...en la conquista y población destos reinos* (ca. 1553); CLDRHP, 1 ser., 1 (1916):111–190; BAE (CONT.) 209 (1968): 56–96.

Molina, Cristóbal de (of Cuzco), *Relación de las fábulas y ritos de los Incas* (1573); CLDRHP, 1 ser., 1 (1916):1–103. Trans. C. R. Markham, *The Fables and Rites of the Incas*, HAKL. SOC., 2 ser., 48 (1873).

Montesinos, Fernando de, *Memorias antiguas historiales y políticas del Perú* (1630); CLERC 16 (1882). Trans. P. A. Means, HAKL. SOC., 2 ser., 48 (1920).

Murúa, Martín de, *Historia general del Perú, origen y descendencia de los Incas* (1590–1611); ed. Manuel Ballesteros Gaibrois, 2 vols., Madrid, 1962, 1964 (Wellington Ms.); CLDRHP, 2 ser., 4, 5 (1922, 1925); ed. Constantino Bayle, 2 vols., Madrid, 1946 (Loyola Ms.).

Ortiz de Zúñiga, Íñigo, *Visita a la provincia de León de Huánuco en 1562*; ed. John V. Murra, 2 vols., Huánuco, Peru, 1967.

Oviedo y Valdés, Gonzalo Fernández de, *La historia general y natural de las Indias* (Seville, 1535; including section on Peru, Salamanca, 1547), Valladolid, 1557; ed. Juan Pérez de Tudela Bueso, BAE (CONT.) 117–121 (1959).

Pizarro, Hernando, "Letter to the Oidores of Santo Domingo" (Panama, November 23, 1533), in Gonzalo Fernández de Oviedo y Valdés, *La historia general y natural de las Indias*, bk. 46, ch. 10, BAE (CONT.) 121 (1959):84–90. Trans. C. R. Markham, in *Reports on the Discovery of Peru*, HAKL. SOC., 47 (1872):113–127.

Pizarro, Pedro, *Relación del descubrimiento y conquista de los reinos del Perú* (1571); BAE (CONT.) 168 (1965):159–242. Trans. P. A. Means as *Relation of the Discovery and Conquest of the Kingdoms of Peru*, New York: Cortes Society, 1921.

Poma de Ayala, see Guaman Poma de Ayala.

Ramos Gavilán, Alonso, *Historia del célebre santuário de Nuestra Señora de Copacabana*, Lima, 1621.

Ruiz de Arce, Juan, *Relación de servicios. Advertencias que hizo el fundador del vinculo y mayorazgo a los sucesores en él* (ca. 1545); BRAH 102 (1933):327–384.

Sancho, Pedro, *Testimonio de la acta de repartición del rescate de Atahualpa* (1533). Trans. C. R. Markham, HAKL. SOC., 1 ser., 97 (1872):131–143.

—*Relación para S.M. da lo sucedido en la conquista y pacificación de estas provincias de la Nueva Castilla y de la calidad de la tierra* (1543); CLDRHP, 1 ser., 5 (1917):122–202. Trans. P. A. Means, New York: Cortes Society, 1917. (The original Ms. is lost but was translated in Giambattista Ramusio, *Delle navigationi e viaggi*, 3 (1559), from which subsequent texts are derived.)

Santacruz Pachacuti Yamqui, Joan de, *Relación de antigüedades deste reyno del Perú* (ca. 1615); ed. M. Jiménez de la Espada, in *Tres relaciones de antigüedades peruanas* (Madrid, 1879); CLDRHP, 2 ser., 9 (1927); BAE (CONT.) 209 (1968):279–319. Trans. C. R. Markham, HAKL. SOC., 1 ser., 48 (1873):67–120.

Santillán, Hernando de, *Relación del origen, descendencia, política y gobierno de los Incas* (ca. 1563); ed. M. Jiménez de la Espada, in *Tres relaciones de antigüedades peruanas* (Madrid, 1879), 1–133; CLDRHP, 2 ser., 9 (1927):1–117; BAE (CONT.) 209 (1968):97–150.

Sarmiento de Gamboa, Pedro, *Historia indica* (1572); BAE (CONT.) 135 (1960):189–279. Trans. C. R. Markham, *History of the Incas*, HAKL. SOC., 2 ser., 22 (1907); also trans., Mineola (NY): Dover, 1999.

Titu Cusi Yupanqui (Inca Diego de Castro), *Relación de la conquista del Perú y hechos del Inca Manco II; Instrucción para el muy Ille. Señor Ldo. Lope Garcia de Castro, Gouernador que fue destos rreynos del Pirú* (1571); CLDRHP, 1 ser., 2 (1916). Trans. as *Titu Cusi: A 16th-Century Account of the Conquest*, Cambridge (MA): Harvard University, David Rockefeller Center for Latin American Studies, 2006.

Trujillo, Diego de, *Relación del descubrimiento del reyno del Perú* (1571); ed. R. Porras Barrenechea, Seville: Escuela de Estudios Hispano-Americanos de Sevilla, 1948.

Vázquez de Espinosa, Antonio, *Compendio y descripción de las Indias Occidentales* (1628); BAE (CONT.) 231 (1969). Trans. Charles Upson Clark, Washington, DC: Smithsonian Collections, vol. 102, no. 2646 (1942).

Zárate, Agustín de, *Historia del descubrimiento y conquista del Perú* (Antwerp, 1555; Seville, 1577); BAE (CONT.) 26 (1947):459–574. Trans. J. M. Cohen, *The Discovery and Conquest of Peru*, Harmondsworth (Middx.): Penguin, 1968.

Modern Works

Agurto Calvo, Santiago, *Cuzco: la traza urbana de la ciudad Inca*, UNESCO, Peru 39 Project, Cuzco, 1980.

—*Estudios acerca de la construcción, arquitectura y planeamiento incas*, Lima: Cámara Peruana de la Construcción, 1987.

Alcina Franch, José, "Excavaciones en Chinchero (Cuzco): Informe preliminar," XXXVIII Internationalen Amerikanistenkongress (Stuttgart, 1968), *Verhandlungen I* (Munich, 1969):421–428.

—"Excavaciones en Chinchero (Cuzco): Temporadas 1968 y 1969," *Revista Española de Antropología Americana*, Madrid, 5 (1970):99–121.

—"El sistema urbanistico de Chinchero," RMN 37 (1971):124–134.

—and Manuel Ballesteros Gaibrois, *La arqueología en Chinchero*, Madrid, 1976.

Angles Vargas, Victor, *P'isaq, metrópoli Inka*, Lima, 1970.

—*Machupijchu, enigmática ciudad inka*, Lima, 1972.

—*Historia del Cusco*, Lima, 1978.

Angrand, Léonce, notes on Choquequirao, in Ernest Desjardins, *Le Pérou avant la conquête espagnole* (Paris, 1858), 137–145.

—*Imagen del Perú en el siglo XIX*, Lima: Editor Carlos Milla Batres, 1972.

Ballesteros Gaibrois, Manuel, *Sencilla historia de Chinchero*, Cuzco, 1971.

Bandelier, Adolph Francis, *The Islands of Titicaca and Koati*, New York: De Vinne Press, 1910.

Barreda Murillo, Luis, *Cuzco, Historia y Arqueología*, Cuzco: Instituto de Arqueología Machupiqchu, 1994.

Bauer, Brian S., *The Sacred Landscape of the Inca: the Cusco Ceque System*, Austin: University of Texas Press, 1998.

—*Ancient Cuzco: Heartland of the Inca*, Austin: University of Texas Press, 2004.

—and Charles Stanish, *Ritual and Pilgrimage in the Ancient Andes: the Islands of the Sun and the Moon*, Austin: University of Texas Press, 2001.

Bedoya Maruri, Ángel Nicanor, *La arqueología en la región interandino del Ecuador. Puebla*, Mexico: Editorial José M. Cajica Jr., 1974.

Béjar Navarro, Raymundo, *Arquitectura inka: el Templo del Sol o Corikanka*, Cuzco: Consejo Nacional de Ciencia y Tecnología, 1990.

Bingham, Alfred, *Portrait of an Explorer: Hiram Bingham, Discoverer of Machu Picchu*, Ames (IA): Iowa State University Press, 1989.

Bingham, Hiram, "The Ruins of Choqquequirau," AA vol. 12, no. 4 (October 1910): 505–525.

—"Vitcos, the Last Inca Capital," *Proceedings of the American Antiquarian Society*, Worcester (MA), April 1912, 135–196.

—"The discovery of Machu Picchu," *Harper's Monthly*, vol. 127, April 1913, 709–19; reproduced in Richard L. Burger and Lucy C. Salazar (eds.), *Machu Picchu, Unveiling the Mystery of the Incas*, New Haven (CT) and London: Yale University Press, 2004, 7–18.

—"In the Wonderland of Peru," "The story of Machu Picchu," "Further explorations in the Land of the Incas," *National Geographic Magazine*, April 1913, 387–573; February 1915, 172–217; May 1916, 431–473.

—*Inca Land: Explorations in the Highlands of Peru*, Boston (MA): Houghton Mifflin, 1922.

—*Machu Picchu: A Citadel of the Incas*, Yale University, Memoirs of the National Geographic Society, New Haven: Yale University Press, 1930.

—*Lost City of the Incas: The Story of Machu Picchu and its Builders*, London, 1951. Recent editions include: with an introduction by Hugh Thomson, London: Weidenfeld & Nicolson, 2002; with an introduction by John Hemming, London: The Folio Society, 2004.

Burger, Richard L., and Lucy C. Salazar (eds.), *The 1912 Yale Peruvian Scientific Expedition Collections from Machu Picchu*, New Haven: Yale University Press, 2003.

—*Machu Picchu: Unveiling the Mystery of the Incas*, New Haven and London: Yale University Press, 2004.

Buse de la Guerra, Hermann, *Machu Picchu. Antología*, Lima, 1963.

Busto Duthurburu, José Antonio del, *Perú incaico*, Lima: Libreria Studium, 1980.

Chávez Ballón, Manuel, "El sitio de Raqchi en San Pedro de Cacha," *Revista Peruana de Cultura*, Lima, 1963, 105–111.

—"Ciudades Incas: Cuzco, capital del imperio," *Wayka*, Cuzco, 3 (1970):1–14.

Cornejo Bouroncle, Jorge, "Huakaypata, la Plaza Mayor del viejo Cuzco," RU vol. 35, nos. 90–91 (1946):85–116.

Covey, R. Alan, *How the Incas Built their Heartland: State Formation and the Innovation of Imperial Strategies in the Sacred Valley, Peru*, Ann Arbor (MI): University of Michigan Press, 2006.

Dean, Carolyn, "Creating a ruin in colonial Cusco: Sacsahuaman and what was made of it," *Andean Past*, 5 (1998):161–83.

—"The Inka married the earth: integrated outcrops and the making of place," *The Art Bulletin*, September 2007.

Dearborn, David S. P., Matthew T. Seddon, and Brian S. Bauer, "The sanctuary of Titicaca: where the Sun returns to Earth," *Latin American Antiquity*, vol. 9, no. 3 (1998):240–258.

Donkin, Robin A., *Agricultural Terracing in the Aboriginal New World*, Viking Fund Publications in Anthropology, 56, Tucson (AZ): University of Arizona Press, 1979.

Duffait, Erwan, "Choquequirao en el siglo XVI: etnohistoria e implicaciones arqueológicas," *Bulletin de l'Institut Français d'Études Andines*, vol. 34, no. 2 (2005):185–196.

Enock, C. Reginald, "The Ruins of Huánuco Viejo or Old Huánuco," *Geographical Journal*, London, 26 (1905):153–179; also in *Boletín de la Sociedad Geográfica de Lima*, 3 (1904): 317–324.

—*The Andes and the Amazon: Life and Travel in Peru*, London, 1913.

Fejos, Paul, *Archaeological Explorations in the Cordillera Vilcabamba, Southeastern Peru*, Viking Fund Publications in Anthropology, 3, New York, 1944.

Flores Espinoza, Javier, and Rafael Varón Gabai (eds.), *El Hombre y los Andes. Homenaje a Franklin Pease G.Y.*, 2 vols., Lima: Fondo Editorial de la Pontificia Universidad Católica del Perú, 2002.

Flores Ochoa, Jorge A., Elizabeth Kuon Arce, Roberto Samanez Argumedo, Luis Federico Barreda Murillo, and Catherine Julien, *Cuzco, del Mito a la Historia*, Lima: Banco de Crédito, 2007.

Franco Inojosa, José María, and Alejandro Gonzales, "Los trabajos arqueológicos en el Departamento del Cusco. Informe,…sobre, las ruinas incaicas de Tarawasi (Limatambo)," RMN 6 (1937):66–80.

—and Luis A. Llanos. "Trabajos arqueológicos en el Departamento del Cusco. Sajsawaman: excavación en el edificio sur de Muyumarca," RMN vol. 9, no. 1 (1940):22–32.

Frost, Peter, *Exploring Cuzco*, Lima, 1979.

—*Machu Picchu Historical Sanctuary, Cusco, Peru*, Lima: Nuevas Imágenes, 1995.

García Rosell, César, *Los monumentos arqueológicos del Perú*, Lima, 1942.

Gasparini, Graziano, and Luise Margolies, *Arquitectura Inka*, Caracas, 1977. Trans. Patricia Lyon, *Inca Architecture*, Bloomington (IN): Indiana University Press, 1980.

Gibaja, Arminda, and Roberto Samanez, "Ollantaytambo, Cuzco, Perú," *Revista Architectura Panamericana de Asociaciones de Arquitectos (Ciudades de América, 1)*, Santiago de Chile: Ministerio de Vivienda y Urbanismo, 1992.

González, Elena, and Rafael León (eds.), *Machu Picchu. Santuario Histórico/Historical Sanctuary*, Lima: Integra AFP, 2001.

González Carré, Enrique, Jorge Cosmópolis, and Jorge Lévano, *La ciudad inca de Vilcashuamán*, Ayacucho: Universidad Nacional de San Cristóbal de Huamanga, 1981.

Guillén, Victor M, "El gran templo de Huiraccocha," RU 2 (1937):82–97.

Gutiérrez, Miguel F., "Monolitos y petroglitos de Say-hui-te antes de Concacha," RIAC 4, nos. 6–7 (1939):91–96.

Hagen, Victor Wolfgang von, *A Guide to Ollantaytambo*, New York, 1949; Lima, 1958.

—*Highway of the Sun*, New York and Boston, 1955; London, 1956.

—*The Royal Road of the Inca*, London: Gordon and Cremonesi, 1976.

—ed., *The Incas of Pedro de Cieza de León*, trans. Harriet de Onis, Norman: University of Oklahoma Press, 1959.

Hardoy, Jorge Enrique, *Ciudades precolombinas*, Buenos Aires, 1964.

—*Urban Planning in Pre-Columbian America*, London: Studio Vista, 1968.

Harth-Terré, Emilio, "Incahuasi—ruinas incaicas del valle de Lunahuana," RMN 2 (1933): 99–125.

—"Fundación de la ciudad incaica," *Revista histórica*, Lima, 16 (1943):11–123.

—"El pueblo de Huánuco Viejo," *Arquitecto Peruano*, Lima, 320–321 (1964):1–20.

—"Técnica y arte de la cantería incaica," *Revista Universitaria*, Cuzco, 51–52 (nos. 122–3 and 124–5) (1965):152–168.

Hemming, John Henry, *The Conquest of the Incas*, London: Macmillan; New York: Harcourt, Brace, Jovanovich, 1970; revised 1993, London: Papermac and later editions by Pan.

—*Machu Picchu*, New York, 1981; revised, London: Papermac, 1993.

—and Edward Ranney, *Monuments of the Incas*, Boston: New York Graphic Society, 1982; revised, Albuquerque: University of New Mexico Press, 1990.

Horkheimer, Hans, "Guía bibliográfica de los principales sitios arqueológicos del Perú," *Boletín Bibliográfico de la Biblioteca Central de la Universidad Nacional Mayor de San Marcos*, Lima, 20, nos. 3–4 (1950):181–234.

Hyslop, John, *The Inka Road System*, New York and San Francisco: Academic Press, 1984.

—*Inka Settlement Planning*, Austin: University of Texas Press, 1990.

Julien, Catherine, *Reading Inca History*, Iowa City: University of Iowa Press, 2000.

—"Inca estates and the encomienda: Hernando Pizarro's holdings in Cusco," *Andean Past*, 6 (2001):229–275.

Kalafatovich Valle, Carlos, "Geología del grupo arqueológico de la fortaleza de Saccsayhuaman y sus vecinidades," *Saqsaywaman. Revista del Patronato Departamental de Arqueología del Cuzco*, 1 (July 1970):61–68.

—"Geología de la ciudadela incaica de Machupicchu y sus alrededores," RU 1963.

Kauffmann Doig, Federico, *Arqueología peruana*, Lima, 1971.

—*Machu Picchu, tesoro inca*, Lima: Editora Cartolan, 2005.

Kendall, Ann, *Everyday Life of the Incas*, London and New York: B. T. Batsford Ltd. and G. P. Putnam's Sons, 1973.

—"Aspects of Inca Architecture," 2 vols., doctoral dissertation, University of London, 1974.

—"Architecture and Planning at the Inca Sites in the Cusichaca Area," Baessler-Archiv, Neue Folge, Berlin, 22 (1974):73–137.

Kosok, Paul, *Life, Land and Water in Ancient Peru*, New York: Long Island University Press, 1965.

—"Inca planning north of Cuzco between Anta and Machu Picchu and along the Urubamba valley," in Nicholas J. Saunders and Olivier de Montmollin (eds.), *Recent Studies in Pre-Columbian Archaeology* (Oxford: B.A.R., 1988), 457–488.

Kubler, George Alexander, *Reconstruction of Cuzco and Restoration of its Monuments*, Paris: UNESCO, 1952.

—"Machu Picchu," *Perspecta*, 6 (1960):49–54.

—*The Art and Architecture of Ancient America: The Mexican, Maya, and Andean Peoples*, Harmondsworth: Penguin, 1962.

Ladrón de Guevara Avilés, Oscar, "La restauración del Ccoricancha y templo de Santo Domingo," RIAC 21 (June 1967).

Laurencich Minelli, Laura (ed.), *The Inca World: The Development of Pre-Columbian Peru, A.D. 1000–1534*, Milan: Editoriale Jaca Book, 1999.

Lee, Vincent R., *The building of Sacsayhuaman*, Wilson (WY): Sixpac Manco Publications, 1987.

—*The lost half of Inca architecture*, Wilson: Sixpac Manco Publications, 1988.

—*A study of function, form and method in Inca architecture*, Wilson: Sixpac Manco Publications, 1988.

—*Design by numbers: Architectural order among the Incas*, Wilson, 1996.

—*Inca Choqek'iraw*, Wilson: Vincent R. Lee, 1997.

—*Forgotten Vilcabamba: Final stronghold of the Incas*, Cortez (CO): Sixpac Manco Publications, 2000.

Lehmann-Nitsche, Robert, "Coricancha, el Templo del Sol en el Cuzco y las imágenes de su altar mayor," *Revista del Museo de La Plata*, La Plata, Argentina, 31 (1928):1–260.

Llanos, Luis A., "Informe sobre Ollantaytambo," RMN 5, no. 2 (1936):123–156.

Lumbreras, Luis Guillermo, Walter H. Wust, and Renzo Uccelli, *Choqequirau: santuario histórico y ecológico*, Lima: Fundación Telefónica, 2001.

McEwan, Gordon, and Maarten van de Guchte, "Ancestral time and sacred space in Inca state ritual," in Richard F. Townsend (ed.), *The Ancient Americas: Art from Sacred Landscapes* (Chicago: Art Institute of Chicago, 1992), 359–71.

MacLean, Margaret G., *Sacred Land, Sacred Water: Inca Landscape Planning in the Cuzco Area*, doctoral thesis, University of California, Berkeley, 1986.

Martínez Martínez, Valentín, *Monografía de Ollantaytambo*, Lima, 1966.

Mason, J. Alden, *The Ancient Civilizations of Peru*, Harmondsworth: Penguin, 1957.

Matos Mendieta, Ramiro, *Pumpu. Centro administrativo Inka de la Puna de Junín*, Lima: Editorial Horizonte, 1994.

Mesa José de, and Teresa Gisbert, "La arquitectura incaica en Bolivia," *Boletín del Centro de Investigaciones Históricas y Estéticas*, Caracas, 13 (1972):129–168.

Middendorf, Ernst W., *Peru, Beobachtungen und Studien über das Land und seine Bewohner*, 3 vols., Berlin, 1893–95.

Millones, Luis, "Machu Picchu between heaven and earth," in Elena González and Rafael León (eds.), *Machu Picchu. Santuario Histórico/Historical Sanctuary* (Lima: Integra AFP, 2001), 193–255.

Moorehead, Elizabeth L., "Highland Inca Architecture in Adobe," *Ñawpa Pacha*, Berkeley, 16 (1978):65–94.

Morris, E. Craig, "El tampu real de Tunsucancha," CIAH 1 (1966):95–107.

—*Storage in Tawantinsuyu*, doctoral dissertation, University of Chicago, 1967.

—"Master Design of the Inca," *Natural History*, New York, December 1976, 60–66.

—"The Identification of Function in Inca Architecture and Ceramics," XXXIX Congreso Internacional de Americanistas (Lima), *Actas y Memorias*, 3 (1971):135–144.

—"State Settlements in Tawantinsuyu: A Strategy of Compulsory Urbanism," in M. P. Leone (ed.), *Contemporary Archaeology: A Guide to Theory and Contributions*, Carbondale (IL), 1972. Spanish trans. in RMN 39 (1973).

—and Donald E. Thompson, "Huánuco Viejo: An Inca Administrative Center," *American Antiquity*, 35, no. 3 (1970):344–362.

—and Donald Thompson, *Huánuco Pampa: An Inca City and its Hinterland*, London: Thames & Hudson, 1985.

Murra, John V., "Rite and Crop in the Inca State," in Stanley Diamond (ed.), *Culture in History: Essays in Honor of Paul Radin* (New York, 1960), 394–407.

—"Cloth and its Function in the Inca State," AA 64, no. 4 (1962):710–728.

—and G. J. Hadden, "Informe presentado al Patronato Nacional de Arqueología sobre la labor de limpieza y consolidación de Huánuco Viejo (20 de julio a 23 de noviembre 1965)," CIAH 1 (1966):129–144.

—and E. Craig Morris, "Dynastic Oral Tradition, Administrative Records and Archaeology in the Andes," *World Archaeology*, London, 7, no. 3 (February 1976):267–279.

—ed., see Ortiz de Zúñiga in "Early Works" section.

Niles, Susan A., "The provinces in the heartland: Stylistic variation and architectural innovation near Inca Cuzco," in Michael A. Malpass (ed.), *Provincial Inca: Archaeological and Ethnohistorical Assessment of the Impact of the Inca State* (Iowa City: University of Iowa Press, 1993), 146–76.

—*The Shape of Inca History: Narrative and Architecture in an Andean Empire*, Iowa City: University of Iowa Press, 1999.

—"The Nature of Inca Royal Estates," in Richard L. Burger and Lucy C. Salazar (eds.), *Machu*

Picchu: Unveiling the Mystery of the Incas (New Haven and London: Yale University Press, 2004), 49–70.

—and Robert N. Batson, "Sculpting the Yucay Valley: Power and Style in Late Inka Architecture," in Richard L. Burger, Craig Morris, and Ramiro Matos Mendieta (eds.), *Variations in the Expression of Inka Power* (Dumbarton Oaks: Harvard University Press, 2007), 185–222.

Nordenskiöld, Erland, "Incallajta, una ciudad fortaleza edificada por Tupaj Yupanki Inka," *Yoner*, Stockholm, 2 (1915).

Núñez del Prado, Oscar, "Chinchero, un pueblo andino del sur," RU 38 (1949):177–230.

Pardo, Luis A., *La metrópoli de los Incas*, Cuzco, 1932.

—*Ruinas precolombínas del Cuzco*, Cuzco, 1937.

—"Exposición de las ruinas del santuario de Huiraccocha," RIAC 2, no. 2 (1937):3–32.

—"La ciudadela de Sacsaihuaman," RIAC 2, no. 3 (1938):3–18.

—*Machupijchu, una joya arquitectónica de los Incas*, Cuzco, 1944.

—"Los grandes monolitos de Sayhuiti," RSAC 1 (1945):6–28.

—"Ollantaitampu, una ciudad megalítica," RSAC 2 (1946):43–73.

—*Historia y archeología del Cuzco*, 2 vols., Callao: Imprenta del Colegio Militar Leonico Pardo, 1957.

—*Historia y arqueología del Cuzco*, 2 vols., Cuzco, 1957.

—"La fortaleza de Saccsayhuaman," *Saqsaywaman: Revista del Patronato Departamental de Arqueología del Cuzco*, 1 (July 1970):89–157.

—and Oscar Ladrón de Guevara Avilés, "Trabajos de limpieza y consolidación, estudio e investigación," *Saqsaywaman*, 1 (July 1970):21–42.

Paternosto, César, *Piedra Abstracta: La escultura Inca, una Visión Contemporana* (Lima: Fondo de Cultura Económica, 1989). Trans. Esther Allen, *The Stone and the Thread: Andean Roots of Abstract Art*, Austin: University of Texas Press, 1996.

Porras Barrenechea, Raúl, *Antología del Cuzco*, Lima: Fundación M. J. Bustamante de la Fuente, 1992.

Protzen, Jean-Pierre, "The fortress of Saqsa Waman: was it ever finished?," *Ñawpa Pacha*, 25–27 (1987–89):155–177.

—*Inca Architecture and Construction at Ollantaytambo*, New York: Oxford University Press, 1992.

—"Inca Architecture," in Laura Laurencich Minelli (ed.), *The Inca World* (Milan: Editoriale Jaca Book, 1999), 193–218.

—and Stella Nair, "Who taught the Inca stonemasons their skills? A comparison of Tiahuanaco and Inca cut-stone masonry," *Journal of the Society of Architectural Historians*, vol. 56, no. 2 (1997):146–67.

Raimondi, Antonio, "Ruinas de Huánuco Viejo," *Boletín de la Sociedad Geográfica de Lima*, 11 (1901):397–400.

—*El Perú*, 6 vols., Lima, 1874–1913.

Regal, Alberto, *Los puentes del Inca en el antiguo Perú*, Lima, 1972.

—*Los trabajos hidráulicos del Inca en el antiguo Perú*, Lima, 1970.

Reinhard, Johan, "House of the Sun: the Inka temple of Vilcanota," *Latin American Antiquity*, vol. 6, no. 4 (1995):340–9.

—*Machu Picchu: the Sacred Center*, Lima: Nuevas Imágenes, 1991; revised as *Machu Picchu: Exploring an Ancient Sacred Center*, Los Angeles: Cotsen Institute Publications UCLA, 2007.

—"The Temple of Blindness: an investigation of the Inca shrine of Ancocagua," *Andean Past*, 5 (1998):89–108.

—*The Ice Maiden: Inca Mummies, Mountain Gods, and Sacred Sites in the Andes*, Washington, DC: National Geographic Society, 2005.

Rivero, Mariano E., and Johann Jakob von Tschudi, *Antigüedades peruanas*, 2 vols., Vienna, 1851. Trans. Francis L. Hawks, *Peruvian Antiquities*, New York, 1854.

Rostworowski de Diez Canseco, María, "Nuevos datos sobre tenencia de tierras reales en el lncario," RMN 30 (1962):130–159.

—"Dos manuscritos inéditos con datos sobre Manco II, tierras personales de los Incas y mitimaes," *Nueva Corónica*, 1 (1963):223–239.

—"Nuevos aportes para el estudio de la medición de tierras en el Virreynato e Incario," RMN 28 (1964).

—"Las tierras reales y su mano de obra en el Tahuantinsuyu," XXXVI Congreso Internacional de Americanistas, Actas, y Memorias (Seville, 1966), 31–34.

—"El repartimiento de doña Beatriz Coya en el valle de Yucay," *Historia y Cultura*, 4 (1970): 153–267.

—*Historia del Tawantinsuyu*, Lima: Instituto de Estudios Peruanos, 1988.

—*Incas* (Enciclopedia Temática del Perú, 1), Lima: Empresa Editorial El Comercio, 2006.

Rowe, John Howland, "An Introduction to the Archaeology of Cuzco," *Papers of the Peabody Museum of American Archaeology and Ethnology*, Cambridge (MA), vol. 27, no. 2 (1944).

—"Inca Culture at the Time of the Spanish Conquest," HSAI 2 (1946):183–330.

—"What Kind of Settlement Was Inca Cuzco?," *Ñawpa Pacha*, Berkeley, 5 (1967):59–76.

—"Urban Settlements in Ancient Peru," in John H. Rowe and Dorothy Menzel (eds.), *Peruvian Archaeology: Selected Readings* (Palo Alto, CA, 1967), 293–319.

—"La arqueología del Cuzco como historia cultural," *Revista del Museo e Instituto Histórico del Cuzco*, 32, year 10, nos. 16–17 (1967).

—"Machu Pijchu a la luz de documentos del siglo XVII," *Kultur*, 4, Lima, March–April 1987, 12–20; also *Histórica*, vol. 14, no. 1, Lima, 1990, 139–154.

—"Las tierras reales de los Incas," in R. Varón Gabai and J. Flores Espinoza (eds.), *Arqueología, antropología e historia en los Andes. Homenaje a María Rostworowski* (Lima, 1997), 277–287.

Rozas L., Edgar Alberto, *Cuzco, ciudad monumental y capital arqueológica de Sud América*, Cuzco, 1962.

Salazar, Lucy C., "Machu Picchu: mysterious royal estate in the cloud forest," in Richard L. Burger and Lucy C. Salazar (eds.), *Machu Picchu: Unveiling the Mystery of the Incas* (New Haven and London: Yale University Press, 2004), 21–48.

Samanez A., Roberto, and Julinho Zapata R., "El conjunto arqueológico inka de Choquequirao," *Andes. Revista de la Facultad de Ciencias Sociales*, Universidad Nacional de San Antonio Abad, Cuzco, vol. 94, no. 2, 1995.

—"El centro ceremonial inka de Choquequirao," *Arkinka. Revista de Arquitectura, Diseño y Construcción*, 46, 1999.

Sasser, Elizabeth Skidmore, *Architecture of Ancient Peru*, Lubbock (TX), 1969.

Sawyer, Alan R., "Squier's 'Palace of Ollantay' revisited," *Ñawpa Pacha*, Berkeley, 18 (1980): 63–73.

Shea, Daniel, "El conjunto arquitectónico central en la plaza de Huánuco Viejo," CIAH 1 (1966):108–116.

Squier, Ephraim George, *Peru: Incidents of Travel and Exploration in the Land of the Incas*, New York: Harper & Brothers, 1877.

Stanish, Charles, and Brian S. Bauer, "Pilgrimage and the Geography of Power in the Inka Empire," in Richard L. Burger, Craig Morris, and Ramiro Matos Mendieta (eds.), *Variations in the Expression of Inka Power* (Dumbarton Oaks: Harvard, 2007), 45–83.

Thompson, Donald E., "Incaic installations at Huánuco and Pumpu," XXXVII Congreso Internacional de Americanistas (Buenos Aires), *Actas y Memorias*, 1 (1968).

—"An Archaeological Evaluation of Ethnohistorical Evidence of Inca Culture," in Betty S. Meggers (ed.), *Anthropological Archaeology in the Americas* (Washington, DC: Smithsonian Institution, 1968).

—"Huánuco, Peru: A Survey of a Province of the Inca Empire," *Archaeology*, Brattleboro (VT), vol. 21, no. 3 (1968).

—and John V. Murra, "The Inca Bridges in the Huánuco Region," AA 31, no. 5 (1966).

Thomson, Hugh, *The White Rock: an Exploration of the Inca Heartland*, London: Weidenfeld & Nicolson, 2001.

—*Machu Picchu and the Camera*, London: Penchant Press, 2002.

Ubbelohde-Doering, Heinrich, *The Art of Ancient Peru*, New York, 1952.

—*Auf den Königstrassen der Inka*. Trans. Margaret Brown, *On the Royal Highways of the Inca: Civilizations of Ancient Peru*, London: Thames & Hudson, 1967.

Uhle, Max, "Fortalezas incaicas: Incallacta-Machupicchu," *Revista Chilena de Historia y Geografía*, Santiago, 21 (1917):154–170.

—*Las ruinas de Tomebamba*, 2 vols., Quito, 1923.

—"El Templo del Sol de los Incas en Cuzco," XXIII International Congress of Americanists (New York, 1928), *Proceedings* (New York, 1930), 291–295.

Valcárcel y Vizcarra, Luis Eduardo, "Arquitectura de Tampu," *Revista Universitaria*, Cuzco, vol. 11, no. 51 (1926):1–3.

—*Cuzco, capital arqueológico de Sudamérica, 1534–1934*, Lima, 1934.

—"Los trabajos arqueológicos del Cuzco," RMN 3 (1934).

—"Cuzco Archeology," HSAI 2 (1946):177–182.

—*Machu Picchu, el mas famoso monumento arqueológico del Perú*, Buenos Aires, 1964.

—*Historia del Perú antiguo*, 3 vols., Buenos Aires, 1964.

Valencia Zegarra, Alfredo, *Excavaciones arqueológicas en Machupijchu: Sector de la "Roca Sagrada,"* Cuzco: Instituto Nacional de Cultura, 1977.

—"Complejo arqueológico de Yucay," *Arqueología del Cusco. Revista del Instituto Nacional de Cultura, Región Cusco*, 1982, 65–80.

—and Arminda Gibaja Oviedo, *Excavaciones y Puesta en Valor de Tambomachay*, Cuzco: Instituto Nacional de Cultura, 1990.

—*Machu Picchu: La investigación del monumento arqueológico después de Hiram Bingham*, Cuzco: Municipalidad del Qosqo, 1992.

—"Recent archaeological investigations at Machu Picchu," in Richard L. Burger and Lucy C. Salazar (eds.), *Machu Picchu: Unveiling the Mystery of the Incas* (New Haven and London: Yale University Press, 2004), 71–84.

Van de Guchte, Maarten, *Carving the World: Inca Monumental Sculpture and Landscape*, PhD dissertation, University of Illinois at Urbana-Champaign, 1990.

—"The Inca cognition of landscape: archaeology, ethnohistory and the aesthetic of alterity," in Wendy Ashmore and A. Bernard Knapp (eds.), *Archaeologies of Landscape: Contemporary Perspectives* (Malden (MA) and Oxford: Blackwell Publishing, 1999), 149–168.

Wiener, Charles, *Pérou et Bolivie: récit de voyage*, Paris, 1880.

Wright, Kenneth, and Alfredo Valencia Zegarra, *Machu Picchu: a Civil-Engineering Marvel*, Restone (VA): ASCE (American Society of Civil Engineers) Press, 2000.

Wright, Ruth, and Alfredo Valencia Zegarra, *The Machu Picchu Guidebook: A Self-guided Tour*, Boulder (CO): Johnson Books, 2001.

Zuidema, Rainer Tom, *The Ceque System of Cuzco: The Social Organization of the Capital of the Inca*, Leiden: International Archives of Ethnography, 50, E. J. Brill (1964).

—"El ushnu," *Revista de la Universidad Complutense*, Madrid, vol. 28, no. 117 (1964):317–362.

Credits

WE ARE MOST GRATEFUL to the following authors and publishers for kindly donating or granting permission to use or adapt their plans, maps, drawings, or pictures:

—Víctor Angles Vargas: from *Machupijchu, enigmática ciudad Inka*, ills. 97 (pp. 118–19), 150 (p. 164); from *P'isaq, metrópoli Inka*, ills. 59 (p. 80), 64 (p. 84).

—Hiram Bingham (Bingham Archive and National Geographic Society): ill. 98 (p. 120).

—Martín Chambi Archive, Cuzco (courtesy Teo Allain Chambi, Director): ills. 16 (p. 21), 52 (p. 68), 105 (p. 128), 107 (p. 129), 114 (p. 133), 153 (p. 167), 154 (p. 168), 155 (p. 169).

—Graziano Gasparini and Luise Margolies, plans and reconstructions from *Arquitectura Inka*: ills. 30 (p. 38), 41 (p. 52), 53 (p. 70), 54 (p. 73), 86 (p. 106), 87 (p. 107), 92 (p. 112), 188 (p. 198), 193 (p. 204), 194 (p. 205), 204 (p. 218).

—John Hyslop, from *Inka Settlement and Planning* (copyright, University of Texas Press, 1990): ill. 69 (p. 90).

—Vincent Lee, from *Forgotten Vilcabamba*: ills. 142 (p. 156), 148 (p. 162).

—Craig Morris and The American Museum of Natural History, New York: ill. 196 (p. 208).

—Susan Niles, from *The Shape of Inca History*: ill. 68 (p. 89).

—Hugh Thomson, from *The White Rock*: ills. 157 (p. 172), 158 and 159 (p. 174).

—Drawings from Felipe Guaman Poma de Ayala, *Nueva corónica y buen gobierno*: ills. 6 (p. 12), 24 and 25 (p. 33), 32 (p. 41), 33 (p. 42), 44 (p. 57).

Passages quoted from the following works are reprinted by permission of the publishers:

—Hiram Bingham, *Lost City of the Incas*, E. P. Dutton, Inc., New York (for Duell, Sloan & Pearce), and J. M. Dent & Sons Ltd., London, 1951.

—Pedro de Cieza de León, *The Incas of Pedro de Cieza de León*, translated by Harriet de Onis, edited and with an introduction by Victor W. von Hagen, University of Oklahoma Press, Norman, 1959.

—Garcilaso de la Vega, *Royal Commentaries of the Incas*, translated by Harold V. Livermore, copyright © 1966 by the University of Texas Press, Austin.

This book was originally designed by Eleanor Caponigro, working with Janet Swan Bush of the New York Graphic Society and Edward Ranney. Their design was used in the first edition for the New York Graphic Society (1982) and for the slightly revised version by the University of New Mexico Press (1990), and formed the basis of the present, substantially rewritten and enlarged edition.

We both wish to give our sincere thanks to the many people and institutions who inspired, helped, and befriended us during many years of study of the Incas and travel in Peru. Edward Ranney gratefully acknowledges support on two occasions from the Fulbright Exchange Program, and from the National Endowment for the Arts, Washington, DC.

Index